Chasing Ladybirds

Chasing Ladybirds

How Irish Players Scaled Golf's Summit

Dermot Gilleece

RED STRIPE PRESS

Published by
Red Stripe Press
Dublin
Ireland
email: info@redstripepress.com
www.redstripepress.com

Paperback ISBN 978-1-78605-266-7
ePub ISBN 978-1-78605-267-4

Typeset by www.typesetting.ie

Printed in the EU

To my wonderfully supportive children, Tara and Mark

Acknowledgements

My thanks to Tourism Northern Ireland for their help during the Open Championship. To Royal Portrush GC for their photographic support. To Shay Smith for background graphics in the chapter on Christy O'Connor Snr. To Royal Dublin GC for their contribution to the Michael Moran chapter. To the late John Glover, rules secretary of the R&A, for his enlightenment on Harry Bradshaw's 'bottle incident.'

'Dad, can we put ladybirds into the trophy [the Claret Jug]?'
– Three-year-old Paddy Harrington to his father, Pádraig, after he won the Open in 2007

Foreword

Dr Bob Rotella

When I was contacted about the possibility of writing the foreword to this book, my immediate reaction was positive. I welcomed the opportunity of noting my involvement with Irish players who have had remarkable success in the game.

I've said many, many times over the last few years that someone really needs to write about this phenomenon. I worked with Graeme (McDowell) when he won the US Open and I've worked with Darren (Clarke), Pádraig (Harrington), Shane (Lowry) and Rory (McIlroy). I've also tried to help Seamus Power and I spent a little bit of time with Leona Maguire.

What's unbelievably impressive, is that they're all very much down-to-earth people and very appreciative of what I've tried to do for them. They all tell me the same thing: in Ireland, if you become very good as a kid, and you begin to get a big head as you grow up, people will let you know. Effectively, players are very confident by the time they reach the competitive arena where they emerge as just good guys.

One of the first things you note is that all the good Irish players are very supportive of the other good Irish players. It's amazing to me how close-knit they are, and how they cheer for each other.

My involvement with them has been based largely on word of mouth. They've told their friends to come and see me. I don't ever walk up to somebody and suggest that they should come and work with me. That's not how it works. It's pretty much word of mouth.

That becomes part of the contagion I often refer to, especially the influence Pádraig had on those who came after him, when he made the breakthrough at Carnoustie. And thinking of that memorable occasion for all of us, the title of this book as *Chasing Ladybirds*, brings back wonderful images of little Paddy and his first sight of the Claret Jug.

It's nice to be able to reflect on what proved to be crucial exchanges with the top Irish players. Like telling Darren at Royal St George's:

> You are unstoppable if you are unflappable. And if you let it happen, it will be party time.

If you were looking for a common denominator in their success, I think a key factor must be growing up in a lot of wind, rain and cold weather. It's the ideal way to learn how to play golf.

There's been a lot of great players from Texas, where it's kind of windy and the ground is firm and fast. Where you have to play golf. Too often in other parts of the world, they try to make it a perfect game. No wind, 75 degrees of weather, hit it in the air and stop it on a dime.

In the Open, you've got to play golf. All the guys from Ireland can hit golf shots. Even Rory, as beautiful as his swing is, you put him in trouble, that's when he's really magical.

I started working with Shane about a year and a half ago. I've known him for a long time because he and Pádraig are always having these short-game contests. Which is part of the magic. When they play these contests, it's always the worst lie – downhill, uphill. They're always having contests.

For me, too many players are trying to make golf a neat, over-controlled game, whereas all the Irish guys can really play. Try growing up in Palm Springs, California, where the temperature is 80 degrees every day and there's no wind and the grass is perfect. Too often, perfect turf in perfect practice conditions will produce a different kind of golfer.

In writing this piece, I'm thinking that perhaps Ireland has the right environment because of the weather, which forces you to become a real player and a more complete golfer.

I grew up in the little town of Rutland, Vermont, in a population of 17,000. My dad was a barber. I started caddying in fifth grade and found myself working for Bobby Locke, who married a girl from my hometown. I caddied quite a lot for him when he came visiting our part of Vermont during the summer months.

You talk about a guy who could play! He would just hook the ball around the golf course and make putts from everywhere. Like the Irish golfers I've come to know and admire, he wasn't trying to hit it straight. I remember as a kid thinking that he didn't look that athletic. Big jowls and a long-sleeved shirt which he'd roll up and shoot 63.

All these years later, I find it fascinating that my first experience with the game of golf was with a man who won the Open Championship four times. Playing the Irish way.

Contents

INTRODUCTION

When the Open Championship returned to St Andrews in 1955, the decision had been made to televise it for the first time. We're informed that the breakthrough was achieved by placing a camera on a mound at the 'loop' end of the course, from where play at the 6th, 7th, 8th, 9th, 11th and 12th holes could be filmed.

Though viewers were treated to some interesting spectacle, it was soon realised that the score at the end of a round was what really mattered. So, a camera was installed at the 18th and programme schedules were adjusted so as to facilitate end-of-round coverage. As it happened, this included the moment of triumph for Peter Thomson, who was capturing the title for a third time.

This was very much a time of development for the Royal and Ancient where the Open was concerned. Though it remained the world's oldest and most revered Major championship, it wasn't attracting a sufficient number of the game's leading players, especially from the United States, to give it truly international status.

For instance, in 1955, the top 20 finishers included only one American, and that was Ed Furgol, who was tied 20th. One suspects his decision to make the trip was due largely to have been nominated 'Player of the Year' on the US Tour in 1954. In the event, Furgol wasn't overly impressed by the player facilities at the Home of Golf.

On complaining to an employee about the lack of showers, he was told snootily: 'Their lordships are accustomed to repair to their castles to bathe after a round of golf.' One can only imagine the impression this made on the country club community back home, when Furgol returned to the US.

We know that Ben Hogan made a victorious trip to the 1953 Open at Carnoustie, largely because of the persuasive powers of the 1946 champion, Sam Snead, who persuaded his friend and rival that he couldn't expect to be rated the best in the game without the Open on his CV.

The fact was that for Americans, the event was a very significant undertaking from a travel standpoint, with precious little cash on offer at the end of the day.

So, one can imagine the delight of the R&A when, for their centenary staging in 1960, Arnold Palmer challenged for the title as that year's Masters and US Open champion. And having his own private aircraft allowed him to take in the Canada Cup at Portmarnock in Dublin en route, where he won in partnership with Snead on his first experience of links terrain.

As it happened, Palmer finished runner-up at St Andrews to the surprise winner, Kel Nagle of Australia, while the holder, Gary Player, was seventh. Palmer's presence was huge. Pat Ward-Thomas described him in *The Guardian* as simply 'the most formidable competitor in the world today.' The real bonus for the R&A, however, was that Palmer returned in triumph the following year at Royal Birkdale, where Dai Rees was runner-up and the Irish flag was flown, almost predictably, by Christy O'Connor in a share of third place with Neil Coles.

As a further boost, the man who would become the popular king of golf retained the title at Troon in 1962, this time by the crushing margin of six strokes over Nagle.

His impact on the Open drew this accolade from Ward-Thomas:

> Palmer's presence these last three years has brought greatness once more to the old Championship. It has inspired others to compete and has set a new standard which can only benefit all

who follow. Now, the organisation of the Championship must match the quality of a great champion.

Which is what happened in the persons of successive champions such as Bob Charles, Tony Lema, Thomson, Jack Nicklaus and Roberto de Vicenzo over the following five years. Predictably, Ward-Thomas reserved some special words for Nicklaus and his final round at Muirfield in 1966:

> As he strode purposefully up the 17th fairway, he said with a smile: 'Interesting position, isn't it?' It was one of the most dramatic I have known. He had used a three-iron from the tee and then hit a deathless stroke with a five-iron 25 feet from the hole. A one-iron from the last tee, a three-iron wonderfully judged to use the wind from the right, left him 25 feet from the hole. He walked into the great gathering of people and a noble victory was his.

This priceless endorsement from Nicklaus completed the wonderful rehabilitation embarked upon by Palmer, six years previously. And the Bear's use of irons off the closing tees at Muirfield emphasised the extent to which his play of links terrain had been influenced by Joe Carr.

We had entered a new era, where full-time tournament professionals were emulating the lead of Bobby Locke (four wins) and Thomson (five wins) in dominating the event. Club professionals were effectively frozen out of contention and these included the Irish contingent, for whom O'Connor Snr was a shining light for decades.

Indeed, a significantly heightened standard was reflected in a fairly stark statistic. Remarkably, between 1960 and the surprise victory by Paul Lawrie in 1999, no player succeeded in winning the Open without first managing to be successful in the US. For Sandy Lyle, this happened to be a non-PGA Tour event, the Kapalua International, which he captured in Hawaii in 1984, some months prior to his victory in the 1985 Open at Royal St George's.

All of which illustrates the difficulty which Ireland's modest representation faced in securing a breakthrough to match that of Fred Daly in 1947. The key would be self-belief. And it would be 2007, 60 years after Daly's triumph, before a determined Dubliner would show them the way.

1

Links

'I love the name links, which conjures up stirring images of battling nature over classic golfing terrain. For my part, I didn't grow up in wind and had to learn how to play in it. And I know I learned a lot from watching Joe Carr play links golf. Watching him hit an awful lot of two-, three- or four-irons off the tee, I came to realise that this was a pretty good way to play those courses. It was the only way you could be certain of avoiding the bunkers.'

– Jack Nicklaus

• • • •

Over the classic, out and back links terrain of Royal Troon in the 1982 Open Championship, a young American named Bobby Clampett caused a sensation by sweeping clear of a quality field with rounds of 67 and 66 to be 11 under par. He also prompted quite a degree of schoolboy tittering in the media centre when references were made to his plus-twos as 'knickers', a term more associated with women's underwear on this side of the Atlantic.

From bitter experience that particular weekend, it could be said that Clampett knew precisely what he was talking about when he said of links courses: 'You hit the wrong spot in a bunker and it will cost you four or five shots.'

As it happened, Clampett's halfway lead of five strokes was trimmed to a single shot after a third-round 78. Then his opening drive plunged into sand in the final round, culminating in a dispiriting 77 and a tumble down to a share of tenth place with Jack Nicklaus, behind the winner, Tom Watson.

Clampett, who came to Troon believing that golf could be reduced to mechanics, departed the scene as a chastened soul. 'Through a horrendous emotional battering, Clampett discovered that technique alone is not enough for the last round of an Open', observed the eminent British scribe Peter Dobereiner.

Writing, as he put it, for the benefit of the uninitiated, Henry Longhurst once observed that golf was 'essentially a business of starting here and finishing there, overcoming as best you may all the hazards encountered on the way and endeavouring to get your ball into the hole in fewer strokes than the other man.'

Naturally, all of us committed golfers would claim it to be a lot more serious than that. Still, it is how the game evolved from rather rudimentary beginnings back in the fifteenth century, when King James II saw fit to ban it, alleging a detrimental effect on archery practice.

At that time, the game was a decidedly haphazard affair, played on courses light years removed from the manicured layouts we enjoy today. The usual setting was what the Scots called a machair, which was the low-lying area of fescue grass, heather and whins between arable land and the seashore.

Suitable for little more than drying clothes or mending fishing nets, it became a favoured location for hitting a ball with a stick. And very fine machairs or linksland were to be found in such places as Leith, Musselburgh, St Andrews, Montrose and Dornoch, which would eventually become home to some of the game's most celebrated links courses.

It was a time long before the advent of golf course architects, who would later be dismissed by Sam Snead as 'guys who don't know how to play golf – and they're gonna make damn sure no one else is allowed to play.' Ironically, when they did arrive on the scene towards the end of the nineteenth century, they were mostly golf professionals, pioneers of Snead's craft.

These early courses had neither putting greens nor tees and the hole was a crude affair. Not only did it serve as the ultimate resting place of the ball, but as the source of a continuous supply of sand for the building of a tee from which to play the next drive.

In his book *The Encyclopedia of Golf*, Malcolm Campbell reasons that:

> The area between the sandhills developed into smooth stretches of turf, probably as a result of continual tracking over the decades by animals such as rabbits and foxes, and by the men who hunted them. These tracks developed into the fairways, while the areas around the holes, worn out by continual play, were expanded to form greens.

As the game became formalised, it was determined that the hole should measure 4¼ inches in diameter. Interestingly, this was not based on mathematical factors; it just happened to be the size of the most popular implement which was used during the nineteenth century for creating holes for stake-posts.

In those early days, the Leith course had only five holes whereas St Andrews had 22. In 1764, however, the course at St Andrews was reduced to 18 holes, so creating a precedent which would be followed eventually throughout the golfing world more than a century later.

We are told that the original course was very much narrower than the present Old Course, which still measures only 83 acres. During the eighteenth century, the North Sea came right up to the edge of the first fairway and the 11 outward holes were played in the reverse order on the homeward journey, with only one flag in each green. Players homeward-bound always had the right of way over those going out, which is a tradition preserved to this day.

In his book *The Game of Golf*, published in 1896, Willie Park Jnr, the Open champion of 1887 and 1889 and a leading golf course architect of that time, wrote: 'The laying out of a golf course is by no means a simple task. Great skill and judgement and a thorough acquaintance with the game are absolutely necessary to determine the best positions for the respective holes and teeing grounds, and the situations of the hazards.'

Meanwhile, the eminent golf writer Bernard Darwin, who was chairman of the Rules Committee of the Royal and Ancient from 1946 to 1949, once suggested that 'golf is not a funeral, but both can be sad affairs.' Through the years, there have been errant practitioners who have attributed much of the grief in the game to the introduction of those wretched rules.

More objective minds, however, would have welcomed the initiative of the R&A in producing, in 1897, a uniform code of rules in response to public demand. A game which had already been more than 400 years in the making was eventually formalised.

Then, as the 1890s gave way to a new century, it was recognised that virgin stretches of fir and heather around London were ideal golfing terrain, because of the sandy, quick-draining nature of the soil which encouraged grass of a linksland texture.

So it was that the game moved inland, where an exciting, new world was opened up. Still in organising their Open Championship, the Royal and Ancient remained faithful to links terrain, concentrated largely in Scotland and England.

In 1951, however, Royal Portrush marked the first staging of the Open outside of mainland Britain. The event then returned there in 2019 when Ireland's Shane Lowry emerged victorious, and it was back again for a third staging this year. And plans are at an advanced stage to bring the event to Portmarnock GC within the next decade.

All as a consequence of the R&A's loyalty to links terrain.

2

St Andrews

'You can play a damned good shot and find it in a damned bad place.'

– George Duncan, the 1920 Open champion, talking about St Andrews

• • • •

With the sun high in the heavens and Edinburgh Airport disappearing in the rearview mirror, my vision was soon dominated by the suspension towers of the Forth Road Bridge. 'Head for the East Neuk of Fife,' I had been instructed. I would find it by following the signs for Kirkcaldy and Leven and Lundin Links and Largo.

My home for Open week would be in Anstruther, a thoroughly delightful fishing village situated on the north shore of the Firth of Forth and nine miles to the south-south-west of St Andrews. I had stayed there in 2000, the last time the great event was staged in the Auld Grey Toon.

No longer was there any sign of the *QE2*, which had been berthed offshore then. And this year's accommodation was also different – a charming, two-room fisherman's cottage down a little side street which carried no identification other than the intriguing sign 'Formerly Witches Wynd'.

My first visit to St Andrews was in 1981 for the British Amateur Championship in which John Carr lost to the eventual runner-up, Philippe Ploujoux, in the semi-finals. It had made a huge emotional impact, just as I had been promised it would by John Redmond of the *Irish Press*, who became my guide, from the Old Course itself to the grave of Young Tom Morris and the iconic old Royal and Ancient clubhouse.

There would be countless further visits, for Open Championships and the Dunhill Cup, which had become something of an institution since the inaugural victory by an Australian team represented by Greg Norman, Graham Marsh and David Graham. Remarkably, they had outclassed an US team comprising Mark O'Meara, Raymond Floyd and Curtis Strange, 3–0 in the medal match play final.

Open Championships over the Old Course had begun for me in 1984 with the thrilling triumph of Seve Ballesteros. Then there was Nick Faldo's second Open win in 1990 and John Daly's victory in 1995, followed by the anticipated dominance by Tiger Woods who became the fifth winner of the Career Grand Slam in Millennium Year. Now I was back in iconic surroundings in 2005, when Jack Nicklaus would be departing a scene he had graced with so much distinction. It would be his 38th Open, including three wins, seven runners-up and eighteen top 10s.

The nine miles from Anstruther into St Andrews were negotiated between fields of gold. In 20 minutes, I was at the course, knowing traffic wouldn't be so simple later in the week. About mid-morning, looking back towards the ancient clubhouse and relishing a glorious spectacle which never seems to fade, I came upon Jock Howard, a senior editor with the magazine *Golf World*, who talked about having a particularly early start to the day, which explained his harassed look. As he explained:

> We heard rumours last night that Jack [Nicklaus] and Tiger were going off together at 6:00 a.m. So I got up at 5:30 out at Kingsbarns where our house is. Which meant I had about two hours sleep because of a party that went on until 3:30.

Myself and a colleague got to the course at 6:00, dropped our bags in the media centre and walked straight out to the 9th hole, asking people as we went if Tiger was out there. Nobody seemed to know. The upshot of it was that we had a five-mile walk by about 7:00, two-and-a-half miles out and two-and-a-half miles back.

And I thought 'ah! the industry of youth.'

At about 2:00 p.m., a Welsh marshal working on the second hole informed me conspiratorially that El Tigre would soon be starting his practice round. 'I've got to be nice to you Irish because I want to do this job at the Ryder Cup at The K Club next year', he said. Sure enough, Woods, coach Hank Haney and Mark O'Meara were seen heading down the first at about 2.50 p.m. I met Howard not long afterwards. Nine hours behind schedule, he'd missed his quarry once more. And cursed quietly.

Driving to Anstruther that evening, I dropped in at the local nine-hole course and saw numerous visitors, including British and American journalistic colleagues. 'Eight ho-hum holes but the 5th is sensational', one of them volunteered. This was a 235-yard par-three, played downhill to what appeared to be a tiny target with the North Sea on the left. Everybody seemed to be playing golf during Open week at St Andrews. Memo to self: Next time, arrange schedule so as to join the happy throng.

Seventeen years later in the calm of a chilly April evening, the Old Course projected its unique appeal as a fourball hit their approaches to the famous 17th. It was weather for windcheaters and woolly hats, not unlike the conditions we encountered in the October days of the fondly remembered Dunhill Cup.

I was there, three months before the 150th Open in 2022, experiencing once more the vibrant atmosphere of a location inextricably linked to golf. As Shane Lowry observed: 'St Andrews is probably the only spot in the world where you can carry your clubs down the street and not look out of place.'

It was close on 6:00 p.m. when the quartet reached the 17th green like straggling schoolboys. And as if the stress of the golfing challenge weren't enough in itself, they were suddenly assailed by the clanging of metal against metal as workers resumed the construction of spectator seating behind this iconic Road Hole.

From there, the players progressed up the 18th and the end of a special experience, on towards the Royal and Ancient's clubhouse bathed in the half-light of evening. To the left, a grandstand beside the first fairway proclaimed '150' in large, white lettering. And the addition of a smaller, lower-case 'th' emphasised that, unlike the Centenary Open of 1960, this celebration had to do with numbers rather than years.

For such an occasion, St Andrews couldn't be matched. There was an appealing constancy about the place, reflecting much credit on the local planning authorities. Less appealing, however, is the cost to visitors. Over the years, I have found it to be one of Europe's most expensive golf tournament venues, possibly matched only by Switzerland.

As an exercise during that particular visit, I had my hotelier research accommodation around St Andrews for that year's Open in July. He sourced three options for a week's stay. One was £8,670 for a newly refurbished house in the city centre; another was £5,600 for a two-bedroom ground apartment and the third was £22,400 for the Old Toll House, just outside the royal burgh.

Revisiting the 17th brought memories flooding back of stirring happenings in the heat of battle. And older observers seem to retain a special feeling for the 1984 Open and the two-stroke victory by Ballesteros over Watson and Bernhard Langer.

On the Monday of my 2022 visit, there was a charming memorial service in St Andrews for the distinguished golf journalist Renton Laidlaw, who had passed from us six months previously. And from the broadcaster himself was a taped reflection on 1984 and the magic of the Spaniard's triumph while his mother watched from a window in Rusack's Hotel.

For Watson, seeking a record-equalling sixth Open, there was the crushing disappointment of a bogey on the 17th where an ill-judged two-iron second shot of 210 yards scampered through the green before coming to rest two feet from the spectator wall at the back.

With its record attendance of 187,753, this happened to be Michael Bonallack's first Open as secretary of the R&A. 'We had a heatwave which added to its appeal and everything seemed to go like clockwork,' he recalled.

And it remained his favourite, not least because of his special affection for the Old Course where he first came to prominence in 1958 when losing to Joe Carr in the semi-finals of the British Amateur, then played over 36 holes. Bonallack said:

> In the morning round, I got off to a good start and having gone out in 33, found myself three-up on the 12th tee. As we were waiting to drive, Joe remarked to his caddie [Andy Doherty] in a voice loud enough for me to hear, 'Don't worry; the wind's from left to right now, and he can't handle that.'
>
> Needless to say he was right, and I duly went down by 4 and 3 and Joe went on to win his second Amateur Championship.

Despite this prominence, it would be 1964 before Bonallack made the Eisenhower Trophy for the first time. Which meant that he missed its inaugural staging in 1958 and the hugely emotional presence of Bobby Jones, who was there for the last time as non-playing captain of the US team.

Not even the ravages of a rare spinal disease could dim the great man's keen sense of fun. 'The provost,' said Jones, 'has given me permission to tell you that lacking a middle initial of his own, he will, in future, be known as Robert T. Leonard. I consider that the greatest triumph I have ever won in Scotland.'

It was 9 October and Jones was addressing a capacity audience of 1,700 in the Younger Graduation Hall, St Andrews, where he received the Freedom of the City. Not since Benjamin Franklin 199 years previously had an American been so honoured.

I got a firsthand account from Joe Carr, who was among those privileged to witness a truly extraordinary occasion. Jones embraced it as 'my last opportunity to revisit the city and golf course that I love so well.'

And interest was such that we're told the hall could have been filled three times over, while, at the end of the ceremony, hundreds gathered outside for a glimpse of their hero.

To mark the occasion, the provost was gowned in a crimson robe with a wide ermine collar, adorned with the magnificent chain of office. And the crippled champion, accompanied by his wife, son and daughter, approached the top table from the wings to a rapturous reception.

Typically dignified and often self-deprecating, Jones emphasised friends and friendship while recalling key moments in the Auld Grey Toon, culminating in his last round there in 1936. He admitted: 'I said to myself, "this is an awful thing to do to my friends if they have come to see me golf, with the dreadful stuff I am playing."'

When word spread of his presence, the crowd had doubled from 2,000 to 4,000 by the time he had played only two holes. 'Such a spontaneous show of warmth and affection I have never known in my life,' said the focus of their attention. Whereupon the Old Course worked its magic in some glorious shot-making which brought him to the turn in 32 strokes, after a birdie on the short eighth.

'A great day for me', was how the great Bobby described it. 'Now I have this,' he went on. 'I could take out of my life everything except my experience at St Andrews and I would still have had a rich and full life.' That last line, which has since become a treasured part of golfing history, was greeted with sustained applause.

Then, draped in the Georgia flag and holding a small, silver casket containing the ceremonial scroll and adorned with the seal of St Andrews, he rode in an electric golf cart down the centre aisle. As Carr remembered it: 'Suddenly, people around me started singing "Will ye no' come back again?" and I found myself joining them in full voice. It was an unforgettable moment.'

So, with tears flowing freely, St Andrews bade farewell to one of its favourite golfing sons. And he, in turn, treasured their gesture as 'the finest thing that has ever happened to me.'

Rusack's remains a wonderful vantage point for its guests, given that it overlooks the first and 18th holes. But protecting the turf against the proliferation of visitor rounds, quite apart from regular competitions such as the Dunhill links, has led to very different playing conditions.

Veteran scribe John Ingham recalled an interview he had with Jones, reflecting on his triumph in the 1927 Open at St Andrews. 'He requested that we meet in room 19 in Rusack's,' said Ingham. 'Apparently, there had been little rain that year and the grass was brown and dusty dry.

'When I holed the winning putt, the *Press* claimed I dried my eyes from emotion,' said Jones. 'Not so. I was wiping the grass dust out of my eyes, so I didn't look too dusty at the prize-giving!' For the record, he carded rounds of 68,72,73,72 for 285, to win by six strokes.

By then, golf's celebrated Claret Jug was, of course, very much a part of the Open scene. And it got quite an airing around Clara and its environs after Shane Lowry brought it home from Royal Portrush in July 2019. Yet the Irish sojourn, though much longer than normal because of Covid and the cancellation of the 2020 Open, could still only match the one accorded to Pádraig Harrington, who also retained it for two years, but as a back-to-back champion.

And to enhance the Irish connection, the plinth carries in its various inscriptions a fascinating spelling error. When Fred Daly's name was engraved as the winner in 1947, the venue was spelt 'Holylake' instead of Hoylake.

In its various travels through the decades, the 1928 replica of the original created a much greater stir than would be expected with other awards. There was the occasion when it returned from the US, somewhat the worse for wear, after being in the possession of Tom Lehman, the 1996 winner at Royal Lytham.

'The jug has been through a few scrapes but I'm sure no more than with any other winner', said Lehman when he handed it back.

> Like when my kids got a hold of it when I was out of town one week and accidentally bent it. But it was fixable.
>
> Then there was the situation where I was playing in a tournament in Minneapolis. After a late dinner, Alysia Herron [sister of Tour player Tim Herron] was given the trophy to take home with

her. But the owner of a place we call the Brits Pub saw her and called the police.

The cop thought she'd stolen it, so he came out and grabbed her. Eventually they called me at 2:00 in the morning and said, 'We have somebody here with the British Open trophy.' When they described her I knew it was Alysia. The upshot was that the police and the TV people all got their picture taken with the trophy.

As it happened, the resumption of the Open in 2021 marked the centenary of the first trip the original Claret Jug made to the New World. It was in the 1921 baggage of a proud American-based Scot by the name of Jock Hutchison. To make the circumstance all the more notable, he happened to be a native of St Andrews, which played host to the Open that year.

Steeped in so much golfing history, very little happens in the Auld Grey Toon that hasn't found its way into the annals of the game. A lasting memory of Ireland's Dunhill Cup triumph over the Old Course in 1988 is of university students mocking Faldo with a banner hung from a window of Hamilton Hall, the imposing, red-stone building overlooking the 18th green.

'Can you see this, Nick?', the printed banner taunted, after the Englishman had declined to finish his semi-final battle with Des Smyth because of an all-enveloping Scottish haar. It descended as he and Smyth came up the 18th fairway in the decisive match between Ireland and England, late on Saturday afternoon.

Though the green presented only a vague outline to him, Smyth opted to play on and hit an approach shot which came to rest 54 feet behind the hole. Faldo, however, insisted that he owed it to his English teammates to wait until the following morning to finish the match.

In their mischief, it is unlikely the students would have known they were occupying the former Grand Hotel, which was sold for an undisclosed sum to the University of St Andrews in September 1949. Or that a local man of an earlier generation used to hit golf shots over its five storeys for bets.

Their education would have been greatly enriched by a marvellous book, *Links with the Past*, written with great affection by Bob MacAlindin about the spiritual home of golf. Especially appealing are stories of a local character named Hutchison with the sobriquet of Peg. He was a one-time professional who had fallen on hard times and lived in an abandoned cottage on the neighbouring Eden Course. And he happened to be Jock Hutchison's brother, with comparable gifts for the game but lacking his sibling's renowned sense of purpose. In fact, Peg was essentially a vagrant.

During the years after World War I, you could imagine him living on his wits, dependant on the generosity of visitors to his native place. A favourite ploy was to position himself strategically behind the famous 18th green where tourists would be asked: 'What would you give me if I could hit a ball from here, over that building [Grand Hotel] and land it on the back lawn of the Scores Hotel [next door]'.

'Impossible,' was the pretty standard reply. Though he rarely had a penny to his name, Peg would confidently pledge to cover any bet the visitor cared to make. 'But how do we know the ball you hit is the one we'll find on the lawn?'

'Mark the ball any way you like.'

With that, the old pro would produce an ancient golf club, open its face and whack the ball unerringly over the roof, as promised. It was said that he never had a mis-hit, which was probably just as well for the safety of hotel guests.

Indeed, there were those who claimed that when the mood took him he could play more impressively than his illustrious brother. Peg was certainly a wonderful teacher, by all accounts.

There's the story of how he came upon a woman golfer playing the 16th hole of the Eden Course and, after giving her a demonstration of his skill, invited her to 'walk a way out' with him. Sometime later, she ran across Tom Ritchie, a member of the St Andrews grounds staff.

'Who was that trampy man?' she enquired. When enlightened about Peg, she declared: 'Well, I've learned more about golf in these last few holes than I learned in 10 hours with Laurie Auchterlonie [the best-known local teacher at that time].'

Jock Hutchison was born in St Andrews in 1884 and captured the American PGA Championship in 1920. This significant success prompted him to enter the 1921 Open Championship, not least because it was being staged in his hometown. It meant he could also rekindle family links, including an often-strained relationship with Peg.

Though tied with Roger Wethered after 72 holes of the Open, Hutchison crushed the English amateur by no fewer than nine strokes in a 36-hole playoff. His final round of 70 raised quite a few eyebrows, including some in the Royal and Ancient, who declared his deep-grooved irons illegal. But his victory stood.

That was in June, when the competitive effort, coupled with the demands of transatlantic travel, seemed to have taken their toll. Returning to the US where the original Claret Jug was paraded for the first time, Hutchison was beaten in a head-to-head at the Sound View GC in New York by the newly crowned US Open champion, Jim Barnes. It was a big-money challenge, flagged to decide the unofficial supremacy of world golf.

Still, in a highly successful career, Hutchison won eight times in the US, including the prestigious Western Open and the North and South at Pinehurst. He later won the US PGA Seniors, in 1937 and 1947, and was inducted into the PGA Hall of Fame in 1959.

In the meantime, he became a familiar face to American golf fans as an honorary starter, with Fred McLeod, of the Masters at Augusta National.

With two Major titles to his credit, Hutchison was undoubtedly one of the finest players to leave Scotland for the New World. Still, many around St Andrews would insist that the more gifted of the Hutchison brothers had stayed at home, though possession of the Claret Jug, however, suggested otherwise.

Meanwhile, from an overall length of 6,933 yards in 1984, the Old Course measured 7,313 for the 2022 Open, incorporating the latest increase of only 16 yards.

As Bonallack pointed out: 'They simply haven't anywhere else to go.'

Though the great man was seriously ill at the time of my interview, he remained happy to talk of a place he loved so well. 'When the course was originally designed, you could move naturally from green to the next tee,' he went on. 'Now, you have to go back 40 or 50 yards in places.'

So, could it survive much longer as an Open venue? There was a marked pause before his measured reply. 'As long as they set it up with firm and fast greens, the rough is up and there's a bit of a breeze, the Old Course will remain a very good test', he said. 'Though it's very vulnerable in still conditions, I feel confident it can survive for some more years. But the greens have got to be firm and fast.'

Its unique place in the game has been acknowledged by Nicklaus, who won the Open there in 1970 and 1978. 'Isn't it great to think of Tiger Woods playing the same course that Lloyd Mangrum [1946 US Open champion] played', the Bear suggested. 'About the only course in the world where that can happen is St Andrews. And about the only way St Andrews holds up is because of the weather and getting the greens as hard as a rock.'

During that particular week in 2005, I had an appointment with Robert Trent Jones II, the distinguished golf course architect, who was anxious to see Nicklaus begin his final Open. When we met up, he pointed to a face in the crowd. Doug Sanders, the nearly man from 1970, the so-called Peacock of the Fairways, was wearing a suitably garish shirt.

'There he is', said Jones, 'looking at the man who took his golfing life away.' He was referring in typical language to the Bear's playoff win after his rival had pushed a two-and-a-half-foot putt ruinously past the 72nd hole in the 1970 Open over the Old Course. Jones added thoughtfully: 'Doug still seems happy to have his spirit moved by images of the Auld Grey Toon.'

The American then presented me with a DVD, having earlier given another copy to Barbara Nicklaus, to mark her husband's swansong. Titled *St Andrews – A Poem*, it was an evocative tribute to the Old

Course, written and read by Jones to appropriate images and the sound of a traditional Scottish fiddler.

Having given me permission to use the poem in Joe Carr's biography a few years previously, he had now, as he mischievously put it, produced 'a golfer's answer to Madonna.' He dedicated the production to Tommy Armour, the so-called Silver Scot and 1931 Open champion whom he got to know as the professional at Winged Foot, many years previously. 'It was Tommy who urged me to make a trip to St Andrews, which I did in 1961 when, as a 21-year-old, I took the train up from London and loved the place at first sight,' he says. Through this poem, Jones was the first to make me aware that the Old Course was laid out in a mere 83 acres.

This is it:

Round and round we go
in the calm and in the gale
gentle air suddenly impaled.

Round and round we go
always back as first I came
among true spirits of the game.

A barren, timeless land tolled by bells,
Carved by wind and shepherds on watch,
Given to humble folk by noblesse oblige,
A low links from receding seas;
They walked the crook rounded at the estuary.
By ancient and royal measure, 83 acres without a tree
Evolving to 18 shots of whisky and holes of golf
A field of such complexity;
With but 11 greens and 16 fairways
The Old Course confounds to create,
A profound test for all full rounds.
For half a millennia in all seasons
Inhaling pure air at Sea's end.

In summer full joy at the long solstice light,
In winter girded against the cold wind and early sight
The same friends passed by unrecognised
Except by the manner of the other's swing and stride;
Unseen bunkers evoked anger and mirth
For tall and slim or stout of girth.

Baptised upon our journey begun,
When life and all is lost and won,
Return we from whence we come.
Again the wee burn bids us in faith to cross
To safe home as did St Andrew upon his cross.

Round and round we go
in the calm and in the gale
gentle air suddenly impaled.
Round and round we go
always back as first I came
among true spirits of the game.

At lunchtime on the Friday, the 27th staging of the Open at St Andrews was nearing the halfway stage and Barbara Nicklaus was waiting for her husband by the 18th, as she had done dutifully for 45 years. 'I feel my age every day, every minute out there', the Bear says, having hit average drives of 280.5 yards en route to a disappointing 75. 'But if I wasn't prepared I wouldn't be here.'

Half an hour later, Tiger Woods carded nine strokes better with a 66, having smashed average drives of 339.5 yards. Which called to mind the words of American senior professional Larry Ziegler, who, on being asked what he did better now that he did twenty years ago, replied: 'Probably sleep.'

When the cut was made on Friday evening, the survival of Darren Clarke, Graeme McDowell and Paul McGinley into the weekend was clearly welcomed by Irish observers. Though Carr captured the British

Amateur there in 1958, it struck me that Irish players had generally tended to fare best on the Old Course when operating in threes. As in the Dunhill Cup triumphs by Smyth, Eamonn Darcy and Ronan Rafferty in 1988 and by David Feherty, Philip Walton and Rafferty two years later.

Almost predictably, Nicklaus was gone, for the last time. Only four months previously he had bade an emotional farewell to the Masters, having spoken movingly about his 17-month-old grandson Jake, who had died in a tragic accident earlier in the year.

Now, the emotion took the form of a salute to a peerless talent. And it was impossible to imagine a more appropriate setting as Nicklaus bade goodbye by holing an 18-foot birdie putt down the slope of the final green which he had driven on his way to victory in 1970. Standing in front of the R&A clubhouse, Barbara and their children Jackie, Gary, Nan and Michael watched and applauded. Then the Bear hugged his other son, Steve, little Jake's father, who had caddied for him.

'Jack never fails us', said Dave Anderson, Pulitzer Prize-winning sportswriter of the *New York Times*, capturing the moment perfectly. And after Nicklaus had embraced Watson and hugged Barbara, he headed past the first tee for a string of farewell interviews, brushing tears from his eyes.

Later, he said: 'On the 18th, I tried to treat the crowd to the real Jack Nicklaus. And when I birdied it, they saw a little bit of me.'

After signing the umpteenth autograph a while later, he looked up, smiled and gave a nod to what the future held for him when he added: 'I was at Killeen Castle [the course he was designing near Dunshaughlin] last Sunday, and it's looking good.'

One wondered how he would handle the loss, 41 years after his St Andrews debut. 'I think Jack is a very well-rounded individual, with his design work and plenty of other things to keep him going,' said Tony Jacklin, the 1969 Open champion. 'Sadly, his body is no longer supple, which means he can't swing the club as he'd want to. So what's the point?'

How hard is it to let go? 'It's a helluva lot harder to keep going and make a fool of yourself', Jacklin replied. 'I still have all the mental discipline that golf taught me. So I know it's time to quit. So does Jack. He's going to be fine.'

Ten years later, I was back at St Andrews, revelling in further dips into golf's illustrious past. This time, the Irish link was with 1960, when Arnold Palmer won the Canada Cup with Sam Snead at Portmarnock and then travelled to St Andrews for his first experience of the Open. He didn't win it on that occasion, but transformed the fortunes of the Championship by returning in triumph at Royal Birkdale the following year and again at Troon in 1962.

For me, 2015 was my seventh Open at the Home of Golf and its appeal hadn't waned. I thought of the way it had burnished some glittering talent over the years, like a youthful Michael Campbell in 1995 and the imperious Woods in Millennium Year.

Significant structural changes had seen the construction of a two-tier grandstand behind the 18th green, virtually blocking out the imposing terracotta structure of Hamilton Hall. But overall, the passing years had not diminished the enduring wonder of the place.

The well-worn cliché of walking in the footsteps of golfing giants seemed to retain a profound significance for the living legends who assembled on the Wednesday for the so-called Challenge of Champions. It certainly meant a lot to Nick Price, who was there, even though he couldn't participate because of a nagging elbow injury. The 1994 champion at Turnberry told me:

> My first Open at St Andrews was in 1978, when I finished maybe two hours ahead of Jack [Nicklaus]. I waited around the clubhouse, where we'd have sandwiches back then. And when Jack was coming up the 18th for the last time, I went out to the steps to see him playing the final hole.
>
> As he walked off the green as the champion, I could see a tear in his eye. And I wondered why it was so emotional for him. I couldn't understand why such a tough competitor would have reacted that way. Over a period of time, however, I learned.

Price went on: 'I really came here just for the Champions' Dinner last night [Tuesday].' Then, looking wistfully down towards the Swilcan Bridge, he said:

> All of us who have loved the Open would really love to have won it here. All of us. The atmosphere, the aura of this place is just phenomenal.
>
> The first time you come here, there's an initial awe, but you don't really feel much. You don't feel any huge buzz until you get a little older, more mature and you've learned more and more about your craft. That's when you come to realise how important this place is in the history of the game.

The sun had broken through on the Friday evening when I met a blonde 31-year-old Australian with a remarkable story. 'I'm Alicia Nagle,' she said, 'and my grandfather won the Centenary Open here in 1960.' She then recounted the extraordinary circumstances which prompted her presence at this latest staging.

Kel Nagle, who shared a birthday with Christy O'Connor Snr on 21 December, had died the previous January in a hospital in Sydney, aged 94. Ten days earlier, Alicia, who worked in advertising in London, responded to a call from her mother and flew back to Australia to be with him and the extended family:

> It was an amazing time for me, with him telling jokes; completely lucid. In fact, when I walked through the door of the hospital ward, he said to a nurse 'Hey, she's back from London.'
>
> He was always a great family man, devoted to his children and grandchildren; very proud of us all. Though he would talk about golf if journalists contacted him and loved to watch it on television, he preferred to talk about life when he was with us. He felt he'd had a great innings and seemed pleased we were all there for him at he neared the end of the road.

She went on:

> In my final conversation with him, I said I would go to the Open at St Andrews this year in his honour, knowing what he'd done here in 1960. This golf course meant the world to him and he meant the world to me, so they were my final words. I left him with that.

When I enquired, gently, if he had responded, her eyes welled with tears. 'I wasn't too sure if he had heard me,' she said, 'but he looked at me, leaned forward and gave me a kiss on the cheek. So he knew all right. It was wonderful.'

In keeping her promise, she talked of being treated royally at St Andrews, with so many people talking affectionately about the departed champion, including Arnold Palmer, who had finished runner-up to Nagle in 1960.

Other devotees of The Old Course had very different experiences. Especially interesting was the reaction of the Dane Soren Kjeldsen, who was the newly crowned Irish Open champion at Royal County Down. 'People who play the game in Denmark know that the Irish Open is a big tournament, but golf is not big in the Danish media,' he said.

'But here at St Andrews, they know about links golf and just how good Royal County Down is. They know that to win around there, you've got to be able to play. That's a nice feeling for me.'

There was also the joy of showing his 12-year-old son, Emil, around St Andrews for the first time, including the closeness of the 18th green to the surrounding buildings. 'He could see the way everything about this place is different,' said the Dane. 'That they haven't spoiled it, which is a great achievement when you think of what might have been done in the name of progress.'

Events on an Open weekend would embellish the St Andrews mystique and its unique place in golfing lore. Yet in quieter moments, players will insist that there's much, much more to it than simple tradition. It remains a seriously searching test of skill and temperament.

'Whenever I played here, I found I had to concentrate much harder than on a lot of other courses,' said Des Smyth, who is working as an on-course commentator:

> Being out there this week, I can see the additional challenge of hitting approach shots off sand-filled divots, where the ball can go anywhere if you're not careful. You have to play smart, knowing that a visit to one of those bunkers is going to cost you a shot, maybe more.
>
> To be able to say that I was part of winning something at St Andrews, like I did in the 1988 Dunhill Cup, remains one of the highlights of my career. Simply because of where it happened.

3

Scheffler supreme

'You can see why they're pros.'
– Young Open observer enthuses
at Royal Portrush

• • • •

During a range of post-championship interviews, Scottie Scheffler uttered a simple sentence which captured the very essence of his being.

'I felt a good amount of peace today,' said the 29-year-old American after a closing 68 for a 17-under-par aggregate of 267, had secured the 153rd Open title, four strokes clear of fellow countryman Harris English, his closest challenger.

The word *serenity* could have been used instead of peace, though it wouldn't have quite fit his image. Yet he felt the need to convey something of the spirituality which has dominated his life as a PGA Tour player.

He even found the presence of mind, having partnered Shane Lowry for 36 holes, to wait back on Friday evening as they approached the 18th green. Thoughtfully, he wanted the winner from 2019 at Portrush to be on his own when greeted by the gallery.

'All I'm trying to do is glorify God, and that's why I'm here,' said the champion, emphasising his strong Christian faith. Scheffler's belief in God plays a significant role in his life and golf career. He credits his wife, Meredith, a fellow Christian, for calming him down before critical rounds, while adding: 'God is in control and the Lord is leading me; and if today is my time, then it's my time' – which was the source of his Portrush peace.

Even his trusty caddie, Ted Scott, was met at a Bible study group, so it's clear that Scheffler's faith is a prominent element of his life.

Against this background and the often-dismissive role that religion is accorded in modern living, it is hardly surprising that the nature of Scheffler as the world's leading golfer seems to pose so many problems for professional observers of the game. How can such inflexible steel be present in such a warm, amenable exterior? How is there never even the hint of ruthlessness within? How did he come to be described as a lethal closer? How can rivals be treated apparently with disdain? The answer, as we observed at Royal Portrush, lies in Scheffler's stated priorities of family and faith before golf. And to save possible embarrassment to his inquisitors, he tends to protect these as private issues.

~

Even the new-look Dunluce Links had a warm familiarity about it, thanks to the indelible memories Lowry had left us from his triumph in 2019. Now, on the Tuesday prior to the 153rd Open, even the weather had resonances of six years ago in the sometimes-fierce rain showers which swept the North Antrim coast. Thankfully, Wednesday was a very different sort of day.

From my standpoint, however, there was a special atmosphere about Tuesday evening and the annual dinner of the Association of Golf Writers, which currently has its first Irish chairman in Philip Reid of the *Irish Times*.

Highlight of the evening was the appearance of Rory McIlroy, resplendent in a beautifully fitting Green Jacket earned three months previously at Augusta National.

McIlroy has had to cope with much pain since a disastrous opening shot in the 2019 Open. 'When I put the tee in the ground and my name was called on the Thursday morning, I had no idea how I was going to feel', he had admitted. 'I made a mess of the first hole.' There was really no other way of describing a wretched eight which culminated in a crushing 79 he had hoped would be so much different.

In speaking to the assembled golf writers and their guests, he didn't run from that potentially damaging memory. Then, when asked who he would be rooting for at the weekend, should he himself fail to make amends for 2019, we were given an insight into a truly wonderful, sporting heart. 'I would like Justin Rose to win,' he said, referring to the player he had beaten in a playoff for the coveted Masters title.

Other award winners on the night included such notable practitioners as Catriona Matthew for her services to golf and Francesco Molinari, whose remarkable 2018 season earned him the Arnold Palmer Open Award. So, it was a special thrill to be included in such company by the Royal and Ancient, who informed my peers that they wished to honour me with an inscribed silver quaich to mark my fortieth Open Championship. Their chief executive, Mark Darbon, did the honours.

'I'll bet those years went by in a blink', remarked a colleague of comparable vintage. And of course he was right. Indeed, there has been much change, yet other key elements have remained largely the same.

Like, for instance, the Irish line-up at Portrush, where the island had five representatives in McIlroy, Lowry, Pádraig Harrington and Darren Clarke, all as former Open champions, who were joined by Tom McKibbin of the LIV Tour.

Back in 1980 at Muirfield, the Irish representation comprised Des Smyth and John O'Leary, who were both exempt. With them were Christy O'Connor Jnr, Eamonn Darcy, David Jones and Ronan Rafferty, who came through final qualifying.

Even at that early stage of his development, Rafferty had already made quite an impact on the amateur scene in these islands as a prolific winner. He won the British Boys Championship in 1979 and when qualifying for Muirfield was just six months beyond his 16th birthday.

Preparing for an Open can take many forms. Few of us were aware, for instance, of what Tom Watson did in the build-up to the 2011 Open at Royal St George's, the one which Darren Clarke captured in such style. This was only two years after Watson had rocked the golfing world by challenging to the point of victory in the 2009 Open at Turnberry. Enthusiasts of a certain age, myself included, still retain profound disappointment about Watson's playoff defeat by Stewart Cink on that occasion.

On his way to the 2011 Open at Royal St George's, Watson took advantage of its proximity to France by making a trip to the Normandy coast, which was the scene, on 6 June 1944, of the largest amphibious invasion in modern times. Watson explained:

> I visited the British military grave site at Ranville first and then I went to Sword Beach, which was the eastern flank. And then we over-nighted in Caen and then the next day we went to the US cemetery and Nointe du Hoc and Omaha Beach. It was very emotional.
>
> I wanted to see, first of all, Point du Hoc. It was man against man and gun against gun. Talk about a disadvantage! It was like me playing Phil Mickelson on this [Royal St George's] golf course. The Rangers, the Second Battalion Rangers, had to go up 115 feet in the air, straight up, and the Germans were up there shooting at them. And they managed to do it.
>
> To see the cemetery there and the 9,000-plus marble crosses, is a striking reminder of what the human condition can do.

In that 2011 Open, where Mickelson was tied second with Dustin Johnson behind Clarke, Watson shot rounds of 72,70,72 and 72 for an aggregate of 286 and a share of 22nd place, a stroke ahead of Rory

McIlroy among others. This little-known excursion emphasised the pride in his homeland exemplified by Watson, two months prior to his 62nd birthday.

In the 2011 Open, another very significant development was the reliance by the champion, Clarke, on the mental guidance of Dr Bob Rotella. Recalling their exchanges on the Sunday morning of the decisive final round at Sandwich, Rotella told me:

> Darren was paired with Dustin [Johnson] and we had been talking all week about looking at your target and letting the swing happen. And you had to accept the outcome of your actions, and have fun.
>
> So I walked with him to the first tee, and we embraced. Darren looked at me and said: 'Doc, if I go out there and have fun today and just look at my targets and let it go, then I'm going to be a happy man no matter what happens.' Then he just gave me the biggest smile and a high five. That night at the celebration party, the first thing I said after hugging him was: 'That was music to my ears when you said that to me this morning.
>
> Because if you had looked at me and said 'Doc, at 42 years old, if I don't win the Open today I might never win one,' I'd have felt I hadn't got my job done. While I didn't know he was going to win, I knew he was in the right place. And it obviously worked out.

Since my Open debut 45 years ago, the R&A have found themselves coping with vast changes in those anxious to attend their great event. And one of the most significant areas of growth has been in applications for accreditation from mind gurus, of whom Dr Rotella has emerged as the most respected.

In their endless search for an edge, players will have their mental adviser close by on the practice ground, thereby encouraging colleagues to follow suit. Though there were a few of them around in the early eighties, their impact had yet to become a key element of a player's challenge, especially in the top events.

It is more than 20 years since I first became aware of them, plying their wares to anyone interested. The key difference with Dr Rotella when he came on the scene was that he would work with a player only on being invited, generally through a friend.

But Jos Vanstiphout had no such inhibitions. He was the little Belgian who passed from us at the cruelly early age of 62 in December 2013. And he holds the distinction of having helped Ernie Els to victory in the 2002 Open Championship at Muirfield, without uttering a word.

Details of this fascinating story were disclosed to me back in 2003 when Jos and I chatted on a Tuesday morning during the one-hour train journey from downtown Chicago to Olympia Fields for the 2003 US Open.

This, we are told, is the championship of pressure, patience and pars, an event in which nerves are stretched to breaking point by the fiendish stratagems of the USGA Championship committee. As it happened, Jos was the first familiar face I saw at Van Buren Street station.

'I've no diploma,' the former pop singer reminded me with a ready smile. Yet his psychological skills couldn't be doubted after his success with Retief Goosen, who captured the US Open in a playoff at Southern Hills in 2001, and with South African compatriot Els in the Open a year later.

'I'm the garbage can into which the stressed player can deposit all his negative feelings', he went on.

Vanstiphout and Goosen parted company in November 2002, after the South African had retained the European Order of Merit title. But Els remained a client at the time of our meeting, along with Thomas Bjørn and Justin Rose.

The Belgian's wordless contribution occurred after the 72 holes at Muirfield had ended in a four-way tie between Els, Thomas Levet and the Australian pair, Stuart Appleby and Steve Elkington. From having the title in his grasp with a one-stroke lead on the 16th tee, Els proceeded to double-bogey the par-three from a seven-iron tee shot.

Vanstiphout recounted how he stood around the area of the first tee waiting for the playoff, which Pádraig Harrington, incidentally, missed by a stroke. That's when Els spied him. 'What the fuck do you want?' snapped the South African, clearly at odds with his world.

The Belgian said nothing, though he felt he had to do something. So he bought Els a sandwich. There still wasn't a word exchanged as Els proceeded to munch absent-mindedly. Gradually his mood changed and by the time the playoff was called, he had become a different person. The simple process of eating had transformed him into a winner.

After the four-man playoff had developed into sudden death between Levet and Els, the South African captured the title with a beautiful bunker recovery to four feet for a par-four at the 18th, the first extra hole.

Opening day

Though there was a fair sprinkling of fives and sixes on the treacherous opening hole, nobody managed to equal the wretched eight that Rory McIlroy carded there in 2019. The closest anyone came to that horrendous number was Rikuya Hoshino, who ran up a triple-bogey seven. And for him the potentially crushing pain was eased with the delivery of an eagle three at the long second.

One can imagine the pressure McIlroy endured as he stood on the opening tee in the company of Justin Thomas and Tommy Fleetwood. Discomfort was clearly in evidence when his driving iron was pulled into the left rough; not enough to be threatened by the out-of-bounds markers, but quite uncomfortable just the same.

And old ghosts seemed determined to haunt him as he proceeded to miss a three-foot par putt. Which may have explained why he tapped down a perceived spike mark, before looking back on three occasions at the scene of the miss, while walking away.

A further hook was in evidence off the tee at the long second, putting the green out of reach in two. But he proceeded to pitch to 12 feet and then sank the putt for a very timely birdie four.

Those opening holes set the pattern for McIlroy's worst-ever driving round at Portrush, where he hit only two out of 14 fairways. Yet with an opening 70, he was surprised afterwards to be only three strokes out of the lead. Which was quite an achievement. As he later observed: 'This place can be visually very intimidating off the tee.' Especially in gusting winds and intermittent rain.

Fans in their thousands followed their favourite in his six-hour trek around this iconic links, often braving decidedly mixed weather. And an indication of the testing nature of the challenge was the sight of Bryson DeChambeau making three desperate hacks in attempting to shift his ball from deep rough to the right of the testing fourth. McIlroy said:

> It was a tough enough day, especially either chopping out of the rough or out of the fairway bunkers most of the time. So to shoot under par was a good effort, though I'm surprised four-under is leading. I thought someone might have gone out there and shot six or seven under today. Only three back with 54 holes to go, I'm really happy with where I am.

Out on the course, there was evidence of what leading players have to put up with these days from smart lads in their galleries. Like Zach Johnson, winner of the 2015 Open but beaten American skipper from two years ago, being informed with heavy irony: 'Thank you for the Ryder Cup.' To which the response was an angry expletive. Still, these same lads had the good grace to commend the cooperation of most competitors, including the Americans, when they went seeking post-round photographs. Indeed, DeChambeau came in for special praise.

There were other, more appreciative young observers, who marvelled at the quality of the ball-striking they were witnessing. 'You can see why they're pros,' one of them remarked in awe.

By the halfway stage, McIlroy and Lowry were the only Irish survivors when the cut was made on 143 – one over par. And even when the world number one, Scheffler, was relentlessly dominating proceedings, there was no dampening the appeal of McIlroy to huge local galleries. In fact, since the enforced absence of Tiger Woods, I cannot remember a tournament at home or abroad with so much attention focused on an individual player.

The highly emotional nature of McIlroy's Masters triumph seemed to stir competitive hearts like few others in recent time. Even the game's supreme competitor, Jack Nicklaus, couldn't resist expressing his feelings. The Bear commented:

> I've never seen a tournament with so many good shots and so many bad shots and so many changes of this and that. I'm delighted for Rory. I know that he's had a lot of pressure on him. He's had the world on his shoulders. So it was wonderful to see him win.
>
> When he had to make a shot, he made it. You look at the shot at 15 [a remarkable, hooked second around trees], the shot at 17 [a magnificently judged approach]. Just remarkable shots.
>
> And then he turns right around and hits a shot like he hit at 13 [a duffed pitch into water] and I'm sitting there saying, 'What are you doing? This will take the world off his shoulders and I think you'll see a lot more great golf out of Rory McIlroy.'

There is little doubt but that McIlroy's very special appeal at Portrush had to do with his recently acquired status as the game's sixth winner of the Career Grand Slam where, after much torment, he had joined the elite group of Gene Sarazen, Ben Hogan, Jack Nicklaus, Gary Player and Tiger Woods to have secured this distinction. And it is widely acknowledged that Rotella played a key role in allowing him to become mentally capable of doing it.

When I discussed the process with the good doctor, he said:

> About a week before Augusta, Rory and I went over things we'd been talking about for a long time. We decided that when you're chasing dreams, you've got to be like steel. You can't let anything bother you or upset you. At Augusta, you've got to get lost in your own little world, knowing you're going to make mistakes.

On the Thursday, he played the front nine nicely and was in the process of playing a wonderful back nine. Then, decent shots on 15 and 17 both ended in double-bogeys. They weren't terrible shots but they still ended up as double-bogeys for a level-par round. That couldn't have been more crushing.

On Friday morning, our conversation centred essentially on the fact that most of the great stories in sporting history are great comeback stories. So you must set yourself up for a great comeback. You've got to be strong. You've got to be unflappable.

Rotella went on:

The front nine is always a hard nine and he played it great on Friday. I thought that's where he really got back into the tournament. Obviously on Sunday he played some wonderful shots. But the truth is that he's really good with recovery shots. Put him in the woods and he's a creative artist.

There really isn't a shot he can't hit, but to have the confidence to take them on on a Sunday at the Masters is pretty impressive.

There was a remark about what people say about him online, to which Rory responded: 'I've decided that what people say about me online is none of my business.' That was a great response, the measure of a Grand Slam winner.

The fairytale duel between McIlroy and Scheffler at Portrush never materialised. The standards set by the American were simply too forbidding. By the halfway stage, he had become the first world number one to lead the Open since Tiger Woods went on to win at Hoylake in 2006. And in his only significant stumble on the Sunday, he would become the only champion with a double-bogey on his card, just like Harrington did in his triumph at Carnoustie in 2007.

Still, in its sometimes cruel way, golf offered hope. DeChambeau scoffed at the notion of Scheffler being unbeatable. 'I beat him quite a lot when we were at college in Texas', he said. But he felt obliged to add with a grin: 'Perhaps I need to step up my game.' The truth is that until the last few years, Scheffler was perceived as vulnerable on the greens. That was when he went to work with English putting guru Phil Kenyon, and the evidence at Portrush of their splendid collaboration could be seen in Scheffler's dominance of the first three days.

Indeed by Saturday evening, the 153rd Open was as good as over. It seemed that the only reason to complete the 72 holes was as a gesture to the thousands of golf fans from all over Ireland and further afield who closed on Dunluce with undimmed enthusiasm in delightful weather.

McIlroy, meanwhile, contemplated his prospects with 18 holes to play, by which stage he was six strokes adrift of the American. Keenly aware of what his supporters wanted to hear, you couldn't help feeling that he was being suitably optimistic. 'I feel I have a better than half a chance', he said without any real conviction. Then, as if suddenly aware of the challenge he faced, he added: 'But I can't expect any favours. Scottie is the best player in the world.' Indeed he is.

As an American scribe remarked: 'For all the good things Scheffler does, what he may be best at is burying hope among his challengers.'

On Sunday at Portrush, they didn't have to wait long for the process to begin. With a beautifully judged iron to the first, he set up a tap-in birdie from little more than a foot. From then on, not even the serious sceptics among us could convince ourselves that an upset might just be possible.

Absolute confirmation of this came in his play of three holes approaching the middle of the closing round. That was when his lead was reduced from a maximum of seven to a minimum of four.

After a poor tee shot at the short sixth, he proceeded to sink a 16-foot putt to save par, the importance of which was emphasised by his surprisingly vigorous fist-pump. Then came a 15-footer for another par save on the seventh, before his first serious stumble of the Championship. This was an over-ambitious fairway bunker recovery on the eighth, where his ball remained in the sand: an ugly, double-bogey six.

Then, as they have done so often in similar circumstances, he and Ted Scott knew what was called for at the next. Almost predictably, a birdie on the ninth repaired some of the damage and he could face the homeward journey with precious peace restored.

In his moment of victory nine holes later, there was none of the histrionics we had come to expect from Woods in such circumstances. Instead, Scheffler tapped in his final shot from around a foot and then began to look around, bemused. It was only when Meredith and their son, Bennett, appeared on the scene that we knew what the champion had been looking for.

'This is amazing to win the Open Championship', he said, with the coveted claret jug by his side, 'but at the end of the day, having success in life, whether it be in golf, work, whatever it is, that's not what fulfils the deepest desires of your heart. It's just tough to describe when you haven't lived it.'

McIlroy, for his part, simply didn't have the necessary stuff to make a fight of it. With rounds of 70,69,66,69 for 274, he was tied seventh with Robert MacIntyre and Xander Schauffele, the defending champion. Admirably dignified after enduring one of the most emotional cauldrons imaginable, he acknowledged the superior skills of a highly competitive opponent. 'All you can do is admire what Scottie does and how he does it', he said.

> What he does is one thing but how he does it is another. He just goes about his business, doesn't do anything flamboyant, but he's the best at executing in the game right now. All you can do is tip your cap and watch in admiration.

4

Michael Moran

'Bobby Jones and Harry Vardon combined exquisiteness of art with utterly relentless precision in a way not given to other golfers.'

– Bernard Darwin, the father of modern golf-writing

Cast in bronze and sitting on a wooden base, it measures less than five inches in diameter. Yet for what it conveyed in terms of pain and loss from horrific events of more than 100 years ago, the so-called Widow's Penny evoked profound emotion.

Not surprisingly, it became the centrepiece of a remarkable evening, organised by Royal Dublin to mark the centenary of the death of a favoured son. Indeed, Michael Moran gained the unique distinction of being appointed professional on the site of his first home.

Through some admirable research by the club's 2017 captain, Peter Finnegan, who is sadly no longer with us, five relatives of Moran attended a special function organised by the club to receive framed photographs of their ancestor. Even more remarkable was that they were meeting each other for the first time.

Bernie O'Shaughnessy, whose father, John Dearl, was once the caddie master at Clontarf GC, brought along the cherished memento. Similar in design to an old penny coin, the plaque was also known chillingly as the 'Dead Man's Penny', because of the circumstances in which it was acquired.

Raised lettering on the right-hand side carried the name: Michael Moran. As with all of the other plaques, no rank was added so as not to distinguish between the sacrifices of the fallen. A total of 1.355 million of them were issued to the next of kin of British service personnel killed in World War I.

'I had never seen Molly Perry before, and my first thought was that she was a ringer for my aunt', said Mrs O'Shaughnessy. Of the relatives present, Mrs Perry was the closest to Moran, who was, in fact, her uncle.

The winner of five successive Irish Professional Championships was an acting lance corporal in the 7th Battalion Royal Irish Regiment, when he died of battle wounds in a German field hospital at Le Cateau, France on 10 April 1918.

'I'm now 84, living in Rathfarnham and the youngest and last survivor of seven children,' said Mrs Perry. Then came the stunning disclosure: 'My mother, Mary, was Michael's sister. There was just the two of them and I remember Mammy talking about a fire in Royal Dublin and everything to do with Uncle Mike was destroyed in it.'

This was the fire of 2 August 1943, when the old clubhouse was burnt to the ground along with the adjoining dwelling-house of the club professional. She went on:

> Mammy didn't even know about the Moran Cup. After she died, an insurance man was talking to me about golf and I told him I had an Uncle Mike who died years ago. With that, he tells me that the Cup was being played for out in Sutton.
>
> Up to that point, I had no idea my Uncle Mike was remembered, so it was a lovely surprise when my daughter, Linda, told me about Royal Dublin's celebration plans. Though I knew Mammy was reared there, last week was my first time ever at the club. Imagine

that, after 84 years! It was very emotional, thinking of my mother and how she never knew that Uncle Mike's name would live on.

In truth, few personal details were known about Moran until relatively recently. Reference was made to him, however, in Joe Kennedy's Dubliners Diary in the *Evening Press* in August 1983, to mark the return of the Irish Open to Royal Dublin where Seve Ballesteros triumphed.

Kennedy referred in a fascinating tailpiece to a photograph of Moran he had acquired through correspondence from Hugh Perry, Molly's late husband. The caption suggested it was a promotional photograph presumably linked to Moran's use of certain golf equipment.

Dated 1911, it claimed the player had unleashed a drive of '365 yards at Dollymount on May 3rd 1910.' It added: 'He won almost every important event in Ireland during the last two years and has used the Dunlop Junior the whole time.' Which made it quite a golf ball, given that this was only nine years after the introduction of the core-wound Haskell ball in 1901.

In the event, an email from Hugh Perry's daughter, Linda Byrne, to Royal Dublin opened crucial doors to complete Finnegan's research. 'My parents were always very interested in Michael Moran's career', she wrote. 'In 2015, just before my father passed away, they made the trip to visit Michael's grave [in France]. As you can imagine, this was a very emotional experience for them both.'

Her correspondence became a crucial link in bringing together the Moran relatives on the night, comprising herself and Molly Perry, along with Bernie O'Shaughnessy, Ann Hickey and Thomas Curley; the Curleys were the maternal side of the original Moran family. As Bernie explained:

> My mother's father was Patrick Curley. I live in Kilmore near Beaumont Hospital and I always knew about Mike Moran from my mother Margaret [Curley] talking about him. She would say that the Curleys were like the Walton family on TV, the way they took everybody in.

I thought the Royal Dublin occasion was absolutely brilliant and I was really touched by the work that went into it. I found newspaper cuttings about Michael Moran in a box my mother had and I was only too delighted to loan them to Peter Finnegan. His club deserve great credit for what they did.

On leave from the fighting, Michael Moran made his last visit home in August 1917. That's when he played a famous exhibition match in aid of the Red Cross over the original par-35 nine holes of Clontarf GC in the grounds of what is now Mount Temple School.

Attired in full army uniform, even down to his spurs and 'ammunition' boots, he used borrowed clubs to card a remarkable three-under-par 32. None of the enthralled observers could have imagined that eight months later he would be dead.

Wild winds swept the Dollymount links on 27 April 2018, when Clontarf professional Eamonn Brady – twice a winner of the West of Ireland Amateur Championship, who has since moved abroad – won the Moran Cup with an outstanding score of 66, as the high point of the centenary celebrations. On beloved terrain, one could imagine a distinguished ghost from the past, nodding in admiration.

By that stage, Moran had already been honoured at Seaham Harbour GC in the northeast of England. Local dignitaries were involved in a special ceremony to mark the centenary of their one-time professional, who moved to Wearside before the outbreak of World War I.

It was hoped that a ceremony would be held outdoors and accompanied by a golf competition in aid of the British Legion. Wretched weather, however, meant limiting the activities to indoors where the mayor of Seaham, Sonia Forster, officiated at the unveiling of a memorial photograph of the five-time Irish Professional champion, accompanied by copies of his two service medals.

Moran was a relatively short time at Seaham when he answered the call to arms. Three years later, at 31 years of age, he died of battle wounds on 10 April 1918.

Grant Dixon, the captain of Seaham Harbour, accepted an invitation to compete in what became the first such event to be staged on the Dollymount links in more than 30 years.

Relatives of the honouree were in attendance, as were officials of the British PGA and the PGA Irish Region, along with representatives of the Dundalk and Galway clubs with which Michael Moran was also associated. As has been well documented, he was involved with Royal Dublin as a messenger, assistant professional and ultimately clubmaker and resident professional. All of which prompted the club to name their 14th hole 'Moran's' in his honour.

Meanwhile, the Seaham connection sparked the interest of club member Paul Murray, who retired in 2016 as a British army captain. 'I'm delighted our club decided to honour him', he said of their celebrations.

> We had a nice, intimate gathering. I gave an introduction about the German spring offensive of 1918, which became known as the Kaiser's Last Stand, then our captain took over. Grant spoke for about 10 minutes, detailing the skill of a player who finished third in the Open Championship at Royal Liverpool in 1913.
>
> Other information was sourced from the Irish Golf Archive and from Phil Weaver of the PGA. Then we had a bugler who sounded 'The Last Post'. Grant was delighted with the Royal Dublin invitation and as a one-handicapper, looked forward to playing a links with its international reputation. From an historical standpoint, there's also the fact that his age on this occasion happens to be the same age as Moran was when he died.

During Moran's time at Seaham, a particularly notable event was the official opening of the clubhouse in 1914. To mark the occasion, he played an exhibition match with George Duncan, the reigning French Open champion who went on to win the 1920 Open Championship and the inaugural Irish Open at Portmarnock in 1927. Also involved was Douglas Edgar from Northumberland GC in Newcastle-upon-Tyne, who won the French Open that year before going on to win the Canadian Open in 1920.

Later in 2018, Seaham instituted an annual 18-hole medal competition, to be known as the Moran Trophy. The name was chosen so as not to clash with the Moran Cup, which has current Royal Dublin professional John Dwyer on its roll of honour, along with Leonard Owens, Neil O'Briain and Niall Kearney, who are also familiar figures down Dollymount way.

Moran's is a truly wonderful story of a time largely forgotten in Irish golf, though it was well documented elsewhere in these islands. Under the expansive heading 'Recollections of the Game in Ireland', the *Aberdeen Journal* of 20 September 1924 made mention of some notable players from the early decades of the twentieth century. Given that the piece was written by none other than the great Harry Vardon, there was obvious appeal in his observations on Michael Moran.

The fact is that Vardon was quite familiar with Moran's golfing skills, not least for having been tied third with the Dubliner behind J.H. Taylor for the Open Championship at Hoylake in 1913. Noting that Moran had been killed in World War I, Vardon described him as having 'no equal in Ireland, so far as my experience goes.' And in claiming that 'Moran was capable of winning anything in any company', the great man went on to suggest that he would very likely have emerged victorious at Hoylake, 'but for a single, bad hole.'

This was the infamous opening hole of his third round where Moran took a disastrous 10, mainly, as Vardon put it, 'owing to his ball being more or less unplayable in the grip that runs along the right-hand side of the fairway.' Another legendary commentator of that period, Bernard Darwin, described the Dubliner as 'one of the most sparkling of our younger players'.

So, who was this remarkable Irishman about whom very little is known, other than the fact that he is commemorated by the Moran Cup professional tournament and by the term 'Dyke', as representing a birdie two in golf? We know little about his early life other than his birthplace being a very small, one-roomed cottage with a tin roof. It was located in an area now lying between the 3rd and the 13th holes on the Royal Dublin links, which didn't exist when Moran first saw the light in 1886.

When golf eventually came to the island, Moran took a predictable route into caddie ranks and progressed with such proficiency as to be appointed professional at Dundalk GC as a 20-year-old in 1906. It has been speculated that the sobriquet of 'Dyke' was prompted by his diminutive figure bounding over the various streams or dykes on his way each morning to the clubhouse. By June of the following year, he was an assistant at Royal Dublin, prompting a correspondent with *Golf Illustrated* to predict: 'I am convinced that Moran is one of the most consistently brilliant players I have seen on the Royal Dublin course.' A significant breakthrough came a further year on when he succeeded Tom Hood as the club professional, making him master of all he surveyed in his native place.

Meanwhile, the Irish Professional Championship was launched in 1907 at Royal Portrush as a match play event won by James Edmundson, who retained the title the following year. And when Moran swept to victory in match play in 1909 at Royal County Down, he proceeded to achieve total dominance when it changed to stroke play the following year. In fact, his run of five successive titles from 1909 to 1913 has never been equalled, not even when 10-time winners Harry Bradshaw and Christy O'Connor Snr were in their pomp.

Not noted as a student of the golf swing, Moran still managed to develop a very effective method. According to the *Connacht Tribune*:

> He drives almost like a catapult. There is no pause. He draws back with swift deliberation, and seems to follow through with lightning-like rapidity. He preserves a perfect balance on his finish, and the head is only half lifted, as if he were still watching the place where the ball had been.

He was at the peak of his powers on the fateful afternoon of Monday, 23 June 1913 on the Royal Liverpool links at Hoylake. With a superb homeward 33 in the second round of the Open Championship, he had become an improbable hero, notwithstanding his Irish Professional Championship triumphs. It brought him to halfway on 150, placed third, only three strokes behind the holder, Ted Ray, and two adrift of the incomparable J.H. Taylor.

According to the *Irish Times*, the slightly built twenty-seven-year-old drove the ball 'with great power' and his only slip while recording the lowest nine holes of the championship was to three-putt the short 11th, more commonly known as the Alps. Almost incredibly, Moran was a serious challenger at the summit of the game, when he stood on the first tee for the third round the following morning. After a fitful night, however, it took only a few minutes to shatter his dream.

In high winds and driving rain, he knocked his second shot at the opening hole out of bounds and later took four from a pot bunker to run up that wretched 10 [and an outward 48] which would remain etched in Vardon's memory.

The dogleg right configuration of the par-four first made it a forbidding start to a round. On the left was the clubhouse and putting green. On the right, for the full length of the hole, was the sinister 'cop', a bank no more than three feet high which enclosed the practice ground.

Though a good drive could be expected to finish past the corner of the dogleg, a lengthy second shot remained. And to further heighten the pressure, there was the awareness that a shot aimed directly at the target was probably going to finish out of bounds if pushed or cut, given that the green was located hard against the cop. As the renowned British scribe Pat Ward-Thomas famously noted: 'Many a player has been out of bounds with his drive and approach; many have run out of hope or ammunition before completing the hole.'

The (London) *Times* the following morning was cruelly critical of the manner in which the Irishman handled the crisis. 'Moran very quickly fulfilled my prophesy as to his Celtic temperament,' their man reported. '... If he had played with discretion [from the bunker], he could still have holed out in seven, but in his impetuosity he went for the green and this sealed his fate. Four times he lashed at the ball before getting it out.'

Still, the writer – though there was no byline on the piece, we imagine it must have been the iconic Darwin – went on to acknowledge:

> Moran's performance in going round in 74 strokes [in the fourth round] after his most ruinous start of the morning was really a splendid one. At present, he seems fated to have one bad round and 'till he is a little more the master of himself, he probably always will. If he could school himself to take things rather more quietly, he might easily win, for he has grand golf in him.

The *Irish Times* reported: 'After a good five at the second, Moran found the bunker guarding the third green off his cleek and, although he got well out, he took three putts and a seven was recorded. Battling against the storm, the little Irishman now played brilliantly. At the short fourth he got a three, while at the next a good five was the outcome.' Thoroughly soaked by the hostile weather and with the clubs frequently slipping in his hands, Moran battled on and eventually carded an inward 41 for a thoroughly dispiriting 89, compared with an 81 from Ray and a remarkable 77 from Taylor.

As it happened, his closing 74, which included a birdie two at the 11th, gave him an aggregate of 313 for a share of third place with Vardon. Meanwhile, with closing rounds of 77 and 74 for an aggregate of 304, Taylor regained the title which he had won at Sandwich in 1894, at St Andrews in 1895 and at Royal Cinque Ports in 1909. His reward was the famous Claret Jug, a gold medal and £50. Ray, the runner-up on 312, received £25, while Moran and Vardon each received £12.10s. This was to be the first prize money to be won by an Irishman in the Open Championship.

Incidentally, the US Open Championship, immortalised in Mark Frost's *The Greatest Game Ever Played*, in which local amateur Francis Ouimet beat Ray and Vardon in a playoff for the title, took place at Brookline, Massachusetts, on 18–20 September of that year. And an Irishman had a fairly prominent role there, too. Pat Doyle, who was Delgany's first club professional before emigrating to the US, was tenth, for a reward of $30.

Early in 1914, in recognition, one imagines, of his Hoylake endeavours, Moran was appointed professional at Seaham Harbour, where their fine course was designed by Alister Mackenzie, no less. In the event, little more than a year later Moran joined thousands of his fellow countrymen in enlisting in September 1915 in the South of Irish Horse Regiment of the British army and was posted to France, where he transferred to the Royal Irish Regiment.

As it happened, he had the rank of acting lance corporal in the 7th Battalion of the regiment when he died. The Battle of the Lys, 9–29 April 1918, was part of the major spring offensive by the German army on the Western Front. And he is presumed to have been in the frontline of that battle, given that his death was recorded not long after the start of the offensive. He wasn't yet 32, with his golfing prime still ahead of him.

He was buried by the enemy at Le Cateau Military Cemetery, grave IB 32, but the circumstances meant that news of his death didn't reach these parts until December 1918.

Le Cateau, an important hospital centre, was in an area controlled by the Germans until October 1918, which meant that Moran was effectively a prisoner of war when he died on 10 April 1918. On learning of his passing, Darwin wrote in *American Golfer* magazine: 'He was by all odds the greatest golfer in Ireland, and was looked upon as liable at any time to break in upon that wonderful combination of Vardon, Braid and Taylor in the British game.'

In his autobiography, *Golf: My Life's Work*, published in 1943, Taylor wrote: 'Mike Moran, a small, wiry type of Irishman, was a fine player and like most of his race a rare tryer [sic] and typically enthusiastic'. Noting that the Irish challenger had been well-placed going into the third-round gale at Hoylake, Taylor wrote:

> I stopped to watch Moran drive off and play around the corner. Mike was a lightweight, and it is but the exact truth to state that he found it almost impossible to stand up to the ball and swing the club. I saw him play five shots before rounding the bend and a few

> minutes later word came that he had taken 10 for the hole and his chance virtually gone.
>
> I was sorry for Mike then, but was sorrier still when we heard some eighteen months later that he had been killed in the war when fighting as a trooper in the Irish Horse. Mike had shot an 89 in the third round and left himself 14 strokes off the lead. It was to his credit that his final round was the best of the day and reduced the deficit by five strokes tying with Vardon in third place.

Interestingly, he confessed to Taylor that he had no real knowledge of the mechanics of the golf swing. With admirable humility, Moran admitted: 'I do not know how I play the strokes. All I know is that the ball is there and that I hit it.' So his motto for golf was, 'Here's a ball, let's hit it.'

A measure of the esteem in which he was held in the game here was that within four years of his passing, a competition was instituted in his memory. Destined to become one of the major events on the Irish professional calendar, the Moran Cup was won on a record 12 occasions by Harry Bradshaw, between 1940 and 1960. It represented worthy recognition of the first Irish professional to have had his talents acknowledged beyond these shores.

In the course of his *Aberdeen Journal* piece, the great Vardon described Moran as having 'no equal in Ireland, so far as my experience goes.'

And in claiming that 'Moran was capable of winning anything in any company', the great man went on to suggest that he would very likely have emerged victorious at Hoylake, 'but for a single, bad hole.'

According to the legendary Darwin, the Dubliner was 'one of the most sparkling of our younger players.' As for myself, I first became aware of him in a meaningful sense while working on the history of Royal Dublin in the build-up to their centenary in 1985. That was when I gained considerable enlightenment from Colonel Bill Gibson, this country's foremost golf historian.

It emerged only recently, however, that an interest in soldiering also began to dominate his thoughts as early as June 1904, when he enlisted in the 3rd Militia Battalion of the Royal Dublin Fusiliers. His employment was given as 'messenger' to his then 'master', a Mr Hood of Clontarf, who was Tom Hood, Royal Dublin's resident professional.

We're told that Moran graduated to clubmaker by December 1905, when he signed for 'short service' with the 6th Dragoons Cavalry of the Line, which was essentially part-time soldiering, more familiar to later generations here as the FCA.

Meanwhile, his golf progressed with such proficiency as to merit an appointment as professional at Dundalk GC in 1906, when he was only 20. By June of the following year, he was back at Royal Dublin as an assistant professional. In 1908, he joined Galway GC as professional and was still attached there a year later when he played what was described as 'an interesting money match' at Royal Dublin against Bangor's Edmundson, the reigning Irish Professional champion.

Soon afterwards, Moran would usurp Edmundson's crown, leading to a record run of five successive Irish Professional titles up to 1913. As we indicated earlier, it is a dominance that has never been equalled. And during that run, he became professional at Royal Dublin, succeeding Hood, who moved to the newly formed Clontarf club in 1912.

His subsequent standing in golf beyond these shores was reflected in a piece in the *Dundee Courier* of 31 December 1915, which informed its readers: 'Moran received several offers of professional appointments in America, but he has preferred to don the khaki.'

For their part, Royal Dublin decided that for the first time since three stagings of the Irish Open there during the 1980s, the celebratory Moran Cup would be part of a pro-am event. Each team consisted of four players, one PGA professional and three amateurs. There was a morning shotgun start at 9:00 and afternoon shotgun start at 2:30 and the entry fee was €400 per team for the morning to include lunch and €500 per team in the afternoon to include dinner.

The event was viewed as an opportunity for the club to celebrate the memory of Ireland's first truly great professional golfer. Dixon, the

Seaham captain, duly honoured his invitation and as a one-handicapper, thoroughly enjoyed the challenge of Moran's home place.

So it was that with hands stretched from Dublin port to Wearside, the Royal Dublin and Seaham Harbour golf clubs proudly saluted the memory of a gifted sportsman whose heroic achievements, on and off the golf course, continue to warm our hearts.

5

When Irish amateurs made their mark

'Had you ever thought of playing the Tour? You could give everyone lessons on starving to death.'

– Atlanta golf writer Furman Bisher on what professionals really think when they make encouraging remarks to amateurs

• • • •

When the invitation came to compete in the 1938 Walker Cup trial at St Andrews, James Bruen Snr knew there was something he had to do. Permission would be required for time off school for his 17-year-old son.

On being approached by the dutiful parent, however, Brother Pius, the principal of Presentation College Cork, was not impressed, declaring that he had never heard such nonsense. Still, the persuasive powers of a formidable father won the day and Jimmy Bruen duly took his place at the Home of Golf.

Revelling in the challenge, he completed a remarkable total of 282 for four rounds on the Old Course by Saturday, 7 May, the eve of his 18th birthday. His place in the British and Irish team was assured from the opening round where his 68 equalled Bobby Jones's amateur course record, much to the delight of Henry Cotton, who was awestruck by the youngster's stunning skills.

The once sceptical Brother Pius was equally impressed, to the extent that he promptly declared a school holiday in celebration of their pupil's achievement.

Bruen was born on 8 May 1920. And he was five days short of his 52nd birthday when he died far too early, on 3 May 1972. Sadly, there was no formal marking of the centenary of his birth, due to Covid restrictions. 'Cork Golf Club was closed and we couldn't even have a family gathering,' said David, the second youngest of Bruen's six children, three boys and three girls.

Their remarkable mother, Nell, a former president of the Irish Ladies' Golf Union (now part of Golf Ireland) and the Ladies' Golf Union (since absorbed into the Royal and Ancient), was effectively isolated in a nursing home, two months prior to her 102nd birthday. Her one-time residence, appropriately named Birkdale after the venue of Bruen's British Boys and British Amateur triumphs, is now the home of another son, Michael.

Back in 1972, Bruen had joined his son David for one of their regular weekend golf games together when suddenly he felt a sharp pain in his chest. 'He went immediately to hospital, but they couldn't find a problem', David recalled.

> He then had a heart attack on a Wednesday and by the following Saturday, the hospital prognosis was that he would be paralysed. As a family, we prayed that he would be taken peacefully, because the prospect of being incapacitated would have been more than he could have borne.
>
> The following Wednesday, the phone rang and instinctively we knew what it meant. It was obviously a dreadful blow to have him taken from us at such an early age, but he lives on through the pages of a wonderful scrapbook my mother put together of

his career. She looked after it like a baby and with its collection of newspaper cuttings, scorecards, telegrams and other memorabilia it's a wonderful tribute to Dad. My mother gave it to me and I've willed it on to my son, James.

In the scrapbook, there is a scorecard from the Old Course of St Andrews dated 30 June 1939. It is believed to have been a practice round prior to the Open Championship. Duly signed, the figures read: Out – 434,454,434 – 35. In – 333,345,343 – 31. Total 66. With the added handicap of +4, it made for a net score of 70, which was a splendid round of golf, especially for one so young.

Among the gifts that Joe Carr received on his 80th birthday was a wonderful old film which had been shot by Skerries member Gerry Owens, a former Irish amateur international and one-time president of the Golfing Union of Ireland (now part of Golf Ireland). Among the featured players was Bruen, who was watched with particular interest by the birthday celebrant, who remarked: 'I always thought the loop was more pronounced than that.'

The essential difference between these two great Irish amateurs was highlighted, ironically, not by an Irish observer but by Sam McKinlay in the *Glasgow Herald*. He wrote:

> His [Bruen's] record is not as good as that of his great fellow countryman, Joe Carr, partly because he did not have Carr's tremendous competitive compulsion. But when Bruen's imagination was alight and when the 'loop' was working and when he was not breaking steel shafts like matchsticks, he was the most thrilling, accomplished golfer in the world.

Carr did not argue with those sentiments. He explained:

> I have no hesitation is acknowledging Jimmy as the best Irish amateur I ever saw. No doubt about that. I played him three times but I thank God it wasn't in his heyday. I was lucky enough to beat

him in the semi-finals of the Irish Close at Killarney in 1963. And I beat him in a match between Leinster and Munster at Little Island and later when Sutton played Cork GC down there.

Though Jimmy could knock it around there in 61 and 62, I never liked Little Island and on the first occasion we met there, I was at the top of the tree and he was some way past his best. For the interprovincial friendly, the crowds came from everywhere and I remember getting it around in about 76 to beat him on the last green.

But when I was a youngster at Portmarnock, in the years just before World War II, I played a lot with Jimmy. He had started in the insurance business in Dublin and used to keep his game in shape at Portmarnock, where he was accorded the facilities of the course. He would give myself and Billy McMullan four up and beat our better ball – for money.

Of course, he was already a Walker Cup player by then and was way ahead of us and certainly a long way ahead of me. He was long, considerably longer in the air than I was. He played a lot at Portmarnock at that time, and he drove the second and fifth greens and was through the back of the third with another huge drive. Still, I could chase a ball which would run further than Jimmy's best.

People talk about John Burke but he didn't have the shot-making talent of Jimmy who, from 1938 until about 1942, was among the six best players in the world, amateur or professional, in my view. Remember, had the 1939 Open at St Andrews been played over six rounds, he would have gone close to winning it. There was nobody in this country in the same class as him at that stage, myself included.

Carr's views were roundly endorsed by Henry Longhurst, who had the good fortune to witness Bruen at the peak of his formidable powers. In the wake of the 1939 British Amateur in which Bruen lost in the quarterfinals to the eventual winner, Alex Kyle, Longhurst wrote:

> With all due respect to the winner, I have to confess that I shared the general opinion that Bruen stood head and shoulders above them all, British and American ...
>
> For myself, I should rate Bruen in the highest professional class and shall not be in the least surprised if he wins the Open.

Seven years later, the same scribe suggested that the destination of the Amateur was decided on Royal Birkdale's long 15th. Longhurst explained:

> With two shots delivered against the wind and on rain-sodden ground, Bruen carried 520 yards. I should not have believed it if I had not seen it ... and the resultant four made him dormie.
>
> [Bob] Sweeney [his American opponent], who has played with Jimmy Thompson, Sam Snead and all the long hitters in the United States, declared that none of them could have come anywhere near equalling those prodigious strokes. The right man won and hats off to the loser.

Among Bruen's course records were: Portmarnock 70; Royal County Down 66; Muskerry 63; Royal Portrush 71; Baltray 71; Little Island 67; Macroom 67; St Andrews Old 68; St Andrews New 69. While the Bruen loop was a unique contribution to golfing technique, his maturity of mind during his teenage years was truly remarkable, in terms of an unerring instinct to play the right shot.

At his peak between 17 and 19 years, he scaled the heights at a younger age than anyone before him in golfing history, certainly in these islands. Small wonder that those in Cork who remember him as a schoolboy remain convinced that Bruen's impact on the game will never be equalled.

Our focus here is on the 1939 Open, which receives detailed treatment from the late George Crosbie in his wonderfully informative book *The Bruen Loop*.

Referring to the practice round of 66 over the Old Course, Crosbie observed: 'For the next four days, the young Irish boy was to hit the headlines in most newspapers in these islands and probably further afield. The *Irish Press*, for instance, carried the headline "Jimmy Bruen, 69, burns up St Andrews".'

Along with Percy Alliss and the American Lawson Little, he was joint leader after the first qualifying round of the Open with a course-record equalling 69. He had another run of threes around the turn, on the eighth, ninth, 10th and 11th and again finished with a birdie on the 18th.

On the following day, he carded another 69, this time a course record on the New Course. All the while, it seemed that newspaper couldn't get enough of the young Irishman and his family. For instance, the *Scottish Daily Record* reported:

> More shy of publicity than any Garbo of Hollywood is Mrs James Bruen of Cork. Each day at St Andrews, Mrs Bruen has followed her son around the course and then goes back to her hotel overlooking the links where she can watch the other players finish, without getting caught up in the crowd. Her son, on the other hand, walks around the course after his game, chatting with the other players and occasionally going along to try out some new clubs in the large marquee near the course.
>
> Mrs Bruen has her own ideas about publicity and although she takes a keen interest in her son's game, she sometimes wishes he had been just a little older before getting into the limelight of championship golf.

In the event, Bruen led the qualifiers on 138, four strokes clear of his great admirer and mentor, Henry Cotton, who was one of three players on 142. Someway back on 147 in the order was Bobby Locke, a future four-time winner of the title.

Sadly, the magic didn't last and rounds of 72,75,75 and 76 in the championship proper gave Bruen a six-round aggregate of 436, which, as things turned out, was eight strokes lower than the winner, Lancashire's

Dick Burton (444). In fact, Bruen was beaten over six rounds by only one player, America's Johnny Bulla, who returned an aggregate of 435.

For a limited field of 129, the competition was intense, as reflected in a halfway cut of 148 on which only 33 players survived.

Effectively, greater consistency allowed Bulla to finish second overall, while Bruen was tied 13th, with Cotton among others, and he beat the reigning Amateur champion, Alex Kyle, by three strokes in pursuit of the leading amateur's medal.

~

In March 2007, from his home in Florida, Eoghan O'Connell let it be known that as a reinstated amateur, he planned to compete in the Irish Amateur Open Stroke Play Championship at Royal Dublin two months later. And if wild dreams happened to materialise, there was an outside chance he could be involved in the Walker Cup at Royal County Down on 8 and 9 September of that year.

Any doubts about the merit of O'Connell's challenge were removed by a handicap of plus 3.7 and recent amateur tournament victories in the US. In fact, were he American, he would probably have been an automatic choice on their Walker Cup panel for the matches at Royal County Down. This, after all, was the same O'Connell who had stunned the golfing world in 1987 with two rounds of 65 at North Berwick in final qualifying for the 116th Open Championship at Muirfield.

Those rounds were executed on the Sunday and Monday of Open week. And I remember marvelling at Sunday's effort which beat the amateur record for the course by one stroke and was matched by only one professional, the experienced Scotsman Bill Longmuir. As it happened, the Irish challengers included Philip Walton whose one-under-par 69 was quite acceptable among the professionals.

As a 19-year-old with the ball apparently on a string, O'Connell's performance on the second day was truly staggering. On a lively stretch measuring 6,258 yards, another sparkling 65 revived memories of 1981 when Walton, also as an amateur, beat the course record with a 65 at North Foreland in qualifying for the Open at Royal St George's.

It seemed inconceivable that O'Connell could match his effort of Sunday, but he proceeded to card a total of 15 birdies over the two days. And perhaps the most admirable aspect of his play was the thoughtful manner in which he handled the considerable eccentricities of the 150-year-old North Berwick links.

For instance, he took a five-iron off the tee at the first and employed a driver, three-wood or one-iron for tee shots at various other holes, where appropriate. In the process, with six birdies in seven holes, he reached the turn in 29 – six under par – having taken a total of only 12 putts.

'I concentrated on making birdies on the way out and then relaxed a little on the homeward journey,' he said with remarkable maturity for a player of his years. In the event, his 10-under-par aggregate of 130 for the 36 holes left him four strokes clear of his closest challengers, who happened to be three professionals, including Longmuir, on 134.

Almost predictably, the magic deserted O'Connell in the championship proper. With two rounds of 77 at Muirfield for a total of 154, he was 10 strokes outside the halfway cut. But he still had reason to be proud of a wonderful adventure which has yet to be matched by an Irish amateur.

It would be 18 years before O'Connell was ready to make a competitive return to the Irish amateur scene. He was joined at Royal Dublin by a group of elite Americans, including Buddy Marucci, who would captain his country to Walker Cup success at Royal County Down.

'I don't know what the necessary qualifications are, but I wouldn't play for the US,' said the proud Corkman. But what about the British and Irish side? He laughed at the idea of a Walker Cup comeback after playing a key role in the trailblazing team of 1989 at Peachtree, Atlanta, where he was a member of the first Great Britan and Ireland team to triumph on US soil.

'I'm not saying I'd be good enough and I wouldn't expect to be in the panel', he replied. 'But if I happened to win at Royal Dublin, I would give serious thought to playing in other qualifying tournaments this summer.'

As an emerging player in the late 1980s, O'Connell seemed to have everything. Irish Boys champion in 1984, he went on to gain a crucial win over Peter McEvoy when Ireland beat England to capture the European Amateur Team Championship in Austria, three years later.

A year after Muirfield, he was in the victorious British and Irish Eisenhower Trophy team in Sweden. Then a year further on, he was runner-up in the highly regarded North and South Championship at Pinehurst, before gaining a memorable halved singles at Peachtree against a gifted left-hander by the name of Phil Mickelson.

Apart from obvious ball-striking skill and keen, competitive instincts, an astute golfing brain seemed to mark O'Connell for stardom. His subsequent struggle as a professional, however, was attributed by leading coach David Leadbetter to a swing flaw which put excessive pressure on his left wrist.

Eventually, he quit the European Tour in 1996, went to Florida with his American-born wife, and has settled there. Having regained amateur status, he had successful surgery on the sinews and tendons of the left wrist in 2002 and resumed his golfing career with renewed enthusiasm. And strong as the appeal of the Celtic Tiger may have been for other emigrants, it couldn't prise him away from shirtsleeve swinging in Florida's sunshine.

His prominence on the US amateur scene was based on victories in the 54-hole Coleman Cup stroke play event at Seminole in 2005 and 2006. Indeed, from six strokes back in 2006, O'Connell shot a closing 68 to beat US Walker Cup player Trip Kuehne, who was also runner-up in 2005. He also won the Travis at Garden City GC, Long Island and the Palm Beach County Amateur, apart from fourball wins in the Florida Senior/Mid-Amateur and the Floyd Cup. He explained:

> Apart from Seminole, I've played in the Crump Cup at Pine Valley for the last three years and it's a real treat to play these great old courses. Terrific fun. In fact, I put those wins down to the actual

> joy of competing. I didn't win that often when I was young, because I was trying too hard. It's funny how it works out.
>
> I played particularly well in the summer of 2006, back to how I was at my best, between the ages of 19 and 24, when I felt bullet-proof and was thinking of all the Majors I'd win. But the pro tour was always a bit of a struggle because I didn't drive it very well. I didn't hit enough fairways and greens. And there's a huge difference between the amateur and pro games.

By way of illustration, O'Connell recalled a visit to Seminole in 2004, when he played with Darren Clarke and Adam Scott during the weekend of the club championship. Conditions were extremely difficult, with strong Atlantic winds sweeping across notoriously firm and fiery greens. He said:

> The low round in the club tournament that day was 77, but Darren shot 65 and Adam 67. And they made it look so easy that I was quite happy to come home to my day job.
>
> Technology has helped me a lot. I have a Taylor Made railer [three wood] which I've had since 1989 and I can now hit it 20 to 30 yards further in the air. And I know I don't have increased clubhead speed, so it's got to be the golf ball. There has been a marked advance in golf technology over the last five or six years.

Using graphite shafts to reduce the shock to his wrist, O'Connell's later success was not surprising, for though he won remarkably few titles as an amateur, he never lacked the ability to compete. For instance, he once retained his European Tour card by shooting a 67 in the BMW International in Germany and in another end-of-season scramble for survival, he produced three top-10 finishes.

But the suspect wrist made tournament golf an ongoing struggle and failure to regain his card at the 1995 European Tour school resulted in a move to the States, where he also failed in the US Tour School of 1996. He had run out of options.

I later met him in Florida in November 2002, when Des Smyth led the Qualifying School for what has since become the US Champions Tour in which he looked after Smyth's interests. He also established his own travel business, Global Golf Links. From a career perspective, however, the big breakthrough came in 2004 when he got together with some investors and bought The Fox Club.

'As a player, there are a lot of things I'd like to do in golf, but it's not the be-all and end-all anymore', he said. 'If I don't play well, it doesn't bother me too much, which is just as well, given the distances the young guys are hitting the ball these days.'

As things turned out, such thinking stood to him at Royal Dublin, which marked a return to an Irish championship for the first time since 1989 when he finished fourth behind Clarke in the East of Ireland at Baltray.

The switch to links terrain clearly became a struggle. Rounds of 80 and 76 pushed O'Connell somewhat wide of the cut of 152 in an event won by Scotland's Lloyd Saltman on an aggregate of 291 (72,77,66,76). Rory McIlroy, who would go on to be a key competitor in the Walker Cup, was tied fourth and Shane Lowry finished in a share of 12th place, despite the disappointment of an opening 79.

For O'Connell, there would never be a performance to compare with 1987 at North Berwick. But happily, memories of those great deeds still linger.

~

Among the talents that Jimmy Bruen and Joe Carr had in common was a firm belief that they could compete with the game's top professionals. Whether they actually felt they could win in such company was another issue, but it is clear that they didn't feel overawed by such rivalry, whatever the circumstances.

This was certainly true of the Centenary Open at St Andrews in 1960, which marked 100 years since the great event was launched. It was the best opportunity Carr would have of becoming an amateur winner of the title.

Two years after capturing the second of his three British Amateurs on the Old Course, he had carded 72 and 73 going into the final 36 holes on the Friday.

This was the standard arrangement for professional tournaments at the time, so scheduled as to ensure that competing professionals could return to their clubs to take care of their members' needs over the weekend. As it happened, Carr broke the amateur record for the Old Course with a third-round 67, which left him five strokes behind the surprise leader, Kel Nagle of Australia.

Then came a marvellous start of 3,3,3 – birdie, birdie, birdie – to the final round, leaving him tied for the lead with 15 holes to play. As luck would have it, however, the round was abandoned because of a torrential rainstorm and, by the Saturday, the Sutton man had lost the momentum. Beginning 4,5,5, Carr carded a closing 73 and eventually finished eighth behind Nagle.

Even more disappointing was being beaten for the amateur medal which went to Guy Wolstenholme, who closed with a splendid 68 for an aggregate of 283, two strokes ahead of Carr. Interestingly, the amateur duo was split by the defending champion, Gary Player.

It is also notable that Christy O'Connor Snr, who had started with a wretched 80, also scored 67 in the second round, as did Nagle and Roberto de Vicenzo, and the professional target was further lowered by Bernard Hunt with a 66 in the final round.

~

Fifty-five years later, similar weather returned to the Old Course when south-westerly gales swept St Andrews from early Saturday causing significant re-scheduling of the 144th Open Championship. It meant that the fourth round wouldn't be played until the Monday, in a repeat of the weather-affected 1988 staging, when Seve Ballesteros won at Royal Lytham on a Monday.

Of the five Irish challengers, Paul Dunne (-6), Pádraig Harrington (-3), Graeme McDowell (par) and Shane Lowry, who missed the cut on one-over, were left to kick their heels on the Saturday, having completed their second rounds on Friday. But after Darren Clarke was two-over for his remaining three holes when completing the second round on Saturday evening, he, too, departed the scene with Lowry.

An attempt to complete the second round at 7:00 on the Saturday morning, before the players were called in only 32 minutes later, met with an angry response from Jordan Spieth, who would win the Open at Royal Birkdale two years later. And with the benefit of hindsight, R&A chief executive Peter Dawson conceded: 'It would have been better if play hadn't started, but the decision was taken on the evidence at the time.'

Though Spieth secured pars during that period, Dustin Johnson, the championship leader, made a mess of chipping and putting the long 14th for a bogey six. He repaired the damage, however, with a two-putt birdie on the last in a round of 69, after play had resumed at 6:00 on Saturday evening.

As one of the late finishers nearing 10:00 on the Friday evening, Tom Watson bade farewell to the Auld Grey Toon. 'I've taken a lot of time playing golf at Ballybunion and other links courses, prior to the Open Championship,' he reflected. 'All those memories ....'

Much attention also focused on Paul Dunne, whose exploits could hardly have been more appropriate at a venue much loved by the game's greatest amateur, Bobby Jones. And if the 22-year-old from Greystones could maintain his challenge, memories would undoubtedly have been revived of the celebrated comment of Jones's Scottish caddie – 'Aye, you're a wonder sir. A blooming wonder.'

As it happened, Dunne arrived at St Andrews as a player with form. Significantly, he had won the final qualifying event at Woburn for a second successive year. By his own estimation, qualifying success in 2014 'gave me a lot of confidence.' He added: 'Prior to 2015, I had played St Andrews only once in an amateur event where I missed the cut. I didn't particularly like it at first, so I went there feeling like I had something to prove.'

He gave himself the benefit of having his college coach, Alan Murray, as his caddie. On the basis of their experience in practice, Murray convinced Dunne that he had reason to aspire to more than simply making the cut.

'I remember breaking it down in my head that if 16 under was going to win, you would have to shoot four under four times,' he said. 'And I knew I could shoot four under on that course easy enough, the way I was playing. That made it seem much more attainable.'

Remarkably, as the championship unfolded, Dunne found himself on target to achieve his objective when he followed two 69s with a third round 66 to be 12 under for the championship on 204 – a 54-hole record for an amateur. So, he was tied for the lead with Jason Day and the 2010 Open champion St Andrews, Oosthuizen, with 18 holes to play. His final round, however, began with crushing bogeys at the first and second holes and though he went on to get back to level par for the outward stretch by the turn, his earlier confidence deserted him on the homeward journey in a closing 78.

With earlier rounds of 69,69 and 66, it meant an aggregate of 282 for a share of 30th place behind the winner, Zac Johnson, who was -15 after rounds of 66,71,70,66 before beating Marc Leishman and Oosthuizen in a playoff. The amateur award went to American Jordan Niebrugge, who was tied 6th on -11 after rounds of 67,73,67 and 70. Dunne later admitted:

> By the time I reached the turn, I knew my chance of winning was gone. It was a very strange feeling. It was like the disappointment hit me when I still had nine or 10 holes to play. And I kind of wanted the ground to swallow me up. Still, there's a little thing in the back of my head telling me that I wish I could do it again.

Had the five amateur survivors been eligible for prize money in that particular Open, they would have collected an estimated €635,834 between them. And in a fascinating interview I had with Paul McGinley, he expressed the view that he would like to have seen them accept the money – before passing it on to their respective national bodies.

He also claimed that these elite players should be attired in their international apparel with corresponding golf bags. 'I think it's wrong that manufacturers are getting free advertising from amateur players,' he said as leader of the Irish men's and women's golf teams at the 2016 Olympic Games in Rio de Janeiro.

The top five amateurs at the Old Course with their possible prize money were: T6 (271) Niebrugge (US) €271,205; T12 (279) Ashley Chesters (England) and Ollie Schniederjans (US) €143,732 each; T30 (282) Dunne €55,925; and T65 (286) Romain Langasque (France) €21,240. It should be noted that these figures for their respective positions on the leaderboard are enhanced by a greater share of the spoils for the professionals, which was announced by the R&A the previous Sunday, when there was the possibility of Dunne scooping the record top prize of €1,591,255.

It would simply be distributed through the rest of the field, they explained, as does all prize money that would go to amateurs. McGinley went on:

> Why should the pros get additional money that they didn't actually earn? We could have had Paul Dunne's money, for instance, going to the Golfing Union of Ireland, with possibly a share to his American university as a sort of thank you for the investment they made in his career. And obviously the same would apply to the two Americans, to England's Ashley Chesters and to the French contestant.
>
> I'm sure a whole new approach to the involvement of amateurs in the Open could be reached through negotiations with the R&A. Wouldn't it be great to see players wearing the jerseys of their national golfing authority, particularly in challenging positions for the Open, as we saw last weekend? I know it's something I'd love to have experienced.

Against this background, it did seem odd to see Dunne attired in the same Under Armour gear as Jordan Spieth. The Greystones player even highlighted the fact that looking at the familiar logo on his cap, autograph-hunters mistook him for the then world number two, until they got close enough to see his face. The 2014 victorious European captain continued:

> In the Ryder Cup, the guys all use Ryder Cup golf bags and Ryder Cup clothes, but they use their own golf clubs and wear their own shoes. Anything that's deemed equipment they're entitled to use. But there should be certain rules for amateurs.
>
> I thought it was nice to see Chesters in an England sweater. It made me think of what his governing body could do with the prize money he might have earned, reinvesting it in the game at grassroots level. And I'm sure the US Golf Association could have found good use for the sizeable cheque Niebrugge might have got. Where appropriate, you could also involve a player's university. I recall noting the Stanford University cap that Tiger Woods wore when competing as an amateur in the 1996 US Masters.

Meanwhile Dunne had reason to be immensely proud of the way he handled himself in very difficult circumstances on the Monday when the Open drew to a belated conclusion. From the time he became a most unlikely joint leader, the level of expectation, especially on social media, bordered on the ridiculous. Sample: 'Is Paul Dunne the next Bobby Jones?'

Then came a start to his final round which would have unnerved even a battle-hardened campaigner. And he dealt with it superbly. Though we had no right to expect anything special from him as an amateur player, in terms of self-control and general demeanour, he did himself and his country proud by the way he handled those difficult opening holes.

The Dunne story had become very much an Irish story and a player of lesser qualities could have projected a damaging image of his native place. As it happened, he won the unstinting support of sympathetic galleries, right to the end, when a miss-hit approach had him hacking from rough at the back of the 18th green on the way to a closing bogey.

Dunne had a handicap of plus-5 when he turned professional in 2015, and he gained a winning breakthrough in the British Masters where he held off a challenge from Rory McIlroy with a chip-in birdie on the last. Two years later, he lost his playing rights on tour, through injury.

Meanwhile, by way of giving some perspective to Dunne's Open travails, I can recall a very similar St Andrews story in the 1984 Open Championship. That was when an unknown 23-year-old Australian professional by the name of Ian Baker-Finch – he was disparagingly referred to in sections of the media as Ian Baker-Who – found himself tied for the lead with defending champion Tom Watson entering the final round.

Just like Dunne, 31 years on, Baker-Finch was in the last two-ball of the day, and proceeded to make a considerably greater mess of the opening hole than the 22-year-old from Greystones. After a three-wood from the tee, he chose to hit a soft nine-iron for a 120-yard second shot, with the intention of eliminating too much spin.

It was some years later before he discovered that the front of the first green had been over-watered accidentally the previous night. And the upshot was that his approach shot spun back ruinously into the Swilcan Burn for a shattering impact on his fragile confidence.

And the outcome? Baker-Finch, already a three-time winner in professional ranks at the time, proceeded to card a final round of 79, one stroke more than Dunne. 'I reckon a lot of people are waiting to see if I'm a flash in the pan', was his wry reaction.

Dunne, who could reasonably have been confronted by similar doubts, would have known that the Australian proceeded to capture the 1991 Open at Royal Birkdale in the most thrilling style.

Which brought us to the Old Course and its continuing position as a key venue on the Open rota. Quite apart from the considerable moisture which descended upon it before and during that particular weekend, it no longer had the brown links look we saw back in 1990, when Nick Faldo famously holed-out for an eagle two on the 18th with a classic pitch and run from an eight-iron second shot.

The demands of heavy tourist traffic led the greenkeepers, however reluctantly, to pursue a fertilised green look, which inevitably eliminated elements of its original firmness and trickiness. And when you had heavy rain creating soft greens, the Old Course inevitably became the setting for a birdie bonanza.

Which is largely why Zach Johnson, a true master of the wedge and putter, the so-called money shots, emerged victorious. It also explained why we saw so few pure links shots played over the five days of what became the longest Open in history.

'Two things changed, and I should have accounted for them,' McGinley acknowledged. 'One was that the wind never really blew from the west, as it normally does, which is in off the left on the way out. Instead, in a south-west wind and with the ball spinning back on incredibly soft greens, you had guys shooting five, six or even seven under on the front nine. And a huge emphasis on wedge play was right up Johnson's street.'

Of course, we all knew, deep down, that an Irish amateur couldn't win golf's greatest prize. But as Paul Dunne set our hearts racing, dreamers of wild dreams revelled in this place of golfing pilgrimage, this glorious monument to the origins of the game.

6

FRED

'On the greens he appeared uneasy, but in reality he had a wonderful feel for pace and for several years had few equals in this area.'

– Fred Daly, as seen by Peter Alliss

• • • •

On Independence Day in the US, Fred Daly achieved his own sense of fulfilment when he captured the Open Championship at Hoylake on 4 July 1947. In fact, it was a distinction which stayed with him for 60 years, until Pádraig Harrington became only the second player from this island to secure golf's finest prize. Yet Daly still stands apart as the only champion to earn a mention in *Hansard*, the official record of exchanges in the British House of Commons.

It happened in the week after his Open triumph, during a debate on the India Bill. Complaining about too much handshaking over India, Sir Walter Smiles MP was reported in Hansard as saying:

> The situation reminds me of Fred Daly, who won the Open Championship at Hoylake the other day and went over to Northern

> Ireland to compete in the championship [Irish Open] there and was beaten. He said he lost because too many people had shaken him by the hand … I think Lord Mountbatten might lose in the final round because we are all too busy shaking him by the hand.

When informed of the comment, Daly responded: 'I have hit some long tee shots in my time, but I never expected to hit *Hansard* from Hoylake. It's true my hand was not in the best of order after all the hearty shakes, but I was pleased to get them.'

Daly's wonderful breakthrough is often thought of as just that, an isolated day in the sun, when a considerable golfing talent happened to gain the ultimate award. But the scale of his impact on the tournament scene stretched way beyond those exploits at Hoylake, remarkable though they were.

The truth is that he lost much of his golfing prime to World War II, though he captured the Irish Professional title in 1940 and won both the Irish Professional and Irish Open titles in 1946. To fully appreciate Daly's rich talent, however, one need not look beyond his Open performances over a relatively short period of seven years.

When the ending of hostilities in Europe paved the way for the resumption of the championship in 1946, Daly finished eighth behind the great Sam Snead at St Andrews, where he shot rounds of 77,71,76 and 74 for an aggregate of 298, eight strokes behind the American.

If anybody still suspected, however, that his performance at Hoylake may have been something of a fluke, Daly's refutation could not have been more emphatic. He was runner-up to Henry Cotton at Muirfield in 1948; tied third behind Bobby Locke at Troon in 1950; tied fourth to Max Faulkner at his beloved Royal Portrush in 1951; and third behind Locke at Royal Lytham in 1952.

The merit of his Hoylake triumph was accorded considerable emphasis by the report in the *Manchester Guardian*, before it had evolved into simply *The Guardian*. It noted:

> Daly is a worthy champion. As a golfer of undoubted class, he has been for some time on the verge of big things. Today he had his chance and he took it like a man.
>
> ... Any player leading in the final round of a championship who can hole the last nine holes at Hoylake in 34 strokes, including a six, is of the stuff of champions. That is what Daly did, and two strokes at least in those last nine holes he will always remember. Both of them were putts.
>
> The first was the 15-yard putt holed at the 13th for a three he needed desperately, a three which gave him the heart for those last five terrific holes. The second was on the last green where he holed from 10 yards for a three, a putt which made amends for a six on the 17th which, when it occurred, bore all the signs of tragedy.

Apart from Locke, Peter Thomson – whose Open performances marginally overlapped the Daly era – Jack Nicklaus, Tom Watson, Nick Faldo and Tiger Woods, no player has achieved such prominence in the world's leading championship in such a concentrated period. Those fortunate enough to be present at Hoylake on those fateful days in July 1947 would have seen no need to make a case for the champion, but the record is worth noting, just the same.

Indeed, his great affection for the event never waned. And he had the considerable pleasure of sharing a rather special happening in 1973 at Troon, where he appeared on a special invitation from the Royal and Ancient. In the event, he was standing on the tee when Gene Sarazen holed-in-one at the famous Postage Stamp eighth hole and was also present when 'The Squire' holed out of a bunker for a birdie there the following day.

All of which was a long way into the future when, 62 years earlier, he first saw the light in Portrush, where he learned to caddie 'at an age which had just about reached double figures.' That is how the late Eoin McQuillan described Fred's humble beginnings in a splendid biography of his lifetime hero.

McQuillan also suggested that apart from a few tips from his father, who corrected the schoolboy's left-hand-below-right grip with the words 'If you're going to play this game, you might as well start the right way', Fred never had a formal lesson in his life. Like many a great player, he learned from observation of the many fine amateurs who graced the celebrated Dunluce links.

A measure of how well he learned his craft can be gauged from this assessment made years later by Peter Alliss. According to Alliss:

> Daly was a short man who had to strive for length. His swing had some unorthodox features. For a start, his clubs were about two inches longer than standard and he used a driver that weighed 17.5 ounces.
>
> He made a wide arc away from the ball, combined with a pronounced sway to a backswing position well past the horizontal. Nevertheless, he was a superb, straight hitter. On the greens he appeared uneasy but in reality had a wonderful feel for pace and for several years had few equals in this area.
>
> He was also known for his habit of glancing sideways at the hole – as many as nine or ten times – when addressing the ball on the greens. And of whistling between his teeth while he did so.
>
> Alliss was being perhaps a little generous in limiting those glances to nine or ten. One observer told me that during a tournament at Bangor he had counted no fewer than 53 such movements on a single putt.

In 1947, the prize fund for the Open was £1,000, from which the winner received £150. But from what I could gather in conversation with Harry Bradshaw during the 1980s, the Irish haul from Hoylake was significantly higher than the official figures. It seems that, by the standards of the day, substantial bets were placed on Fred by his fellow professionals.

They may have been prompted by the then professional at Portmarnock, Eddie Hackett, who played with Daly in the *Manchester Evening Chronicle* Tournament. Looking towards the Open, Hackett observed:

'The way you're playing Fred, I fancy you at Hoylake and I'm having a few bob on you.'

Heading for the Royal Liverpool Club, Daly couldn't have imagined that he would become the first player since the great James Braid in 1905 to win the Open and the *News of the World* Match Play Championship in the same year. But the manner in which he achieved this superb double, particularly in the execution of majestic two-wood fairway shots, caused him to be described as 'the man who brought the brassie back into golf.'

In the event, he travelled with Bradshaw and Max Faulkner to Hoylake where the three of them stayed in the same guest house. They had their first practice round on the Saturday before the championship with the local professional Cyril Hughes who, apparently, imparted some priceless local knowledge.

Two rounds later, Daly was content with his preparation, particularly the way in which his newly acquired driver was performing. This came from an old friend, PG 'Stevie' Stevenson, the resident professional at Royal Portrush, for whom he had done clubmaking work in his shop.

According to Eoin McQuillan, the club that won the Open later hung horizontally for years in Stevenson's shop until it was passed onto a Portrush member. Patsy McGuckian, a former Antrim and Ulster Gaelic football full-back from Cloughmills, borrowed it for 18 holes and it performed so well that he persuaded the professional to sell it to him.

'It nearly broke my heart,' said Stevenson, years later. 'But to a club professional, his members' needs should always come first.'

Considerable doubt, however, was cast on that charming story by my experience at the 1980 Open Championship at Muirfield. This was my first Open and a special memory was a media centre meeting with the great Newcastle United and England striker Jackie Milburn, who was writing a newspaper column for the *News of the World* at the time. As an 11-handicap golfer, he talked to me about his proudest possession.

'I have the driver which Fred Daly used when he won the Open at Hoylake in 1947,' said Milburn. 'I treasure it so much that I'm afraid to play with it. I take it out every now and again to polish it up.' He went on to tell me that during his spell as player-manager of Linfield from 1957 to 1961 he came to know the bold Fred:

> He sold me a set of clubs for £36. And because of our friendship, he threw in his Open driver for good measure.
>
> Since then, I have become a golf addict, since joining the Holywood club [later made famous by Rory McIlroy]. In fact, golf is now my first love, though I still keep in touch with soccer by reporting on matches. Once I am on a golf course, nothing else seems to matter. It's a marvellous release. I would strongly recommend it to soccer players who want to maintain an interest in sport after they quit the game.

So there. I never saw Milburn again.

The history of Daly's driver reminds me of 1989 and the memorable two-iron shot of 229 yards which Christy O'Connor Jnr famously hit onto the 18th green at The Belfry to beat Fred Couples in the Ryder Cup. Never one to turn up a chance of self-promotion, Christy later told us how he donated the two-iron for a raffle by some missionary nuns. Shortly afterwards, further stories emerged about the same two-iron being donated for auction to other charities. When I gently pointed this out to Christy, his mischievous response was: 'Didn't you know that Ping have had to extend their factory in Phoenix, Arizona to handle the increased demand for two-irons?' All of which was accompanied by a hearty laugh in the belief that where raising money for charity was concerned, the end justified the means.

Back at the 1947 Open, conditions were pleasant for the opening round in which Cotton and fellow Englishman Laurie Ayton shared the lead on 69. The gifted American amateur Frank Stranahan shot 71 while Daly, who extracted precious little reward from the greens, was tied fifth on 73, along with the Belgian Flory van Donck and the 1939 champion, Richard Burton.

Remarkably, Fred signed autographs for admirers after the 16th hole of his second round before going on to finish 4,4 for a 70 and the halfway lead on 143. He went on, however, to seemingly jeopardise a glorious chance of the title by carding a dispiriting third round of 78 which brought him back to a share of the lead on 221 with Cotton (74), Norman von Nida (71) and Arthur Lees (72). The menacing figure of Stranahan was a stroke back on 222.

In fact, any chance of Daly reasserting his early dominance appeared to have disappeared when he reached the turn in 38 in the final round that afternoon (those were the bad old days when the final two rounds of the Open were played on the same day). But he responded dramatically when facing the homeward journey for the last time.

At a time when the leaders didn't necessarily go out last in the final round, the only player out on the course who could catch him was the amateur, Stranahan. Indeed, the situation would be repeated at St Andrews in 1984 when Watson needed a two at the 72nd to force a playoff with Seve Ballesteros.

According due prominence to 'their man', the *New York Times* of 5 July 1947 reported:

> Frank Stranahan, 24-year-old amateur from Toledo, Ohio (home of the Champion spark-plug company which his family owned), lost the British Open Championship by three inches today, but he gained the most important victory of his career when he captured the hearts of embittered Britons with a courageous finish that left him only one stroke behind the new champion, Fred Daly of Belfast, Ireland.
>
> Needing an eagle on the 72nd hole to tie, the powerful youngster hammered his 120-yard second shot straight for the pin on the final green It came to rest exactly hole high, but three inches to the left.

'... Every time I come over here I seem to get in a lot of trouble', said Stranahan at the awards ceremony after sharing second place with Horne. 'This time everyone has been very fair to me.'

All the while, Fred sat in the bar with the Whitcombe brothers who had finished out of contention. 'I could hear the wind rattling the windows,' he would later recall, 'and as far as I was concerned, it would have been all right if it had been strong enough to blow them in.'

In further reflection on the tension of those climactic moments, he added: 'Every year, I hear and read so many post-mortems in which Frank's ball gets an inch nearer the hole, that I'm frightened it will eventually drop in and we'll be sent for to go out in a 36-hole playoff.'

After more than half a lifetime as Ireland's lone winner of a Major championship, Fred died in November 1990; I happened to be covering the 36th World Cup of Golf at Grand Cypress Resort in Orlando when the news reached us. It was Monday the 18th and David Feherty, who was there representing Ireland with Ronan Rafferty, ensured a suitable send-off for his departed fellow Ulsterman by relating marvellous stories from his time as Fred's assistant at Balmoral – 'the greatest two years of my life.'

Typically mischievous, Feherty attempted to familiarise an American audience with his experiences at Balmoral, at a time when Northern Ireland was being ripped apart by civil strife. 'We didn't have too many problems, other than the clubhouse being blown up twice', he remarked in the sort of tone he might have used when describing his choice of approach iron at a particular hole.

One story I remember with particular affection concerned Garth McGimpsey, who went on to win 14 championships, including the British Amateur of 1985 at Royal Dornoch, and who became a Walker Cup captain before reaching senior status with similar success. This particular incident happened in 1979 when Hal McGimpsey, Garth's father, decided that if his richly promising son was to scale the heights of amateur golf, a lesson from Fred was absolutely mandatory.

So it was that the pair made the pilgrimage to Balmoral, where Hal took copious notes for future reference. Near the end of the lesson, the old pro became seriously animated, swishing the driver vigorously with his left hand through rough grass at the edge of a fairway. 'That's it! That's it!' the Open champion exclaimed. Convinced he and Garth were being made privy to a great golfing secret, Hal eagerly enquired: 'What is it, Fred?' Only to be told: 'That's the fucking moss that's destroying our greens.'

Maureen Madill, who became a distinguished golf commentator after winning both the British Amateur Stroke Play and Match Play crowns, recounted a very different experience with Daly, whom she knew about from her earliest days at Portstewart. As a 15-year-old in 1973, she was to realise the dream of every youngster by actually playing with her childhood hero. It was a 36-hole pro-am at Bangor GC where all the amateur competitors were women.

When Daly arrived on the tee, she remembers him as being 'very courteous' while introducing himself to Madill and her local female partner. The girl in question was no more than 20 with a curtain of hair which covered her face when she addressed the ball. 'Then, as we set off up the first fairway, I suddenly noticed she was in her bare feet,' Madill recalled. 'Fred said nothing but I felt I should make some attempt at conversation so I asked her: "Do you always play in your bare feet?" To which she replied "Oh yes", drawing a line under that particular subject of conversation.'

As the older of the two young ladies, she of the bare feet was given the task of marking Daly's scorecard for a professional's individual competition. Poor putting, which had become an ongoing problem by that stage, left Fred none too pleased after a six at a particular par four. 'Fred, what did you have there?' cried Bare Feet after him. 'What did you ...'

Madill takes up the story:

> Fred was getting progressively furious at this and at the eighth hole he told me he was no longer going to communicate with this girl. From then on he would say to me, 'Tell her I had a five; tell you I had a four, etc.' So I would say 'Fred had a five; Fred had a four.' And so on.
>
> Realising what was going on, she wanted to know why Fred wasn't talking to her. And there was I caught in the middle, which

was horrendous. But on we went for what had by then become an interminable round. Little did I realise there was worse to come.

Even off the back tees, Daly's drives were invariably furthest out on the fairway, followed by Madill and then Bare Feet. And given his celebrity, they had attracted a large gallery by the time they reached the 18th. So Madill was delighted when, having walked up to the middle ball, she hit her best shot of the day, a glorious eight-iron to eight feet, which brought enthusiastic applause.

After they had walked the 30 yards to the longest drive, however, Daly looked down at the ball and then at Madill. 'You played the wrong ball, sweetie', he said acidly. 'I was mortified', she recalled:

> Naturally, I had to go back and hit another shot to the green and when it was all over, I remember turning to my father and, close to tears, telling him: 'I can't play with those two ever again.' Now, with the benefit of hindsight, I regret that I was too young to fully appreciate the artistry of a wonderful playing partner.

With his great friend Harry Bradshaw, Daly gained the distinction of completing Ireland's first Canada Cup (World Cup) pairing in Montreal in 1954, when they were tied 11th behind Australia's Kel Nagle and Peter Thomson. And they played again the following year (8th behind Chick Herbert and Ed Furgol of the US). By way of celebrating that link, Feherty did his country proud at Grand Cypress in 1990, where a course record final round of 63 lifted himself and Rafferty to a share of second place behind Germany, represented by Bernhard Langer and Torsten Giedeon. One imagines Daly would have approved.

Ever mischievous, Feherty delighted in telling me years later how he had congratulated Pádraig Harrington as the first Irish winner of the Open at Carnoustie in 2007. Somewhat bemused, Harrington corrected him that Ireland's first Open champion was Fred in 1947, 60 years previously. To which Feherty responded: 'But Fred was British. Everybody knows that Fred was British, even down to the orange Vauxhall Viva he drove.' And there the matter rested.

Though history sometimes tells us otherwise, the appealing notion that sport can transcend all boundaries gained rich credence in the bond between Daly and Bradshaw. It meant not a moment's hesitation in Bradshaw's decision, as a 77-year-old, to travel north from his home in Raheny, Dublin to attend Daly's funeral with fellow professional Paddy Skerritt.

And when The Brad himself died little more than a month later, we knew we had truly reached the end of an era.

Fred and Harry – mention of these old pals creates a charming ring about their exploits in blazing a trail for Harrington and other Irishmen to follow. Sport transcending boundaries can often appear otherwise in this troubled land, though the golfing community have done wonderfully, for the most part, in healing divisions. The fact is that golf remained a 32-county sport through the most difficult times in Irish history, largely through the determination of the Golfing Union of Ireland and the Irish Ladies' Golf Union, which evolved in 2000 into Golf Ireland. I still think fondly of the black humour of Connacht golfer Seán Flanagan in a phone call to fellow interprovincial Cyril Devins, concerning doubts which had been raised as to the staging of that year's Interprovincial Championship at Royal Portrush, with the Troubles at their height. Whereupon Flanagan suggested to his friend, 'Wouldn't it be wonderful to die for Connacht!'

Fred and Harry were born in humble circumstances on either side of the Border, Fred in Portrush, Co. Antrim in 1911 and Harry in the village of Killincarrig, Co. Wicklow two years later. Where religion and political allegiance divided many of their compatriots, this remarkable duo found a common bond in golf, right back to their start as caddies.

The Ryder Cup gave them their greatest experience together, when they formed an unbeatable partnership in the matches at Wentworth in 1953. But they had been keen rivals for a number of years prior to that, stretching back before World War II. With more than a hint of southern bias, their rivalry was captured by the *Irish Independent* of the period in an article which read:

> Admittedly, he [Daly] is a very good golfer but, at the same time, I do not think he is as good as Bradshaw. It must be remembered that in 1941, 1942, 1943 and 1944, Bradshaw won successive Irish Professional Championships and in all four, he had Daly behind him.
>
> Daly's one Irish title was gained on a rock-like course at Little Island, when a wonderful finish enabled him to beat Bradshaw by one stroke. If I were asked to give one broad reason why I consider Bradshaw a better golfer, I would plumb for the Kilcroney man's consistency. Without any doubt, he is the most consistent golfer the country has produced since the days of Michael Moran.

As it happened, the 'many' to whom the writer alluded as considering Daly to be the better golfer proved to be somewhat better judges of golfing skills than the *Independent*'s man.

As a reward for his Open triumph, the Ulsterman became a member of the then exclusively British Ryder Cup team for the matches in Portland, Oregon on 1 and 2 November 1947. And he also played at Ganton in 1949 and at Pinehurst, North Carolina in 1951.

Meanwhile, Bradshaw's prominence in the game in these islands was such that he would certainly have been worthy of selection in 1949, when he forced a playoff in the Open at Royal St George's, Sandwich, only to lose to Bobby Locke. But there was a problem. As a citizen of the Irish Republic, he was categorised by the British PGA as an 'overseas member' and, as such, ineligible for Ryder Cup selection.

The situation was rendered decidedly odd, however, by their decision to select him on a four-man team which toured South Africa in the winter of 1950–51. Daly was also in the team, along with Ken Bousfield (England) and John Panton (Scotland).

It was there that the Daly–Bradshaw partnership was cemented in earnest. The Brad later recalled: 'On one occasion during that trip, me and Fred took on the best ball of four amateurs who played off scratch, one, two and three handicap. And we beat them twice. Fred had nerves of steel when the crunch came and I could always manage to sink the odd putt.'

Against this background, they became a logical partnership for skipper Cotton, when the Ryder Cup was staged at Wentworth in 1953. As it happened, these matches would mark Bradshaw's debut and Daly's swansong in the biennial tournament.

Their opponents on the opening day were the American partnership of PGA champion Walter Burkemo and the 1949 US Open champion, Cary Middlecoff. After a fine morning round of 70, the Irish pair were three up when they went to lunch, but Daly's fine putting touch seemed to desert him in the afternoon. Still, with The Brad lending staunch support, they held on for a one-hole victory – the only win by a home pairing.

In the sports pages of the *Daily Express* the following morning, Desmond Hackett wrote of 'the loveliest sound all day.' This was the plop of a four-foot winning putt from Daly finding the cup on the decisive hole, after Bradshaw had played a delightful recovery from a greenside bunker. Colleague Bernard Hunt recalled standing by the green with the rest of the team and counting Daly's routine of passing the putter head backwards and forwards over the top of the ball before eventually addressing it. 'We counted 12 before he got round to hitting the ball', said the Englishman. 'But it went in.'

A day later, the *Sunday Express* carried a headline at which Feherty would have taken serious exception: 'Britain loses Ryder Cup – but what a day for two Irishmen!' This salute referred to the singles matches of the Saturday, when Daly had a crushing 9 and 7 win over Ted Knoll, and Bradshaw beat Fred Haas by 3 and 2 in the anchor position. Between them, they had contributed three points to the British and Irish total, in a 6.5 to 5.5 win for the Americans overall. A report of Bradshaw's singles match enthused that 'his steadiness flowered into golfing genius when, over the last 11 holes, he returned figures of four under fours.'

The Brad played again at Thunderbird G&CC in 1955 and in the historic victory at Lindrick two years later, but Wentworth marked the end for his partner. 'I was disappointed', the Ulsterman admitted later in his biography. 'I was a pretty good match player and another trip to America would have been a lovely finale to my career.'

Pat Ward-Thomas of the then *Manchester Guardian* paid him this beautiful tribute:

> Perhaps his proudest days have gone with the remorseless years. It seems no time at all since he played the finest golf ever seen in the Ryder Cup in the contest at Wentworth, and it is sad to reflect ... that he may never again play for Britain.

Daly later said of his partner: 'Harry and I were a good combination. We played a lot of people and seldom lost. In Ireland, we never lost at all.' Of all the matches they played together, it is doubtful if any exhibition match meant as much to The Brad as that which marked Fred's 25 years as professional at Balmoral.

On 21 October 1970, the pair of them rolled back the years by delivering a 6 and 4 spanking to Ryder Cup 'youngsters' Eric Brown and Max Faulkner. And an Ulster fan of The Brad's was prompted to remark: 'To see him charm the ball around Balmoral whipped up a host of delightful memories.'

It may not have held the same excitement for the old stalwarts as their battles at Wentworth 17 years previously. But it was a priceless testimony to an enduring friendship.

7

The Brad

'Harry could have been fortunate to find an official who decided on a generous interpretation of Rule 11, covering obstructions. The problem as I see it, however, is the fact that certain objects were listed in the Rule. It would be very difficult to consider a broken bottle as being similar to a hut, a bridge, a seat or a shelter.'

– An R&A Rules expert speaking 40 years after the incident during the 1949 Open

• • • •

In these days when the more sensitive among us rail against the excesses of the internet, it may be appropriate to acknowledge the shortcomings of newspapers as far back as the years following World War II. I'm thinking about a truly remarkable photograph which adorns the official history of Royal St George's GC.

It was of particular interest to me, given that I had written Harry Bradshaw's biography in which the famous ball-in-the-bottle incident from the 1949 Open Championship was given due prominence. The photograph showed The Brad bending over an upturned broken Guinness stout bottle, which had a golf ball lodged inside. Indeed, the same photograph is to be found in the elaborate 2019 history of Royal Portrush GC.

The shot was taken by an admirably inventive snapper from the *Liverpool Echo*. We may well ask ourselves how it was that he happened to have been right there on the spot, when The Brad pushed his second shot at the fifth hole at Sandwich, into what proved to be a dire situation. He would need to have been most fortunate indeed.

The truth is that the picture was actually posed, behind the resident professional's shop at Royal St George's, when news of the incident broke. The Brad later confirmed this to me, almost 40 years after it was taken.

All of which added to the mystique of one of the most fascinating incidents in the history of this great championship. And The Brad did much to gild the lily, as it were, over subsequent years through his splendid gifts as a storyteller.

As to the accusation that he had acted in haste, it should be noted that Bradshaw considered his position for around 10 to 15 minutes in a situation where there were no walkie-talkies nor any buggies in which to ferry a rules official to the incident.

So it was that it became the stuff of legend. Especially the appealing notion of an Irishman being undone by a Guinness bottle.

In carrying out their periodic review of the Rules of Golf in 1946, the Royal and Ancient made no major changes. So the Rules, which were generally geared towards match play at that time, remained decidedly vague in two crucial areas.

Rule 6 stated: 'A ball must be played wherever it lies, or the hole be given up, except as otherwise provided for in the Rules.'

Meanwhile Rule 11, which dealt with the removal of obstructions, stated: 'Any flagstick, guidepost, implement, vehicle, bridge, bridge planking, seat, hut, shelter or similar obstructions, may be removed. A ball moved in the removal of such obstructions, shall be lifted and dealt with as provided for in Rule 8, without penalty.'

It was generally accepted at the time that a ball could be deemed to be unplayable only if the player could not make a stroke at it and dislodge it into a playable position. Under subsequent revisions, however, a player became entitled to declare a ball unplayable at any place on the course except in a hazard. A player became the sole judge as to whether their ball was unplayable.

As could be seen from Rule 11 as things applied in 1949, there was no clear distinction between a movable and an immovable obstruction, and the vague nature of the rules in general caused golfers to accept the safe dictum of 'play it as it lies', except in the most dire circumstances.

Significantly, a clause was added to Rule 11 in the autumn of 1949, presumably as a consequence of Bradshaw's unfortunate experience as few months earlier. It meant that a ball could now be removed from 'any object placed or left on the course', as in broken pieces of glass.

During the early summer of 1949, Bradshaw, by his own estimation, was playing excellent golf, the best in fact since he became a fully-fledged professional. His putting had never been sharper, a fact which promoted the defending Open champion, Henry Cotton, to remark:

> I always thought that Harry Bradshaw's putting slogan of 'hitting and harking' was one of the best I ever encountered. The genial Irishman is certainly a perfect example of not taking the eyes, or the head, from over the spot where the ball is, until it arrives at the hole, or is heard to rattle in the cup. On his best days, he is a superb putter.

Putts were certainly dropping for The Brad when he entertained four distinguished Dutch visitors to Kilcroney under clear summer skies and the backdrop of well-clad sylvan hills. The Brad marked the occasion by covering his home stretch in a sizzling 61 strokes – 12 under par.

'The Dutchmen were so thrilled that they asked me to sign my score-card', Harry later recalled. 'Then they assured me that I would be the winner at Royal St George's. Their request of a signed card was so that they could show it to their friends back home, when I was crowned champion at Sandwich!'

The Brad, too, was confident though his experience of tournament golf left him acutely aware of the difficulty of capturing the biggest prize in the same, irrespective of how well he might be playing. Especially with the prospect of Royal St George's being a new challenge for him. He recalled:

> Nobody noticed me when I arrived there. I didn't expect anything else, particularly with such famous players as Bobby Locke, Arthur Lees, Roberto de Vicenzo, Sam King and the marvellous Anglo-Scot Jimmy Adams in the field. They were the big fish; I was small fry by comparison.

Of the leading challengers, Locke was especially admired by The Brad, whom he had met for the first time at Portmarnock in 1946 when the South African finished runner-up to Fred Daly in the Irish Open.

In this context, Harry was greatly encouraged by developments in the 36-hole qualifying for the Open on Monday and Tuesday 4 and 5 July 1949. His opening 67 was four strokes better than Locke's 71. And when the line-up of qualifiers was completed by the Tuesday evening, Harry, with a total of 139, was in the clubhouse noting the unavailing challenge of Locke and the American Johnny Bulla over the final holes.

The seven leading qualifiers were: 139 – H Bradshaw (Kilcroney) 67,72; 140 – AD Locke (South Africa) 71,69; 141 – J Bulla (US) 72,69; 142 – RW Horne (Hendon) 69,73; 143 – A Murray (New Zealand) 71,72; M Faulkner (Royal Mid Surrey) 72,71; J Panton (Glenbervie) 71,72; K Bousfield (Coombe Hill) 69,74.

By the time the first round proper got under way on the Wednesday, The Brad's qualifying exploits had generated tremendous interest back home. And the news remained heartening when his many admirers listened to radio reports of the opening day. Jimmy Adams of Wentworth led on 67, one stroke ahead of The Brad and deVincenzo on 68, while Locke was in a group of seven on 69 who included Bousfield and the experienced Australian Bill Shankland.

In the process of his splendid effort, Harry equalled a championship record by covering the outward nine in superb 31 strokes – 443 343 433.

His playing partner for what would prove to be a fateful second round on the Thursday was Harry Osborne, an English professional from the Newquay club in Cornwall. In the event, The Brad was not unduly concerned about covering the opening four holes in 4,4,4,5 – two strokes more than he had taken the previous day. 'Then THE THING happened', he recalled with some emphasis. 'There was a strong breeze and my second shot to the fifth was slightly off line, but it was still a reasonably good shot.'

Interestingly, when assessing the challenge of the 422-yard par-four fifth hole, local experts maintained that the second was a problem shot insofar as the ball had to be played through a gap in the sand dunes.

A sharpish dogleg to the left presented quite a deal of featureless green between the dunes and the green. In the process, the casual player was offered a clear view of the North Sea with the cliffs of Ramsgate on the far side of Pegwell Bay.

Mind you, Open competitors would have been in no mood for sight-seeing. 'How is my ball', Harry anxiously asked his caddie. 'All right', came the reply. 'It won't be difficult to make the green.'

As he approached the ball, Harry had quick look towards the green. 'This should be handy enough', he thought. Then he stopped dead in his tracks, speechless. The ball had been pushed into the rough on the right where it came to rest near the road which separated the course from the sea ... in the middle of broken glass.

Much fiction has been written about the nature of that infamous glass. At the time, an appealing, ironic touch was added by reporters who described the glass as the lower part of a Guinness bottle. The truth is that nobody, including Harry, had any idea of the nature of the bottle. Asking Harry to identify it, given his state of mind at the time, would have been like asking a drowning man if the water tasted salty, or if he noticed whether it was polluted.

It was some time afterwards before Harry could fully understand the nature of the newspaper reports, which he was only too happy to embellish. As I have indicated earlier, the presence of a Guinness bottle was the product of a creative photographer.

Playing partner Osborne, who was marking Harry's card, the caddies and a few spectators following the match came to stare in amazement at the Irishman's predicament. Someone made the tasteless comment, 'You won't play that shot from memory.' Osborne advised: 'For your own safety, that's a shot that'll take careful hitting.' Harry saw the danger. As soon as he hit the glass, it would splinter in all directions. It might even cost him an eye.

'Looking back on it now, I feel I could have put the competition committee in a quandary', he reflected. 'Back then, however, it was not easy to get a ruling out on the course. There was no buggies or walkie-talkies.'

After considering his position for between 10 and 15 minutes, Harry took a nine-iron, made a couple of practice swings, closed his eyes, turned his head away and gave ball and glass all he had, with a blind swing. He made good contact, smashing the top part of the broken bottle into little pieces while the neck, which had been stuck into the ground, flew several yards in front of him. The ball travelled about 20 yards from where Harry took three more strokes to hole out for a double-bogey six.

So, what were his options? Under the present rules, the bottle would have been treated as a movable obstruction and, if there were any doubt about the matter, Harry could have dropped a ball, completed the hole with both balls and report the matter afterwards to the Championship Committee. This, however, was not permissible under the rules as they applied in 1949.

It is also important to note that had Harry taken a drop to which he was not entitled after separating ball from bottle, he would have been disqualified. And with so much at stake, he would have been determined not to concede a penalty stroke.

If he had insisted on a ruling, what were his prospects of gaining relief from a championship referee? I have discussed the matter with an R&A rules expert who, after studying the 1949 Rules, came up with this verdict:

> Harry could have been fortunate to find an official who decided on a generous interpretation of Rule 11, covering obstructions. The problem as I see it, however, is the fact that certain objects were

listed in the rule. It would be very difficult to consider a broken bottle as being similar to a hut, a bridge, a seat or a shelter. There was also the point, as Harry proved, that it was possible to dislodge the ball into a playable position. Taking these points into consideration, I believe that it would have been very difficult for an official to grant him relief under the rules of the time.

We take pleasure in issuing our Fourteenth Edition of the Rules of Golf as approved by the Royal and Ancient Golf Club of St Andrews with amendments to May 1946.

May 1946

RULE 6

Ball Played Wherever it Lies
A ball must be player wherever it lies or the hole be given up, except as otherwise provided for in the Rules or Local Rules.

RULE 8

Dropping and Placing
When a ball Through the Green is lifted and dropped under the Rules, it must be dropped as near as possible to the place where it lay, and must come to rest not nearer to the hole.

If the ball, when dropped, comes to rest nearer to the hole, it shall be re-dropped *without penalty*, and in cases where it is impossible owing to the configuration of the ground to prevent a dropped ball from rolling nearer to the hole, the ball shall be placed.

A ball lifted from the Putting Green must be replaced on the stop from which it was lifted, except as otherwise provided for in the Rules. For Hazards see Rule 25.

Penalty for Match Play – loss of Hole.

Penalty in Stroke Play – Two Strokes.

If, in the act of dropping, the ball touches the player, he shall incur no penalty and, if it rolls into a Hazard, the player re-drop the ball *without penalty*.

RULE 11

Removal of Obstructions

Any flagstick, guidepost, implement, vehicle, bridge, bridge planking, seat, hut, shelter of similar obstruction may be removed. A ball moved in removing such an obstruction shall be lifted and dealt with as provided for in Rule 8 *without penalty*.

If the player's stroke be interfered with by any such obstruction which is immovable and which is within two club lengths of his ball, the ball may be lifted and dropped or on the Putting Green placed not more than two club lengths from the obstacle, but not nearer the hole, *without penalty*.

For Hazards see Rule 25.

STROKE RULE 11

Lifting Ball

A ball may be lifted from any place on the Course. If a player lifts a ball under the provisions of this Rule, he shall either –

(1) Play a ball as provided for in Rule 22 or

(2) Tee and play a ball under penalty of two strokes behind the place from which the ball was lifted, if this be impossible he shall tee and play a ball under penalty of two strokes as near as possible to the place from which the ball was lifted, but not nearer to the hole.

In preparing a tee as above authorised, the player is exempted from the restrictions imposed by Rule 25.

Penalty – Disqualification.

The view of the R&A rules expert was borne out by an addition two months after the 1949 Open of a clause aimed at clarifying Rule 11.

SECTION VIII: OBSTRUCTIONS, LOOSE IMPEDIMENTS. GROUND UNDER REPAIR

33 OBSTRUCTIONS (DEF. 23)

1. Movable obstructions may be removed. Any movable obstruction may be removed. If the ball be moved in so doing, it shall be replaced *without penalty.*

2. Ball lying on, touching or within two club lengths. If the player's ball –

(i) lie on any obstruction, (ii) touch an immovable obstruction or (iii) lie within two club lengths of an immovable obstruction,

the player may, *without penalty*, through the green, lift and drop the ball or on the Putting Green, place the ball not more than two club lengths from that point, (i) at which the ball crosses the margin of the obstruction, (ii) at which the ball touched the obstruction, or (iii) of the obstruction nearest which the ball originally lay, but not nearer the hole.

Penalty for breach of Rule: Match play – Loss of hole; Stroke play – Disqualification.

34 LOOSE IMPEDIMENTS (DEF. 20)

1. Removal of loose impediments. Except when both the ball and the loose impediment lie in or touch a hazard, any loose impediment may be removed *without penalty.*

2. Ball moved. If the ball move after any loose impediment lying within a club length of the ball through the green has been touched by the player, his partner or either of their caddies, the player shall be deemed to have caused it to move. The penalty shall be one stroke and the ball shall be played as it lies.

35 GROUND UNDER REPAIR (DEF. 16)

1. Ball lying on or touching (i) Through the green. If the player's ball lie or touch ground under repair, or lie in a hole made by a greenkeeper through the green, the player shall *without penalty* drop a ball not more than two club lengths from the ground under repair, or the hole made by a greenkeeper, but not nearer to the hole.

If the ball lie within two club lengths of ground under repair, the player may, *without penalty*, drop a ball not more than two club lengths from the ground under repair, but not nearer the hole.

(ii) In a hazard. If the player's ball lie in or touch ground under repair in a hazard, the player shall *without penalty* drop a ball in the hazard not more than two club lengths from the ground under repair, but not nearer to the hole being played.

(iii) On the putting green. If the player's ball lie on or touch ground under repair, or lie in a hole made by a greenkeeper, on the putting green the player shall, *without penalty*, lift it and place it in the nearest position to where it lay which is not nearer to the hole being played and which affords a stroke to that hole without ground under repair or a hole made by a greenkeeper intervening.

If ground under repair or a hole made by the greenkeeper intervene between a ball lying on the putting green and the hole being played, the player may *without penalty*, lift it and place it in the nearest position to where it lay which is not nearer to that hole and which affords stroke to that hole without ground under repair or a hole made by a greenkeeper intervening.

The revised Rules of September 1949

~

The largely sympathetic and responsible golf writers of the day considered Harry's plight to have been most unfair. Among them one imagines would have been Henry Longhurst, who was a long-time admirer of The

Brad, despite having what the scribe described as an agricultural swing. Longhurst once wrote: 'He can size up a shot, choose his club, hit the ball and be walking after it, all in the time it takes some to test the direction of the wind.'

Another writer argued rather colourfully:

> If anyone was careless enough to leave a barrel out in the middle of the pitch at Wembley on Cup Final day, and the Wembley officials were careless enough not to notice it and the ball was careless enough to get inside the barrel at the first movement, would the players have to kick the barrel to pieces before the game could proceed? No. Some sensible person, probably the referee, would pick the ball out and remove the barrel. If a large dog swallowed the ball during a Test Match at Lord's, would they bring on Bedser to bowl the ball, dog and all? No. Some sane person would send out another ball and let the battle recommence. What is it that makes golfers act this way and cost a sportsman a title he richly deserved up to that point?

The most enlightened views on the situation were expressed by the noted Scottish golf writer Frank Moran, who was president of the Association of Golf Writers at the time. His article, titled 'Should Bradshaw have played that ball in the bottle?', appeared in the magazine *Irish Golf* in August 1949, a month after Royal St George's. The article is especially interesting for the fact that Moran adopted an admirably balanced view, despite being commissioned to write for an Irish magazine. It read:

> It might have been. The saddest words of tongue or pen, the poet called them, and with Harry Bradshaw at Sandwich tragically fresh in the mind, how right the poet was. Not to many, even once in a lifetime, does the greatest honour of the golfing world come so close. Bradshaw's brilliant failure will go down to posterity as one of the greatest misses ever.

Coming and going in his customary quiet and modest way, Bradshaw built himself and professional's ultimate dream, right to the very brink of reality with a wonderful week's golf. He may, if you like, have had his bit of luck in touching the crest of form just when it was supremely wanted, but had six rounds, including the 36 holes qualifying figures been counted, Bradshaw would have beaten Locke by a stroke. Even over the four counting rounds, he set up the 283 aggregate which has been spectacularly sufficient in three other years to win the Championship by five strokes in two cover cases, four in the other.

In the end, Locke could only tie with it, and the South African looked as if he had thrown away his chance by taking four for the 70th hole, the short 16th, when he had to do the last three holes in the strictest par.

That dramatic error left him to cover the last two holes – stiff par fours – in seven shots and you know that he picked up his lifeline tree at the 71st hole. It was preciously near Bradshaw's title at about that time.

It was awfully near Kilcroney's turn to house the Cup too at the last gasp of Bradshaw's final round for his first putt on the home green needed only two or three more tolls and there would have been no tie.

The bottle incident

Now I must refer to what will be historically known as the Bradshaw bottle incident. Without hesitation, I enter upon this controversial subject in the knowledge that angels with their sense of fairness would not fear to tread.

It is, in my opinion, no overstatement to say that but for the unconsidered action of some person unknown, and no doubt a non-golfer who 'could not care less', as they say, Bradshaw might well have been Open Champion today. The fifth hole in his second round where he found his ball in a broken bottle, cost him a six.

I have no idea who had the bottle party, but Bradshaw certainly endured the hangover!

There were those at Sandwich who pooh-poohed the idea that Bradshaw's lost title should be pinned down to that accident. Locke, they pointed out, had a seven at the 14th hole. But you must get behind the figures for a just comparison. After all, Locke took the seven entirely by his hand and without any extraneous interference with his play. He drove out of bounds. Bradshaw on the other hand was a victim of circumstances absolutely outside his own control.

Now the question arises: did the Kilcroney man handle the situation to his best possible advantage? Let us glance at the options open to him. There were four, including the one he adopted of playing the ball where it lay, bottle and all. The others were, lifting and teeing behind the place under two strokes penalty (Stroke play Rule); deeming the ball unplayable and going back to where he played the shot and playing again under stroke and distance penalty; and (this alternative has been rather overlooked) removing the bottle as a loose impediment within a club length of his ball and counting one penalty stroke for moving the ball. The last two come under General Rules.

I have heard yet another option argued – that he could have removed the bottle as an obstruction with no penalty at all. But that can be ruled out, for I have the authority of the R&A Secretary for saying that the bottle could not be considered an 'obstruction' in the sense in which the Rules use that term.

By playing ball and bottle together, Bradshaw took the risky but economic line, for there was no penalty. But he was able, amid flying glass splinters, to knock only 20 yards or so.

Had he treated the bottle as a loose impediment, he would have been playing his fourth shot to the green, and it is possible that he might still have saved the all-important stroke by squeezing a five out of his problem.

As it was, he had with his bottle-shot played only five, but my theory is that he was upset enough by the whole incident to affect his play at subsequent holes, and taking 39 to the turn he finished no better in that round than 77. So Luck showed its debit side to Bradshaw.

In what I have written, I have tried to take a judicial view of the affair and in the same vein I must add that Locke is the superior golfer. His technique is better; he has a greater command of the shots to the flag, long or short, and he gave himself more chances to hole the first putt than the Irish player did.

Against the South African's masterly exhibition in the playoff, Bradshaw was like a caged man. He could not find a loophole anywhere, even when he was in fighting trim in the earlier phases of the duel. Yet Bradshaw is entitled to echo the sad words of a famous Scottish golfer, beaten in the (British) Amateur Championship final on the 36th green. 'It's hard to get so near and have to start all over again.'

Locke, who is a grand sportsman as well as a great golfer, would be the first to acknowledge that he has had big advantages that have not, of course, been available to Bradshaw whose *proxime accessit* is all the more meritorious for that fact.

As it happened, The Brad was understandably unnerved by the bottle incident and proceeded to run up a round of 77 – 39 out and 38 back – as Frank Moran has indicated. Yet, at the halfway stage, he was level with Locke, who also had a total of 145 after slipping to a second round of 76. They were five strokes behind the leader, Sam King, who recorded rounds of 71 and 69 for 140.

Bradshaw's partner for the two rounds on the final day was another Englishman, Wally Smithers. Among the 31 qualifiers, Fred Daly was a notable casualty on 151. With brilliant third rounds of 68 The Brad and Locke were level with Max Faulkner after 54 holes.

An early starter in the final round, Ireland's challenger displayed admirable confidence to reach the turn in 33 strokes and went on to be still three under fours when entering the loop between the 11th and 15th. Then came his first indifferent shot of the round at the treacherous long 14th where his second shot just managed to clear the canal. But he emerged with a par and he also safely parred the next. From there, he covered the remaining three holes in par figures though he seemed likely to birdie the 18th where an eight-yard putt, dead on line, stopped on the lip of the hole. 'It's dropping, it's dropping', the crowd roared as Smithers playfully stomped the green as if to help the ball on its way. By the time he had signed for a closing 70 and a Championship record-equalling aggregate of 283, his gifted rival, Locke, was entering the back nine.

Trying to relax over a cup of tea, he was kept up to speed on Locke's progress by a stream of caddies who came in with almost stroke-by-stroke reports. After reaching the turn in 32 to be a stroke clear of The Brad, Locke three-putted the 10th. He then negotiated the loop in somewhat stumbling fashion to be left needing a 3,4,4 finish to tie.

Locke's chance seemed to have disappeared the previous evening when he left a long putt four feet short of the target on the par-three 16th and proceeded to card a bogey four. But the 423-yard 17th yielded a most improbable birdie. With a superb second shot from a demanding lie, Locke left the ball five yards from the pin and then sank the putt. Two putts for a par from 25 yards on the last, earned him the first tie in the Open since Craig Wood beat fellow American Densmore Shute in a playoff for the title at St Andrews in 1933.

In the event, the battle for the title on this occasion was anti-climactic. Over 36 holes on the Saturday, Locke produced arguably the best performance of his illustrious career. Having greeted Harry the previous evening with a hearty 'Oh! You tiger you – long live Ireland', Locke now adopted an irresistible mood. Rounds of 67 and 68 against 74 and 73 from The Brad gave him the title by a crushing 12-stroke margin.

There was further disappointment for Harry when he learned he would not be considered for the Ryder Cup at Ganton on 16–17 September, because the British PGA had seen fit to designate him 'an overseas player'.

Meanwhile, Locke was generous in praise of his defeated rival. 'He is a grand fellow to play with', he said, 'always first to congratulate you on a good shot. But I'm afraid he did not have a chance in the playoff. I never made a slip.'

There was a glimmer of hope for The Brad, however, when Locke added: 'He'll have his chance of revenge when we meet in the Irish Open at Belvoir Park next week.'

And so it happened. With rounds of 70,71,72 and 73 for a total of 286 against 71,75,71,70 from the South African, The Brad claimed top prize of £400. The climax was similar, in certain respects, to Sandwich the previous week in that Harry, who was finished at 5.05 p.m., set the target before heading for a wash and a cup of tea.

Three strokes down with nine holes to play, Locke battled relentlessly on the homeward journey and by the 17th he needed to cover the remaining two holes in seven strokes to tie, just as at Sandwich.

On this occasion, however, he had to settle for a par on the 17th and with his rival afraid to look, he missed a birdie on the last by no more than an inch, as a putt of 33 feet slipped past the target. The excitement was palpable as delighted Irish fans revelled in the Brad's revenge.

A few days later, in a further unavailing attempt at exorcising the ball-in-the-bottle incident from his golfing consciousness, Harry presented a friend of his at Kilcroney with a souvenir. He decided to part company with the ball that had been the source of so much heartache.

'And d'you know the funny thing about it', he mused. 'It was a number two. And I always played with a number one.'

Of the leading golf scribes who reported on his achievements, Bradshaw always appeared to have a soft spot for Longhurst. He appreciated how highly regarded the Englishman was, despite sometimes hurtful comments. I always detected a forgiving tone in his voice when he made reference to potentially damaging remarks.

For his part, Longhurst made amends in the wake of the 1958 Canada Cup Mexico where Harry and Christy O'Connor Snr captured the title for Ireland. This is how he reported from Mexico on the stronger half of the Irish partnership:

The journey so far afield as Mexico leaves many impressions on the mind, not all of them related to golf, which was strictly the object of the visit. The first is that having expended the whole of this space a year ago to lifting my hat off to Harry Bradshaw, I cannot refrain from briefly doing so again. Ireland brought the Canada Cup home and Christy O'Connor played a splendid supporting role but Harry was the hero.

I will not harp further on the difficulties of playing golf at high altitudes, but it will hardly be disputed that weight for weight and age for age, they progressively increase. On as course longer than any British championship links and with a strict par of 72, Bradshaw had rounds of 70,70,76 and 70 and he is 45 and carrying 15 stones.

When others were sinking exhausted in the locker room, he was ready with affable conversation and, as for the fears of dysentery, 'I drink the water out of the tap. If you're going to get it, you'll get it anyway.'

A year ago in Tokyo, he had to retire from this tournament through persistent nose-bleeding. I saw him standing cheerfully in the hotel entrance as we left. Only three or four people, of whom I was not one, knew that in the intervening days he had been so near to death that a priest was called to administer the last rites.

My colleagues are due shortly to elect a Golfer of the Year who has done 'most for British golf.' Had they seen him in Mexico, they would look no further than Harry Bradshaw – and never mind what part of Ireland he comes from!

Appreciations hardly come any stronger.

8

Portrush '51

'Mr HS Colt, who designed it in its present form, has thereby built himself a monument more enduring than brass.'

– Bernard Darwin, 1951

● ● ● ●

Though a welcoming hand was extended in a corridor of the Portstewart clubhouse, our meeting still got off to a rather fraught start. 'You had my score wrong', chided Peter Alliss, in a reference to a piece I had written about the 1951 Open Championship. 'It was 69, not 79.'

It was early July 2017 and I was in Portstewart GC for its first staging of the Irish Open. As a special treat, the golfing voice of the BBC had made the trip as a gesture to his son, Simon, who was celebrating his baptism as championship director of the Irish Open. In my anxiety to talk further with this remarkably enduring icon of the game, I held my counsel, thereby ensuring that our introduction didn't become an argumentative exchange.

Maureen Madill too maintained a diplomatic silence when we eased our way into a corner of the upstairs restaurant in what had been a qualifying venue for the 1951 Open at nearby Royal Portrush. Then, having dispensed with his gripe about those happenings of 66 years previously, the great man was ready to talk.

Madill is the club's most celebrated member and, latterly, her work with Alliss for BBC television had been a feature of golf broadcasting. So it seemed like a perfect way of celebrating the arrival of the Irish Open at her club.

'I protested some months ago that I didn't feel up to it', said Alliss, who was 89 when he departed from us on 6 December 2020.

> But he [Simon] came back to me more recently and insisted 'I'd very much like you to come. You'd be doing me a favour.'
>
> That's when I realised it was a big thing for him. So I said that if they didn't mind me shuffling about like a cantankerous old bugger, abusing the invalid loo, I'd come. To support my son.

At 86 for his Portstewart visit, he walked unsteadily with the aid of a stick, but the distinctive voice and eloquent delivery had managed to defy the passing years. And the sense of mischief, apparently inherited from his golfing father, Percy, was also undiminished.

His finest competitive year was 1958 when, after regaining the Spanish Open title he had captured two years previously, he added the Italian and Portuguese Open crowns for good measure. But he is best remembered in Ireland, certainly by my generation, for the 36-hole score of 127 he recorded in the Irish Hospitals Tournament at Woodbrook in 1961.

'I was considered to have had one of the best swings of my time and putting is, I believe, the main reason I never won an Open Championship', he went on:

> Towards the end of the sixties, I began to twitch on short putts and I retired from international matches at the end of the 1969 Ryder Cup.
>
> I made great friendships in Ireland with people like [Christy] O'Connor [Snr]; Mary, his wife; Philomena Garvey; Joe Carr, with

his endless John Player cigarettes; and all sorts of players. As a wonderful character who had played Augusta, Joe had me imagining myself working as an estate agent in a nice area where they turn over houses every three or four years and where there would be nice golf courses. And I'd have a very sympathetic boss who would let me play and I'd be good enough to win a few bits and pieces. That was me, around 1960.

My earliest memory of Christy was that he seemed to appear out of nowhere at the age of 28 or 29 and was attached to Bundoran. He was looked upon as the wunderkind of the day. This fellow from the west coast of Ireland with the most natural swing. He was going to set the world on fire. And he did, of course.

At which point I reminded Alliss of how he had reported for the *Daily Express* on the famous victory by O'Connor and Harry Bradshaw in the Canada Cup at Mexico City in 1958. 'The elevation was 10,000 feet and Bradshaw had the worst varicose veins and flat feet of anyone I've ever seen in my life', he recalled:

It was 100 degrees. At the time, it was one of the greatest golfing feats ever, and I was essentially giving my opinion to the *Express*, as my father had done for the *Sunday Express* on the Ryder in 1930-something.

They were strange times. The Brad was 5ft 9 or 10, overweight a bit and walked bump, bump, bump and told stories about Americans at Portmarnock and doing three rounds in the one day, pulling his trolley. Playing them for £50 and skinning them with ease because they didn't think Harry could play, with the grip he had [three fingers of the right hand overlapping].

I suppose he would be considered a little eccentric these days. We don't have any Harry Bradshaws any more. He played at a time where there were several eccentrics on the circuit.

If I'm not mistaken, Harry went one-and-a-half if not two tournaments, missing maybe one fairway. And I think he went for an entire season without missing a green with anything higher than a seven iron. From 120 yards he never missed a green, and I look at them today missing greens with wedges.

This isn't just a stupid old man talking, but I'm sure the players were more skilful in my day and more skilful still from 1900 to 1930, when you look at the equipment, the balls and clubs they used. They were geniuses.

Today, they're looking at yardages. Like it's 99 yards. What am I going to do? I've got a club that can do 96 or 104. I'm buggered now. I can't play. So why can't you just take a bit ...

Fourteen Irish challengers, five of them amateurs, made the Open field of 98 for the event's first staging at Royal Portrush. Highest finisher among them was local man, Fred Daly, the 1947 champion who was tied fourth behind England's Max Faulkner despite a third-round 75, as an indication of how wonderfully competitive he was at that time.

O'Connor started disappointingly with a 79, but recovered with rounds of 74,72 and 74 for an aggregate of 299, the same score as Australia's Kel Nagle, who would capture this great prize nine years later, in its Centenary staging at St Andrews. Christy Kane was the last of the Irish challengers to complete four rounds on 309.

The leading amateur medal went to the gifted American Frank Stranahan, a shot ahead of The Brad in a share of 12th place. And we're told that Harry retained many admirers from his performance at Portrush only four years previously when he beat Flory van Donck by two strokes to capture the Irish Open title.

Joe Carr was the leading Irish amateur (tied 24th on 300), followed by Cecil Beamish (tied 31st on 303). Jimmy Carroll (76,79), Norman Drew (75,88) and John Glover (80,83) failed to make the cut, along with Irish professionals Sam Bacon, Jimmy Martin, PG Stevenson, Adam Whiston and Christy Greene.

The Open was a very different event back then to what we've become accustomed to in recent decades. Indeed, the gentle nature of life at Portrush in 1951 is captured beautifully by Maurice McAleese in his charming book, *Echoes of Open Glory*, published in 2014, especially in Chapter 16, titled 'There was a great buzz about the clubhouse'.

His piece begins:

> A commercial traveller from Belfast, who regularly stayed at my mother's boarding house in Causeway Street, was a keen golfer and one evening after tea he said to me, 'Maurice, let's take a run down to the golf club and see what's happening with the golf.'
>
> We drove down to the golf club in his little Morris Minor, and if memory serves me right, we were able to drive straight into the clubhouse carpark with no bother at all.
>
> Not too many people owned cars then and the traffic was nothing like today. We were able to watch some of the players, some on the practice ground and others on the putting green. There was a great buzz about the clubhouse but everything was relaxed and there didn't seem to be much security in evidence.
>
> I don't know how much spectators' tickets were in those days, but that wasn't something that worried me unduly because I knew all the best places to sneak onto the course and it was easy to lose myself in the crowds and keep out of the way of the stewards. I offer a belated apology for that now, but I still enjoy telling the story.
>
> In a funny sort of way, my little subterfuge added to the thrill and excitement of the occasion and I remember seeing some of the top players of the day in action. Players like the great Henry Cotton, Bobby Locke, Flory van Donck, Fred Daly and, of course, the winner, Max Faulkner, who cut a flamboyant dash because of the bright colours he wore.

An enduring memory locally was the manner in which Locke handled the treacherous short 14th, known as Calamity Corner, en route to a share of sixth place (71,74,74,74). It seems that his approach each day was to hook a fairway wood into the depression left of the green from where he would chip and putt for par. So it was that 'Bobby Locke's hollow' became one of the legacies of the event.

The splendid history of Royal Portrush by Roger C. Anderson, published in the autumn of 2019, provides some wonderful detail about the 1951 Open. It tells how the staging of the Championship had been a long-term objective of the club, from the time when architect Harry Colt completed his transformation of the Dunluce Links in 1932.

The official announcement came on 24 November 1949, though the *Belfast News Letter* had carried a headline proclaiming 'Open Championship Promise' in its edition of 10 August, 13 years previously. We're told that 'authoritative assurance' had been secured by the highly influential Sir Anthony Babington, who was captain of Royal Portrush for four years from 1932 to 1936. It was agreed that £2,500 would be spent on refurbishing the clubhouse.

On seeing for the first time the masterpiece which Colt had created, the eminent scribe Bernard Darwin wrote that the architect had built himself a monument 'more enduring than brass'. The link with Colt stemmed from his re-design of Royal Dublin after it had been used as a musketry range by the British army during World War I. In this context, a key figure was Babington, a one-time Dublin resident and a graduate of Trinity, who was a prominent member of both Royal Dublin and Royal Portrush.

As Ian Bamford pointed out in his early history of Royal Portrush:

> Only men of perception and foresight would have contemplated improving on a natural championship links which had been the venue of a most successful Irish Amateur Open Championship in 1919 and had been the venue of the 1911 and 1924 British Ladies Championships.

Babington was such a man. Given that both men practised law – though Colt had quit his practice as a solicitor in Hastings, Kent, by that stage to become secretary of Sunningdale – they became firm friends, and the architect was often Babington's guest on visits to this country.

So it was that in 1923, Colt prepared a comprehensive layout for two new courses, though it was eight years later before Royal Portrush acquired leases to the land.

Then there was the price. Though Colt's initial figure for the development was £7,000, he intimated that the eventual cost would probably be closer to £10,000. This was accepted by the club, despite the fact that they had insisted at a general meeting in 1932 that the cost should not exceed £3,200. Little more than a year later, the Dunluce course was formally opened, having been played on as early as Easter of that year. The Valley course, which was a particular favourite of Babington's, took somewhat longer. And when completed, the entire project reflected enormous credit on the determination and foresight of a man who, as we've indicated, was captain of the club for four years and president for eight years, from 1938 to 1946.

Anderson further informs us that the Open field was notable for two debutants in Peter Thomson and Christy O'Connor Snr. As a 21-year-old of formidable promise, Thomson was taken under the wing of fellow Australian Norman von Nida, 16 years Thomson's senior and with three top six finishes from four previous Open appearances.

On first seeing Thomson, the great golf writer Pat Ward-Thomas observed: 'I never saw a golfer who seemed so assured of his destiny. There is about him the unmistakeable air of success.' For the following years up to 1958, Thomson would finish no lower than second in the Open, with four victories. He would secure his fifth triumph in 1965.

As for Portrush '51, *The Guardian* reported:

> With a six strokes' lead over N Sutton and Cerda at the end of the third round, Faulkner had the Championship in his grasp. No one else – though Cerda made a wonderful attempt – could win it if Faulkner played sensibly in the afternoon. And this he did, driving superbly with his wide, shut-face swing and making no real mistakes. Even when a five came at the 15th, and again at the 16th, he remained calm.

A lovely chip to the side of the hole saved a stroke at the 17th and although he cut his second shot to the last green, a safe five proved to be enough.

Incidentally, among the amateur entries, Knock's John Glover had won the British Boys Championship in 1950 and in a distinguished career as a golf administrator went on to become Rules Secretary of the Royal and Ancient. Norman Drew would go on to win the Irish Amateur Open titles in 1952 and 1953 while Joe Carr's experience there was to last a lifetime.

'My favourite Irish course is Royal Portrush', he told me 50 years later. 'It's where a player's shot-making skills are subjected to the ultimate test', he said:

> Portmarnock, which I grew to love from an early age, is the fairest test, but Portrush demands greater shot-making.
>
> I suppose I'm prejudiced, having won my third Amateur there in 1960. Apart from shot-making skills, Portrush tests your temperament, in that you won't necessarily get what you deserve there, whereas the good shot is almost invariably rewarded at Portmarnock. If you don't use your brain and keep your emotions in check while playing the magnificent Dunluce Links, you're going to be dead as a dodo.

The only disappointment in the build-up to 1951 must have been the weak American entry, which was rendered even more so when Jimmy Demaret, Charlie Coe and Jackie Burke scratched from the event.

Faulkner, meanwhile, prospered in dull, calm conditions early on, then in the worst of the weather on the Friday afternoon, and carded no worse than a five in rounds of 71,70,70,74 for an aggregate of 285. Born in 1916 in Boxhill, England, he was only a few weeks away from his 35th birthday at the time. Described by Peter Alliss as the most talented and eccentric British player of his era, he invariably played with an odd assortment of clubs which included a mixture of stiff and whippy shafts. Among his estimated 300 putters was a particular favourite with a driftwood head and a shaft made from a billiard cue.

In the event, putting was a major factor as he became the fourth home-based winner of the title after World War II. In fact, so enthused was he by his performance with the blade around Dunluce that he vowed he would never again miss a short putt. Faulkner also talked about being helped by what he described as 'a mystery guiding light'.

Whatever it was, the Portrush magic seemed to pass on to his son-in-law, Brian Barnes, who won successive Senior British Open titles there in 1995 and 1996.

At this point, it may be appropriate to clear up the slight that Alliss made on my numeracy. A story from the 1951 Championship concerned Alliss just out of his teens, shooting a brilliant opening round of 69 and then celebrating by going out on the town in the company of a winsome local lassie he remembers as Doreen. Which was supposed to have led to a second-round 84 and a missed cut. In fact, the 69 was shot in qualifying and his two rounds in the Open proper were 79 and 80. Which reminds me of the famous line from the movie *The Man Who Shot Liberty Valance* advising us that 'when fact becomes legend, print the legend.'

The *Belfast Telegraph* reported:

> In one crowded half-hour of glorious golf at Portrush, the record of 69 set on Monday by Arthur Lees (Sunningdale), was equalled by the tall, 21-year-old Peter Alliss (Ferndown) and was then twice broken by Bobby Locke with an immaculate 67 and next by Jack Hargreaves (Sutton Coldfield) with a tremendous 66.

Some years later, Alliss informed Maurice McAleese:

> I had just completed two years National Service with the RAF Regiment so I was very much out of practice [for the 1951 Open]. I was chaperoned by my brother Alec.

> I remember the large crowds, the wonderful golf course, the rather dreary weather and Max Faulkner's splendid victory. It was quite a good time for British players – Fred Daly won the Championship in 1947 and Henry Cotton in 1948. In 1949 and 1950 it went to Bobby Locke of South Africa, and then in 1951 it was the turn of Max Faulkner. He was a very flamboyant character who brought a touch of colour to our very dull lives.

Ideally, one imagines the Championship should have been about local hero Daly, who signed more autographs than he would like to have done. But it became the story of Faulkner, who signed autographs he might sensibly not have done.

Though Daly finished strongly, the pressure of having been backed heavily by his many friends clearly affected him. In fact, he was so hotly fancied locally that bookmakers in the town wouldn't lay odds against him. As he admitted afterwards: 'I wasn't the best player at Portrush. I got what I deserved.'

In the end, the 34-year-old Faulker was declared a very worthy winner of the top prize of £300, by a two-stroke margin over Argentinian Antonio Cerda. And out of the total prize fund of £1,700, there was sufficient for a reward of £20 to the virtually unknown professional from Tuam GC, by the name of O'Connor.

The references to autographs stem from the fact that it was estimated Daly signed more than the rest of the field put together, while Faulkner seriously tempted fate by signing himself 'Open Champion 1951', with a final round still to play after lunch on Friday. Granted, he was a comfortable six strokes clear of his closest challengers after 54 holes, but the more superstitious among players known to be notoriously fatalistic were absolutely horrified that he should have been so presumptuous.

Still, we're told that Bernard Darwin of *The Times* quickly brought him back to earth. 'Faulkner', barked the doyen of the golf-writing fraternity within minutes of the final putt finding the cup, 'I understand you've won the Open. Sit there and I'll write about you.' The thoughts of issuing such a command to modern-day practitioners such as Brooks Koepka, Bryson DeChambeau or even the affable Scottie Scheffler, is enough to chill the blood.

Nobody, however, would have dared question Darwin's command of his craft.

From a local standpoint, the reward for all their endeavours was that they became the first and still the only club outside of mainland Britain to stage the Open Championship. Understandably, there was huge excitement in the build-up to the event not only in Portrush, but in the neighbouring resort town of Portstewart. Despite the hardship of the post-war years, golf had become a significant part of everyday life in the area. Principal figures during Open week were former Walker Cup representative and Irish amateur Open champion Brigadier G.N.C. Martin, who was captain of the host club, and Coleraine solicitor Alex E. Martin, who was captain of Portstewart.

As Maurice McAleese indicated, the scale of the Championship was actually quite modest, when compared with present-day stagings at which crowds of more than 40,000 are pretty much routine on a daily basis. Back in 1951, when, incidentally, the last two rounds were staged on Friday, 7 July, attendances were estimated at around 7,000 per day earlier in the week and roughly 8,000 for the climax.

For the avid fan, however, it was an absolute treat, with crowds permitted to walk the fairways which were not roped off. Certain restrictions were still in place, however, to protect the precious dune structure, not unlike the arrangements which were deemed necessary at Ballybunion for the 2000 Murphy's Irish Open.

Stewards had instructions to ensure that the galleries kept to the left at holes two, four, five, six, nine, 10, 12, 13 and 14 and to the right at holes one, three, 11, 15, 16, 17 and 18. And no spectators at all were permitted on the seventh and eighth holes.

With such modest crowds, the nature of these restrictions give a fair indication of the problems organisers faced when the event returned there in 2019, even accepting the significant changes that were made to the course by architect Martin Ebert. His main work, of course, involved the removal of the old 17th and 18th holes and the introduction of a new seventh and eighth.

Faulkner was 88 when he died in February 2005, but it wasn't before he recounted details of one of the most remarkable shots in the history of the Open. It happened on the 16th, which is now the 18th, as the third round was drawing to a close in 1951. 'There was a stile', he recalled:

> I was near out of bounds and a barbed wire fence. And my ball was only a yard away from the stile and I had to swing the club very upright.
>
> I had a little baffy thing, a four-wood in these days, and I was a trick-shot player when I was young and I knew I could do it. I had to hit this ball out of bounds, through a barbed wire fence, and curl it. And I hit this ball with no follow-through, otherwise I'd have torn my hands to pieces on the barbed-wire fence that my bottom was leaning against.
>
> And this ball shot underneath, it didn't rise for 30 yards, hardly at all. It went under the wire and it started to curl and it curled right round, 40 yards or more, onto the green. It was only a six-iron shot but my ball travelled about 180 yards in a big circle. And it pitched on the green, stopped like a niblick and I was only about five yards from the pin.

Faulkner's remarkable shot kept him on course for Open glory and also drew generous praise from his previously silent playing partner. 'The last 36 holes, I played with Frank Stranahan, the American amateur, and I said "Good morning, Frank"', Faulkner added.

> Not a word came back. He never said good morning! I thought 'Ooh, that's it.' And that was it. Never spoke one word, until we got to the 16th on that morning round. And his first words, walking from in front of the crowd were, 'Max – that's the finest shot I've ever seen in my life'. And he shook me by the hand.

When the Irish Open returned to Portrush in 2012, for the first time since 1947, vast golf-knowledgeable crowds turned out to see Welshman Jamie Donaldson claim the title. Throw in the presence of three recent home-grown Major champions in Darren Clarke (then a Portrush resident), Graeme McDowell (a Portrush native) and Rory McIlroy, and the enthusiasm of the Irish nation could surely be taken for granted.

As was often said, and meant as a compliment, 'the Irish will show up to watch the grass grow.' Soon, it would seem, they would be able to do so under the feet of golf's greatest players competing in the game's oldest and most important championship.

Meanwhile, back at Portstewart in 2017, the presence of Ms Madill added a further dimension to what became a lengthy chat about golf and golfers in the west of County Antrim. I was reminded that when I was getting into my stride at golf writing nearly 40 years previously, Madill was putting Portstewart on the map as a gifted player.

'I believe I was the first female along with a Welsh girl to go to the US on a golf scholarship,' she said. 'I had done a year at St Andrews University and was still 18 when I went to Texas. Of course, there was no such thing as emails or texts in those days. You got a phone call only if somebody died.'

She went on:

> Our family had an association with Peter Alliss even before he was aware of it. Patricia, my older sister, went to Edinburgh University and mum wrote to Peter asking if he could recommend a good coach in the Edinburgh area. As I was to discover later on, Peter replied to every letter he ever received, including this one.
>
> He replied to Mum telling her that there was one fellow worth checking out. And that was John Shade, father of RDBM [Ronnie] Shade. So Patricia started having lessons with JS, as we called him. They hit it off. Then, on my first trip away as a 15-year-old, I went to my big sister in Edinburgh where I, too, started getting lessons from John Shade.

> I credit him with taking me to the level which allowed me win the British Match Play title in '79. He was a great, great guy. Sadly he died two months before I won it.

She went on:

> Thirteen months later, I won the British Strokeplay. But I never won an Irish, which was a bit of a disappointment, especially losing two finals. The second of those was particularly painful, given that it was against Mary McKenna at Portrush, where I was two up playing the 13th.

Recalling her decision to turn professional in 1986 prompted Alliss to interject:

> I was the first president of the Ladies European Tour and with 28 or 29 tournaments a year, I felt convinced it had a great future, given the commercial possibilities of the things that women use, like cosmetics, perfumes and clothing. I was sure there would be companies waiting in line to sponsor tournaments. But sadly it didn't happen.

He closed by speaking of the Irish Open host at that time, Rory McIlroy. 'Rory has travelled an enormous distance in the 10 years I've been observing him', said Alliss. 'It must be his background, his schooling, the people he met at school and the efforts his mum and dad put in. Whatever the reasons, his connections here are genuine and robust and he has tried to become part of Irish golf.'

With that, it was time to go. I had imposed enough strain on those mellifluous chords which had enriched so many lives for so long. Not least around those parts. I met him again at Lahinch, two years later. Then, as if in the blink of an eye, he was gone from us. But no commentator on golf has left a richer legacy.

9

Himself

'In golfing terms, Christy had already been canonised for his achievements in the game by the mid-fifties and he was recognised throughout the international golf community as one of the outstanding players of the day.'

– Distinguished British golf writer Peter Dobereiner

● ● ● ●

During a visit Peter Thomson made to Rathsallagh GC in the summer of 1996, there was the opportunity of discussing varied aspects of the tournament game. Among these was the perennial question as to why Christy O'Connor Snr had failed to win the Open Championship.

Nobody was better qualified to provide the answer than the gifted Australian, given his own achievement of five Open triumphs, including 1958 at Royal Lytham, where O'Connor was tied third, and 1965 at Royal Birkdale, where Thomson edged Himself into a share of second place with Brian Huggett.

According to O'Connor, there was no love lost between them as trenchant rivals. Yet Thomson was markedly generous when I talked to him on that June afternoon, by which stage both had eased comfortably into retirement. 'I believe Christy was unlucky in the Open', said Thomson. 'I always felt that if he had won it once, he would have gone on to win it several times.'

As can be seen from the accompanying details, Himself played in 26 Opens, from his debut at Royal Portrush in 1951, to his swansong at Lytham in 1979, when Seve Ballesteros triumphed. He missed three stagings during those years, at Lytham in 1952 when his entry was late, at Carnoustie in 1975 when he failed to qualify, and in 1978 at St Andrews where, in his own words, he declined to enter the pre-qualifying lottery.

Birkdale in 1965 was obviously O'Connor's closest call. The inimitable Pat Ward-Thomas wrote in *The Guardian*: 'The golf of O'Connor and Huggett in setting the final pace is beyond praise. O'Connor has by far the finest record of any home golfer in the last 10 years, and he scored throughout with a consistency that hitherto has escaped him this year.'

Portrush in 1951 reflected the struggle of his early years. In his autobiography with John Redmond, he wrote of his time as part greenkeeper, part professional at Tuam GC, where he received heart-warming support from a group of members led by Jimmy Glynn:

> It was a typical if wholly unexpected gesture, when Jimmy, along with fellow club members Paddy Smyth and Jarlath Canavan, a man who had won fame on Gaelic football fields for Galway, organised a collection to finance my entrance fee at Royal Portrush. They collected the tidy sum of £70 and but for that support, I might never have been launched as a tournament player.

After joining Royal Dublin in April 1959, he remarked to me with a smile that 'there must be some secret in the sand.' He went on:

> People said I was gifted and I was in one way, thank God. I had the ability to do the right things for myself. Nobody told me these things.

> I believe the real secrets in golf are the ones a player discovers for himself. And the more you practise, the more natural you get. A natural swing can only be the result of constant repetition. Hands, legs, eyes, balance, set-up – there you are. And a determination to be successful. If there's a secret, that's it.

From a competitive standpoint, his last serious Open challenge was at Troon in 1973 when Jack Nicklaus was among his playing partners when he finished tied seventh behind Tom Weiskopf. He was then five months from his 49th birthday.

1951

AT ROYAL PORTRUSH

285 - M Faulkner (Unattached)	71, 70, 70, 74
287 - A. Cerda (Argentina)	74, 72, 71, 70
290 - C. H. Ward (Little Aston)	75, 73, 74, 68
292 - F.Daly (Balmoral)	74, 70, 75, 73
292 - J. Adams (Wentworth)	68, 77, 75, 72
293 - A.D. Locke (South Africa)	71, 74, 74, 74
293 - W. Shankland (Templenesan)	73, 76, 72, 72
293 - N. Sutton (Leigh)	73, 70, 74, 76
293 - H. Weetman (Cronham Hurst)	73, 71, 75, 74
293 - P.W. Thomson (Australia)	70, 75, 73, 75
294 - J. Panton (Glenbervie)	73, 72, 74, 75
295 - D.J. Rees (South Herts)	70, 77, 76, 72
296 - H. Bradshaw (Portmarnock)	80, 71, 74, 71
297 - E. Cremin (Australia)	73, 75, 75, 74
298 - A, Waters (Worplesdon)	74, 75, 78, 71
298 - Mr. K. Enderby (Australia)	76, 74, 75, 73
299 - K. Nagle (Australia)	76, 76, 72, 75
299 - C. O'Connor (Tuam)	79, 74, 72, 74
299 - U. Grappasonni (Italy)	73, 73, 77, 76

1952

AT ROYAL LYTHAM AND ST. ANNES

287 - A.D. Locke (South Africa)	69, 71, 74, 73
288 - P.Thomson(Australia)	68, 73, 77, 70
289 - F. Daly (Balmoral)	67, 69, 77, 76

C. O'Connor (Entry went missing)

1953

AT CARNOUSTIE

282 - B. Hogan (USA)	73, 71, 70, 68
286 - Mr. F. Stranahan (USA)	70, 74, 73, 69
286 - D.J. Rees (South Herts)	72, 70, 73, 71
286 - P.W. Thomson (Australia)	72, 72, 71, 71
286 - A. Cerda (Argentine)	75, 71, 69, 71
287 - R. de Vicenzo (Argentina)	72, 71, 71, 73
290 - S. L. King (Knole Park)	74, 73, 72, 71
291 - A.D. Locke (South Africa)	72, 73, 74, 72
292 - P. Alliss (Ferndown)	75, 72, 74, 71
292 - E. Brown (Unattached)	71, 71, 75, 75
294 - F. Daly (Balmoral)	73, 75, 71, 75
295 - M. Faulkner (St. George's Hill)	74, 71, 73, 77
296 - A. Lees (Sunnindale)	76, 76, 72, 72
297 - H. Weetman (Cronham Hurst)	80, 73, 72, 72
297 - J. Jacobs (Sandy Lodge)	79, 74, 71, 73
297 - T.Fairbairn (Redish Vale)	74, 71, 73, 79
298 - H. Hassanein (Egypt)	78, 71, 73, 76
298 - E. Lester (Bristol & Clifton)	83, 70, 72, 73
299 - C. H. Ward (Little Aston)	78, 71, 76, 73
299 - R.W. Horne (Hendon)	76, 74, 75, 74
300 - S. Scott (Carlisle City)	74, 74, 78, 74
300 - H. Themson (Unattached)	76, 74, 74, 76
301 - C.O'Connor (Bundoran) 24th	77, 77, 72, 75

1954

AT ROYAL BIRKDALE

283 - P. W. Thomson (Australia)	72, 71, 69, 71
284 - S. Scott (Carlisle City)	76, 67, 69, 72
284 - D. J. Rees (South Herts)	72, 71, 69, 72
284 - A. D. Locke (South Africa)	74, 71, 69, 70
286 - J. Adams (Royal Mid Surrey)	73, 75, 69, 69
286 - A. Cerda (Argentina)	71, 71, 73, 71
286 - J. Turnesa (USA)	72, 72, 71, 71
287 - P. Alliss (Ferndown)	72, 74, 71, 70
287 - S. King (Knole Park)	69, 74, 74, 70
289 - J. Demaret (USA)	73, 71, 74, 71
289 - F. van Donck (Belgium)	77, 71, 70, 71
293 - C. O'Connor (Bundoran) 20th	74, 72, 72, 75

1955

AT ST. ANDREWS

281 - P.W. Thomson (Australia)	71, 68, 70, 72
283 - J. Fallon (Huddersfield)	73, 67, 73, 70
284 - F. Jowle (Edgbaston)	70, 71, 69, 74
285 - A.D. Locke (South Africa)	74, 69, 70, 72
286 - A. Cerda (Argentina)	73, 71, 71, 71
286 - K. Bousefield (Coombe Hill)	71, 75, 70, 70
286 - H. Weetman (Cronham Hurst)	71, 71, 70, 74
286 - B. J. Hunt (Hartsbourne)	70, 71, 74, 71
286 - F. van Donck (Belgium)	71, 72, 71, 72
287 - C. O'Connor (Bundoran)	71, 75, 70, 71

1956

AT HOYLAKE

286 - P. W. Thomson (Australia)	70, 70, 72, 74
289 - F. van Donck (Belgium)	71, 74, 70, 74
290 - R. de Vicenzo (Argentina)	71, 70, 79, 70
291 - G. Player (South Africa)	71, 76, 73, 71
292 - J. Panton (Glenbervie)	74, 76, 72, 70
293 - T.H. Cotton (Temple)	72, 76, 71, 74
293 - E. Bertolino (Argentina)	69, 72, 76, 76
294 - A. Cerda (Argentina)	72, 81, 68, 73
294 - M. Souchak (USA)	74, 74, 74, 72
295 - C.O'Connor (Bundoran)	73, 78, 74, 70
295 - H. Weetman (Cronham Hurst)	72, 76, 75, 72

1957

AT ST. ANDREWS

279 - A.D. Locke (South Africa) 69, 72, 68, 70
282 - P. W. Thomson (Australia) 73, 69, 70, 70
283 - E.C. Brown (Buchanan Castle) 67, 72, 73, 71
285 - A. Miguel (Spain) 72, 72, 69, 72
286 - D. C. Thomas (Sudbury 72, 74, 70, 70
286 - T. Haliburton (Wentworth) 72, 73, 68, 73
286 - Mr. W. Smith (Prestwick) 71, 72, 72, 71
286 - F. van Donck (Belgium) 72, 68, 74, 72
287 - T.H. Cotton (Temple) 74, 72, 69, 72
287 - M. Faulkner (Selsey) 74, 70, 71, 72
287 - A. Cerda (Argentina) 71, 71, 72, 73
291 - C. O'Connor (Bundoran) 19th 77, 69, 72, 73

1958

AT ROYAL LYTHAM AND ST. ANNES

278 - P. W. Thomson (Australia) 66, 72, 67, 73
278 - D. C Thomas (Sudbury) 70, 68, 69, 71
279 - E.C. Brown (Buchanan Castle) 73, 70, 65, 71
279 - C. O'Connor (Killarney) 67, 68, 73, 71
281 - F. van Donck (Belgium) 70, 70, 67, 74
281 - L. Ruiz (Argentina) 71, 65, 72, 73
283 - G. Player (South Africa) 68, 74, 70, 71
284 - T. H. Cotton (Temple) 68, 75, 69, 72
284 - H. Weetman (Selsdon Park) 73, 67, 73, 71
284 - E. Lester (Hazel Grove) 73, 66, 71, 74
*Play-off scores: 139 Thomson 68, 71
143 Thomas 69, 74

1959

AT MUIRFIELD

284 - G. Player (South Africa) 75, 71, 70, 68
286 - F. van Donck (Belgium) 70, 70, 73, 73
286 - F. Bullock (Prestwick) 68, 70, 74, 74
287 - S. Scott (Roehampton) 73, 70, 73, 71
288 - C. O'Connor (Royal Dublin) 73, 74, 72, 69
288 - Mr. R. Jack (Dullatur) 71, 75, 68, 74
288 - S. King (Knole Park) 70, 74, 68, 76
288 - J. Panton (Glenbervie) 72, 72, 71, 73
289 - D. J. Rees (South Herts) 73, 73, 69, 74
289 - L. Ruiz (Argentina) 72, 74, 69, 74

1960

AT ST. ANDREWS

278 - K. Nagle (Australia) 69, 67, 71, 71
279 - A. Palmer (USA) 70, 71, 70, 68
282 - B. J. Hunt (Hartsbourne) 72, 73, 71, 66
282 - H. Henning (South Africa) 72, 72, 69, 69
282 - R. de Vincenzo (Argentina) 67, 67, 75, 73
283 - Mr. G. Wolstenholme (S/dale) 74, 70, 71, 68
284 - G. Player (South Africa) 72, 71, 72, 69
285 - Mr. J. B. Carr (Sutton) 72, 73, 67, 73
286 - H. Weetman (Selsdon Park) 74, 70, 71, 71
286 - S. Scott (Roehampton) 73, 71, 67, 75
286 - D. J. Rees (South Herts) 73, 71, 73, 69
286 - E. C. Brown (Buchanan Castle) 75, 68, 72, 71
295 - C. O'Connor (R. Dublin) 36th 80, 67, 76, 72

1961

AT ROYAL BIRKDALE

284 - A. Palmer (USA) 70, 73, 69, 72
285 - D. J. Rees (South Herts) 68, 74, 71, 72
288 - C. O'Connor (Royal Dublin) 71, 77, 67, 73
288 - N. Coles (Coombe Hill) 70, 77, 69, 72,
289 - E.C. Brown (Unattached) 73, 76, 70, 70
289 - K. Nagle (Australia) 68, 75, 75, 71
290 - P. W. Thomson (Australia) 75, 72, 70, 73
291 - K. Bousefield (Coombe Hill) 71, 77, 75, 68
291 - P. Alliss (Parkstone) 73, 75, 72, 71
293 - S. Scott (Roehampton) 76, 75, 71, 71
293 - H. Henning (South Africa) 68, 74, 75, 76
295 - R. Sota (Spain) 71, 76, 72, 76
297 - A. Coop (Dean Wood) 71, 79, 73, 74

1962

AT ROYAL TROON

276 - A. Palmer (USA) 71, 69, 67, 69
282 - K. Nagle (Australia) 71, 71, 70, 70
289 - B. Huggett (Romford) 75, 71, 74, 69
289 - P. Rodgers (USA) 75, 70, 72, 72
290 - R. Charles (New Zealand) 75, 70, 70, 75
292 - S. Snead (USA) 76, 73, 72, 71
293 - D. Thomas (Sunningdale) 77, 70, 71, 75
293 - P. Alliss (Parkstone) 77, 69, 74, 73
294 - S. Scott (Roehampton) 77, 74, 75, 68
295 - R. Moffitt (Coventry Hearsall) 75, 70, 74, 76
296 - S. Miguel (Spain) 72, 79, 73, 72
296 - R. Whitehead (B/stead Downs) 74, 75, 72, 75
296 - J. Garaialde (France) 76, 73, 76, 71
296 - H. Weetman (Selsdon Park) 75, 73, 73, 75
297 - C. O'Connor (Royal Dublin) 74, 78, 73, 72
297 - D. Hutchinson (South Africa) 78, 73, 76, 70
297 - R. Foreman (Belfairs) 77, 73, 72, 75
297 - B. J. Hunt (Hartsbourne) 74, 75, 75, 73
297 - J. Panton (Glenbervie) 74, 73, 79, 71
297 - J. Martin (Edmondstown) 73, 72, 76, 76

1963

AT LYTHAM AND ST. ANNES

277 - R. J. Charles (New Zealand)	68, 72, 66, 71
277 - P. Rodgers (USA)	67, 68, 73, 69
278 - J. Nicklaus (USA)	71, 67, 70, 70
283 - K. Nagle (Australia)	69, 70, 73, 71
285 - P. Thomson (Australia)	67, 69, 71, 78
286 - C. O'Connor (Royal Dublin)	74, 68, 76, 68
287 - G. Player (South Africa)	75, 70, 72, 70
287 - R. Sota (Spain)	69, 73, 73, 72
288 - S. Miguel (Spain)	73, 69, 72, 75
288 - J. Garaialde	72, 69, 72, 75

*Play-off scores: 140 Charles 69, 71
148 Rodgers 72, 76

1964

AT ST. ANDREWS

279 - T. Lema (USA)	73, 68, 68, 70
284 - J. Nicklaus (USA)	76, 74, 66, 68
285 - R. de Vicenzo (Argentina)	76, 72, 70, 67
287 - B. J. Hunt (Hartsbourne)	73, 74, 70, 70
290 - B. Devlin (Australia)	72, 72, 73, 73
291 - C.O'Connor (Royal Dublin)	71, 73, 74, 73
291 - H. Weetman (Selsdon Park)	72, 71, 75, 73
292 - H. Henning (South Africa)	78, 73, 71, 70
292 - G. Player (South Africa)	78, 71, 73, 70

1965

AT ROYAL BIRKDALE

285 - P. Thomson (Australia)	74, 68, 72, 71
287 - C. O'Connor (Royal Dublin)	69, 73, 74, 71
287 - B. Huggett (Romford)	73, 68, 76, 70
288 - R. de Vicenzo (Argentina)	74, 69, 73, 72
289 - K. Nagle (Australia)	74, 70, 73, 72
289 - B.J. Hunt (Hartsbourne)	74, 74, 70, 71
290 - S. Miguel (Spain)	72, 73, 72, 73
290 - B. Devlin (Australia)	71, 69, 75, 75
293 - J. Panton (Glenbervie)	74, 74, 75, 70
293 - M. Faulkner (Selsey)	74, 72, 74, 73
294 - N. Coles (Coombe Hill)	73, 74, 77, 70
294 - J. Nicklaus (USA)	73, 71, 77, 73
294 - L. Platts (Wanstead)	72, 72, 73, 77
294 - H. Boyle (Unattached)	73, 69, 76, 76
295 - A. Palmer (USA)	70, 71, 75, 79

1966

AT MUIRFIELD

282 - J. Nicklaus (USA)	70, 67, 75, 70
283 - D. Thomas (Dunham Forest)	72, 73, 69, 69
283 - D. Sanders (USA)	71, 70, 72, 70
286 - G. Player (South Africa)	72, 74, 71, 69
286 - B. Devlin (Australia)	73, 69, 74, 70
286 - K. Nagle (Australia)	72, 76, 68, 70
286 - P. Rodgers (USA)	74, 66, 70, 76
288 - D. Marr (USA)	73, 76, 69, 70
288 - P. Thomson (Australia)	73, 75, 69, 71
288 - S. Miguel (Spain)	74, 72, 70, 72
288 - A. Palmer (USA)	73, 72, 69, 74
290 - R. Sikes (USA)	73, 72, 73, 72
291 - C. O'Connor (Royal Dublin)	73, 72, 74, 72
292 - J. Boros (USA)	73, 71, 76, 72
293 - J. Hitchcock (Cronham Hurst)	70, 77, 74, 72
293 - P. Butler (Harborne)	73, 65, 80, 75

1967

AT HOYLAKE

278 - R. de Vicenzo (Argentina)	70, 71, 67, 70
280 - J. Nicklaus (USA)	71, 69, 71, 69
284 - C. Clark (Sunningdale)	70, 73, 69, 72
284 - G. Player (South Africa)	72, 71, 67, 74
285 - A. Jacklin (Potters Bar)	73, 69, 73, 70
286 - S. Miguel (Spain)	72, 74, 68, 72
286 - H. Henning (South Africa)	74, 70, 71, 71
287 - B. Devlin (Australia)	70, 70, 72, 75
287 - A. Balding (Canada)	74, 71, 69, 73
287 - T. Horton (Ham Manor)	74, 74, 69, 70
287 - P. Thomson (Australia)	71, 74, 70, 72
287 - H. Boyle (Jacobs Centre)	74, 74, 71, 68
289 - G.Wolstenholme (St. George's)	74, 71, 73, 71
289 - S. Peach (Australia)	71, 75, 73, 70
289 - M. Hoyle (Castle Inn)	74, 75, 69, 71
289 - D. Beman (USA)	72, 76, 68, 73
289 - L. Platts (Pannal)	68, 73, 72, 76
290 - B. Coxon (Australia)	73, 76, 71, 70
290 - D. Sanders (USA)	71, 73, 73, 73
290 - H. Muscroft (Moor Allerton)	72, 73, 72, 73
291 - C. O'Connor (Royal Dublin)	70, 74, 71, 76

1968

AT CARNOUSTIE

289 - G. Player (South Africa)	74, 71, 71, 73
291 - J. Nicklaus (USA)	76, 69, 73, 73

291 - R. Charles (New Zealand) 72, 72, 71, 76
292 - W. Casper (USA) 72, 68, 74, 78
293 - M. Bembridge (Little Aston) 71, 75, 73, 74
295 - B. Barnes (Burnham & Berrow) 70, 74, 80, 71
295 - N. Coles (Coombe Hill) 75, 76, 71, 73
295 - G. Brewer (USA) 74, 73, 72, 76
296 - A. Balding (Canada) 74, 76, 74, 72
297 - R. de Vicenzo (Argentina) 77,72, 74, 74
297 - B. Devlin (Australia) 77, 73, 72, 75
297 - A. Palmer (USA) 77, 71, 72, 77
157 - C. O'Connor (Royal Dublin) 76, 81
Missed last two rounds

1969

AT ROYAL LYTHAM AND ST. ANNES

280 - A. Jacklin (Potters Bar) 68, 70, 70, 72
282 - R. Charles (New Zealand) 66, 69, 75, 72
283 - P.Thomson (Australia) 71, 70, 70, 72
283 - R. De Vicenzo (Argentina) 72, 73, 66, 72
284 - C.O'Connor (Royal Dublin) 71, 65, 74, 74
285 - J. Nicklaus (USA) 75, 70, 68, 72
285 - D. M. Love (USA) 70, 73, 71, 71
286 - P. Alliss (Parkstone) 73, 74, 73, 66
287 - K. Nagle (Australia) 74, 71, 72, 70
288 - M. Barber (USA) 69, 75, 75, 69

1970

AT ST. ANDREWS

283 - J. Nicklaus (USA) 68, 69, 73, 73
283 - D. Saunders (USA) 68, 71, 71, 73
285 - H. Henning (South Africa) 67, 72, 73, 73
285 - L. Trevino (USA) 68, 68, 72, 77
286 - A. Jacklin (Potters Bar) 67, 70, 73, 76
287 - N. Coles (Coombe Hill) 65, 74, 72, 76
287 - P. Oosterhuis (Dulwich) 73, 69, 69, 76
288 - H. Jackson (Knockbracken) 69, 72, 73, 74
289 - J. Panton (Glenbervie) 72, 73, 73, 71
289 - P. Thomson (Australia) 68, 74, 73, 74
289 - T. Horton (Ham Manor) 66, 73, 75, 75
290 - A. Palmer (USA) 68, 72, 76, 74
292 - M. Bembridge (Little Aston) 67, 74, 75, 76
292 - J. Richardson (Lee-on-Solent) 67, 72, 76, 77
292 - B. Yancey (USA) 71, 71, 73, 77
292 - R. Charles (New Zealand) 72, 73, 73, 74
293 - R. Bernardini (Italy) 75, 69, 74, 75
293 - W. Casper (USA) 71, 74, 73, 75
293 - R. de Vicenzo (Argentina) 71, 76, 71, 75
293 - C. Clark (Sunningdale) 69, 70, 77, 77
293 - C. O'Connor (Royal Dublin) 72, 68, 74, 79
294 - G. Wolstenholme (Australia) 68, 77, 72, 77
294 - T. Weiskopf (USA) 70, 74, 72, 78
294 - W. Godfrey (New Zealand) 71, 75, 74, 74
* Play-off scores: 72 Nicklaus
73 Sanders

1971

AT ROYAL BIRKDALE

278 - L. Trevino (USA) 69, 70, 69, 70
279 - Lian Huan Lu (Formosa) 70, 70, 69, 70
280 - A. Jacklin (Potters Bar) 69, 70, 70, 71
281 - C. De Foy (Coombe Hill) 72, 72, 68, 69
283 - J. Nicklaus (USA) 71, 71, 72, 69
283 - C. Coody (USA) 74, 71, 70, 68
284 - W. Casper (USA) 70, 72, 75, 67
284 - G. Player (South Africa) 71, 70, 71, 72
285 - D. Sanders (USA) 73, 71, 74, 67
285 - P. Thomson (Australia) 70, 73, 73, 69
294 - C. O'Connor (R. Dublin) 35th 74, 72, 76, 72

1972

AT MUIRFIELD

278 - L. Trevino (USA) 71, 70, 66, 71
279 - J. Nicklaus (USA) 70, 72, 71, 68
280 - A. Jacklin (Potters Bar) 69, 72, 67, 72
281 - D. Sanders (USA) 71, 71, 69, 70
283 - B. Barnes (Fairway DR) 71, 72, 69, 70
285 - G. Player (South Africa) 71, 71, 76, 67
286 - D. Vaughan (North Wales) 74, 73, 70, 69
286 - T. Weiskopf (USA) 73, 74, 70, 69
286 - A. Palmer (USA) 73, 73, 69, 71
286 - G. Hunt (Wentworth) 75, 72, 67, 72
287 - C. Clark (Sunningdale) 72, 71, 73, 71
289 - R. Charles (New Zealand) 75, 70, 74, 70
288 - R. Bernardini (Italy) 73, 71, 76, 68
289 - P. Townsend (Portmarnock) 70, 72, 76, 70
289 - P. Butler (Harborne) 72, 75, 73, 69
287 - D. Marr (USA) 70, 74, 71, 72
289 - J. Dorrestein (Holland) 74, 71, 72, 72
289 - J. Miller (USA) 76, 66, 72, 75
290 - H. Bannerman (Banchory) 77, 73, 73, 67
290 - M. Bembridge (Little Aston) 73, 71, 75, 71
290 - F. Beard (USA) 70, 76, 74, 70
290 - B. Yancey (USA) 73, 72, 72, 73
291 - C. O'Connor (Royal Dublin) 73, 74, 73, 71
291 - D. McClelland (Hartsbourne) 73, 74, 72, 72
291 - C. De Foy (Coombe Hill) 70, 75, 71, 75

1973

AT TROON

276 - T. Weiskopf (USA)	68, 67, 71, 70
279 - J. Miller (USA)	70, 68, 69, 72
279 - N. Coles (Holiday Inns)	71, 72, 70, 66
280 - J. Nicklaus (USA)	69, 70, 76, 65
281 - B. Yancey (USA)	69, 69, 73, 70
286 - P. Butler (Golf Domes)	71, 72, 74, 69
288 - C. O'Connor (Royal Dublin)	73, 68, 74, 73
288 - L. Wadkins (USA)	71, 73, 70, 74
288 - R. Charles (New Zealand)	73, 71, 73, 71
289 - L. Trevino (USA)	75, 73, 73, 68
289 - G. Brewer (USA)	76, 71, 72, 70
289 - H. Henning (South Africa)	73, 73, 73, 70
289 - B. Barnes (Fairway DR)	76, 67, 70, 76
290 - A. Palmer (USA)	72, 76, 70, 72
290 - G. Player (South Africa)	76, 69, 76, 69
290 - A. Jacklin (Potters Bar)	75, 73, 72, 70

1974

AT ROYAL LYTHAM AND ST. ANNES

282 - G. Player (South Africa)	69, 68, 75, 70
286 - P. Oosterhuis (Fiji)	71, 71, 73, 71
287 - J. Nicklaus (USA)	74, 72, 70, 71
309 - C. O'Connor (R. Dublin) 56th	80, 74, 77, 78

1975

AT CARNOUSTIE

279 - T. Watson (USA)	71, 67, 69, 72
279 - J. Newton (Australia)	69, 71, 65, 74
280 - R. Cole (South Africa)	72, 66, 66, 76
280 - J. Nicklaus (USA)	69, 71, 68, 72
280 - J. Miller (USA)	71, 69, 66, 74

*Play-off scores: 71 Watson
72 Newton

C. O'Connor (Royal Dublin), failed to pre-qualify

1976

AT ROYAL BIRKDALE

279 - J. Miller (USA)	72, 68, 73, 69
285 - J. Nicklaus (USA)	74, 70, 72, 69
285 - S. Ballesteros (Spain)	69, 69, 73, 74
155 - C. O'Connor (Royal Dublin)	74, 81

Missed last two rounds

1977

AT TURNBERRY

268 - T. Watson (USA)	68, 70, 65, 65
269 - J. Nicklaus (USA)	68, 70, 65, 66
279 - H. Green (USA)	72, 66, 74, 67
226 - C. O'Connor (Royal Dublin)	75, 75, 76

Missed last round

1978

AT ST. ANDREWS

281 - J. Nicklaus (USA)	71, 72, 69, 69
283 - B. Crenshaw (USA)	70, 69, 73, 71
283 - R. Floyd (USA)	69. 75, 71, 68
283 - T. Kite (USA)	72, 69, 72, 70
283 - S. Owen (New Zealand)	70, 75, 67, 71

C O'Connor (Royal Dublin) Did not enter.

1979

AT ROYAL LYTHAM AND ST. ANNES

283 - S. Ballesteros (Spain)	73, 65, 75, 70
286 - J. Nicklaus (USA)	72, 69, 73, 72
286 - B. Crenshaw (USA)	72, 71, 72, 71
299 - C. O'Connor (Royal Dublin)	79, 73, 71, 76

35th, last time to play in British Open.

10

My first Open

On being asked if he collected anything Scottish for good luck, Tom Watson replied: 'Only Opens.'

• • • •

Thrilling developments in the Open during the 1970s happened to elude, for the most part, Ireland's leading players. Notable exceptions were Christy O'Connor Snr who, five months before his 49th birthday in 1973, gained the distinction of finishing in a share of seventh place behind Tom Weiskopf at Troon.

Three years later, his nephew Christy Jnr demonstrated his liking for the game's oldest event by sharing fifth place behind Johnny Miller in the staging at Royal Birkdale, which was also notable for the emergence of 19-year-old Seve Ballesteros as a Spanish runner-up of immense promise. And in 1978, Troon was granted the royal charter to mark its centenary.

Meanwhile, significant increases in the prize fund were reflected in a reward of £5,500 for Weiskopf (O'Connor received £1,716) and Miller's £7,500 (O'Connor Jnr got £2,820 in 1976). An unexpected bonus for Junior was an invitation to the 1977 Masters Tournament at Augusta National as a joint winner of the Braid Taylor Memorial Medal for the highest Open finisher from Britain and Ireland. It made him the first Irish professional to challenge for that coveted title and only the second Irishman, professional or amateur, to play there after Joe Carr.

On a broader level, the seventies grabbed international attention for the Open successes of Jack Nicklaus, Lee Trevino, Weiskopf, Tom Watson, Miller and Ballesteros. And all of these champions were set to light up the field at Muirfield in 1980, when I would be experiencing the Open for the first time. By then, what had been a gradual increase in the prize fund had surged to a seriously desirable £25,000 for the winner, from £15,000 in 1979.

When a trip to Muirfield was put to me, I became acutely aware of two key elements associated with the home of the Honourable Company of Edinburgh Golfers. One was the cost of accommodation for a travelling scribe, and the other was the notoriously inhospitable club secretary, Captain PWT 'Paddy' Hanmer RN (retd).

If memory serves, the best accommodation I could manage was sharing a bedroom in a local council house with Gerry Noone, sports editor of the *Irish Times*, at a cost to each of us of £40 per night. I imagine this was agreed upon when Gerry trusted me to make the arrangements, which wasn't one of my better decisions. I remember being kept awake for most of our first night together, due to Gerry's snoring. And on the second night, I awoke at 2:00 a.m. to see Gerry sitting on the edge of his bed, smoking a cigarette. 'I didn't want to waken you with my snoring', he explained bleakly.

Still, I was to discover later that year that it was arguably the most valuable experience I could have had at that stage of my career. It transpired that Gerry was on the lookout for a golf correspondent for the *Irish Times* and I was top of his list, provided I didn't mess up my chance. As it happened, the job offer was formally made in November 1980 and my transfer from Middle Abbey Street across the Liffey to D'Olier Street was completed the following March.

As I remember it, accommodation became a dirty word at Muirfield over the four days of the Open. When no less a figure than Jack Nicklaus was asked if there was any truth in the rumour he was going to buy the Grey Walls Hotel adjoining the golf course, he replied with a wry smile: 'No, but it would probably be cheaper to do so.'

In the event, after he had collected £9,250 as tied fourth finisher behind Tom Watson, Nicklaus headed in his private twin-engined executive jet for a fishing holiday in Canada. Whereupon we learned that the craft cost $40,000 per month to run.

Before his departure, however, there was time to renew old friendships on the Saturday evening in a dinner date with J.J. Fitzgibbon, non-playing captain of the Irish international tennis team. Fitzgibbon was at Muirfield for the entire championship, and on this particular occasion the chat was not about golf.

It seems they spent much of the evening reminiscing on a tennis match they played at Muirfield during the 1972 Open which Lee Trevino won. 'It was quite a light-hearted affair, umpired by Arnold Palmer', Fitzgibbon disclosed. 'Jack plays a reasonable game of tennis. He has a strong serve and, of course, he's fiercely competitive.'

Meanwhile, with a retired navy captain at the helm, Muirfield became notorious as 'possibly the rudest club in the world', a reputation which Hanmer seemed to delight in promoting during his reign of almost 20 years. And I was at the Open only a couple of days when his reputation was suitably enhanced.

The embellishment came from Jerry Pate, the 1976 US Open champion, who recalled his first visit to Muirfield as a tourist in 1972. He recalled:

> I was a student at the University of Alabama at the time, and one of the things that sticks in my mind is the fact that myself and a friend had to wait a few hours until fog had cleared from the course.
>
> The other memory is of the club secretary [Captain Hanmer], who had a big Labrador dog by his side as he warned me: 'If you play longer than three hours, we'll pull you right off the course.'

> This is my first time to play here as a competitor and despite my 67 today [Friday], I guess it will take another eight years before I'll really have it cracked.

Pate had fared considerably worse in high winds at Portmarnock the previous year when he carded successive rounds of 77 to depart the scene at the halfway point of the 1979 Irish Open.

Another, personal memory of Muirfield was observing notoriously crusty members attempting to come to terms with the intrusion by so many outsiders into their sacred place. I especially remember two elderly club members standing behind the 18th green where they seemed horrified by ugly, intrusive scaffolding supporting the grandstands. 'Good God! Jeffrey', exclaimed one to the other, 'they've turned our course into a fucking shipyard.'

My assignment at Muirfield was to supply daily reports for the *Evening Herald*, which I would supplement with diary pieces for the *Irish Independent* for which Colm Smith, their golf correspondent, would be doing the main reports.

Though the Irish Open had become a highly ranked European tournament at that stage through the industry of Pat Heneghan of PJ Carroll and Co, I remember being quite staggered by the actual scale of the Open. It was also revealing to have so much access to the leading players, even to the point of receiving printouts of their media centre interviews. These were produced by a veteran English scribe named Alan Booth, who had an enviable command of shorthand. You will have gathered that this was a time before electronic developments made such processes effectively pain-free for all concerned.

A great thrill for me during the practice days was to get up close to the great Nicklaus, whom I was seeing in the flesh for the first time. And I can distinctly recall being decidedly uncomfortable in his presence, like one might be in getting close to a celebrated movie star. Yet he was quite ordinary in how he handled himself.

For instance, I can remember his matter-of-fact reaction on being asked how he had celebrated winning the US Open at Baltusrol the previous month. Did the champagne flow? 'No', he replied. 'I went to McDonald's with my family.' Then, noting our muted reaction, he added: 'You don't have to lay into alcohol to celebrate something, you know.' He even made a point of explaining how he had taken the precaution of making it clear to McDonald's that he would be paying his way, in case they got the idea that he was seeking a handy sponsorship deal.

The main feature in the Open programme that week dealt with the appeal of Muirfield and was written by the prince of scribes, Pat Ward-Thomas. Naturally, the Bear figured prominently in the piece, as in:

> Earlier that summer [1959], a youth of 19 named Nicklaus had fallen in love with Muirfield. He had played in the Walker Cup match there and startled everyone with his awesome power. Seven years later, the rough had been allowed to grow to a greater height and density than ever before for an Open, at least in modern times. This imposed a savage premium on accuracy and patience, the quality which, above all others, enabled Nicklaus to beat Doug Sanders and David Thomas by a stroke [to win the 1966 Muirfield Open].
>
> For all his strength, Nicklaus never attempted to overpower the course, whereas occasionally, Palmer did. I can still see him taking three shots to escape from the rough on the 10th. Jokes about hay concessions were not without point. Few British golfers have ever come as close to winning the Open, and twice failed, as Thomas. Few have driven further and straighter than he did for many years. While Nicklaus and others were using irons frequently from the tees, Thomas, as frequently, used a driver.

Some years later at a function in Dublin, Nicklaus reflected with obvious delight on those precious times and how Joe Carr had taught him to use the driver sparingly on fast, fiery links terrain. 'On seeing Muirfield, I had no idea what I was looking at, but I enjoyed it', he recalled. Then, capturing the essence of the links challenge, he went on:

> We had an east wind all the time we were there in 1959, but when I returned to Muirfield for the British Open in 1966, the wind was from the west – until the last day, when it switched to the east.

That was when he had the first of three Open triumphs and I marvelled at his memory for such detail. 'Oh sure', he said by way of response:

> Wind is a very significant part of links golf. Usually, you find that links golf has two wind conditions, either a shore breeze from the ocean or an offshore breeze. Weather patterns are very different inland, where the wind just goes around the clock.

There were six Irish qualifiers for the 1980 Open – Des Smyth and John O'Leary (both exempt) along with O'Connor Jnr, Eamonn Darcy, David Jones and Ronan Rafferty, who came through final qualifying.

Even at this early stage of his development, Rafferty had already made quite an impact on the amateur scene in these islands as a prolific winner. He won the British Boys Championship in 1979, when he also captured the Ulster Youths and Irish Youths title. And he went to Muirfield as winner of the Irish Amateur Close title at Royal County Down, where he crushed the hapless Michael Bannon by 8 and 7 in the final. This was the same Michael Bannon who turned professional and became coach to Rory McIlroy with whom he is still involved.

From Muirfield, Rafferty flew on the Monday morning to Düsseldorf where he was a member of Ireland's winning team in the European Junior Championship later that week. In fact, Rafferty's mother, Marie, had asked Gerry Noone as a responsible adult to look out for her son en route from Muirfield.

On the Wednesday at Muirfield's practice ground, Rafferty stood a few yards behind Nicklaus, watching intently as the master went through his repertoire of shots from wedge to driver. It was only a short session, but the impact on Rafferty and the large accompanying gallery was electrifying. Cameras whirred and clicked while the champion of

The birth of *Chasing Ladybirds* – Pádraig and Caroline Harrington with their imaginative son, Paddy, holding the Claret Jug in triumph at Carnoustie in 2007

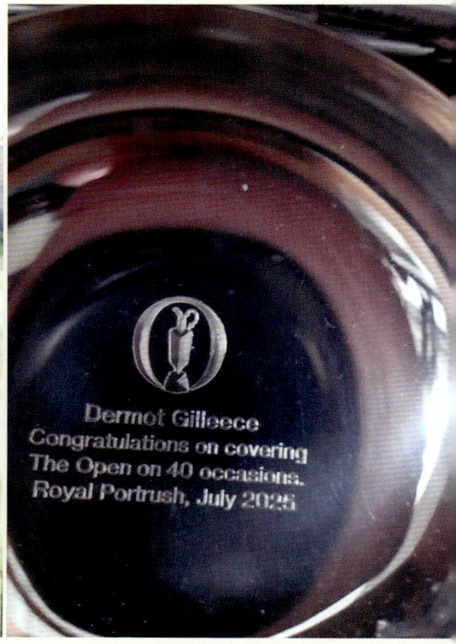

Top left: The author being presented with a traditional Scottish quaich by the impressively tall Mark Darbon, CEO of the Royal and Ancient, during the 2025 Open Championship at Royal Portrush
Top right: The inscription on the quaich, which reads: Dermot Gilleece – congratulations on covering The Open on 40 occasions, Royal Portrush, July 2025
Bottom: Rory McIlroy, resplendent in his Masters jacket, beside *Irish Times* golf correspondent and chairman of the Association of Golf Writers, Philip Reid, at the association's annual dinner at Royal Portrush

A stunning illustration of why the Dunluce stretch at Royal Portrush is widely regarded as the finest piece of links terrain in these islands.

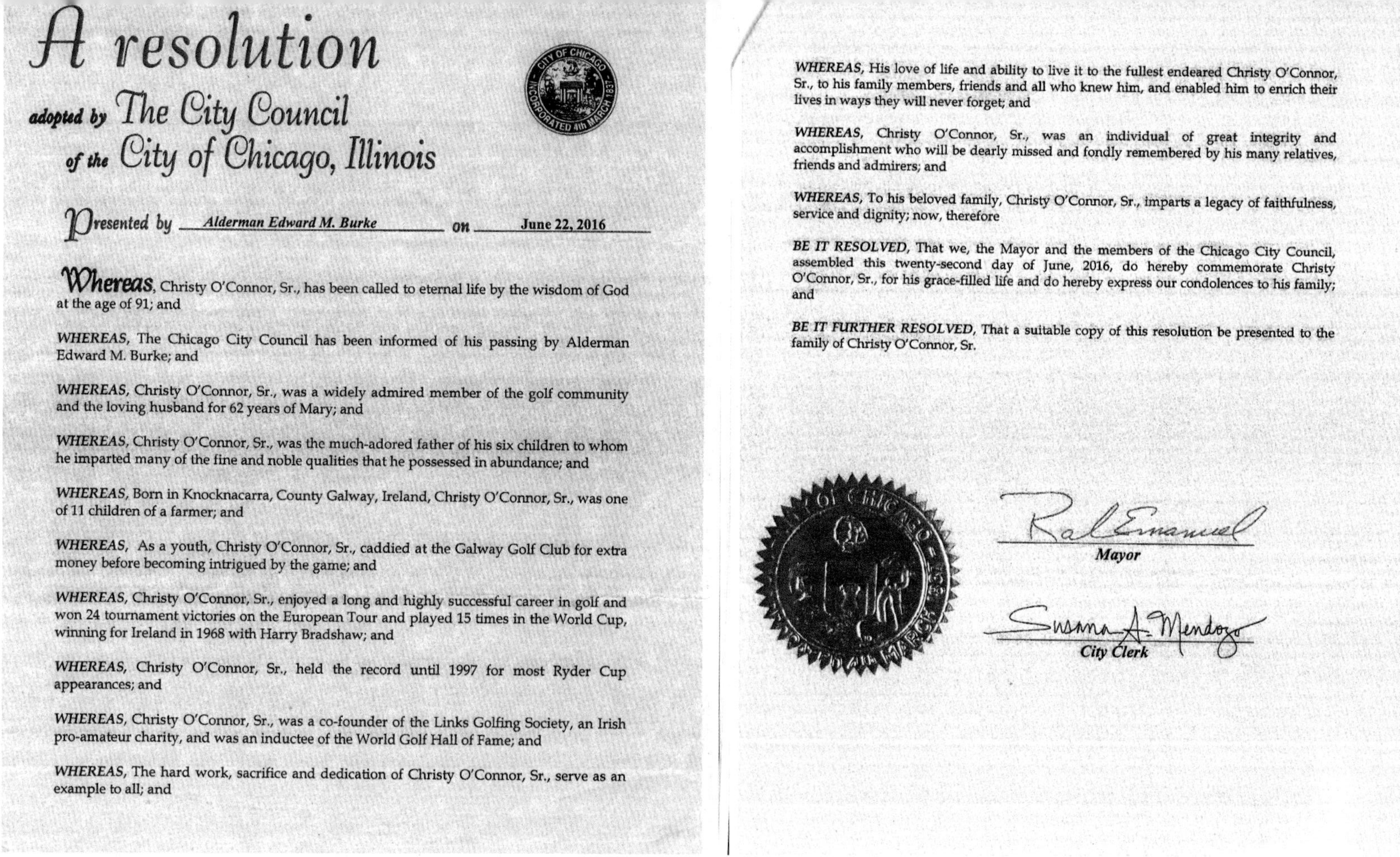

A resolution

adopted by The City Council of the City of Chicago, Illinois

Presented by *Alderman Edward M. Burke* on **June 22, 2016**

Whereas, Christy O'Connor, Sr., has been called to eternal life by the wisdom of God at the age of 91; and

WHEREAS, The Chicago City Council has been informed of his passing by Alderman Edward M. Burke; and

WHEREAS, Christy O'Connor, Sr., was a widely admired member of the golf community and the loving husband for 62 years of Mary; and

WHEREAS, Christy O'Connor, Sr., was the much-adored father of his six children to whom he imparted many of the fine and noble qualities that he possessed in abundance; and

WHEREAS, Born in Knocknacarra, County Galway, Ireland, Christy O'Connor, Sr., was one of 11 children of a farmer; and

WHEREAS, As a youth, Christy O'Connor, Sr., caddied at the Galway Golf Club for extra money before becoming intrigued by the game; and

WHEREAS, Christy O'Connor, Sr., enjoyed a long and highly successful career in golf and won 24 tournament victories on the European Tour and played 15 times in the World Cup, winning for Ireland in 1968 with Harry Bradshaw; and

WHEREAS, Christy O'Connor, Sr., held the record until 1997 for most Ryder Cup appearances; and

WHEREAS, Christy O'Connor, Sr., was a co-founder of the Links Golfing Society, an Irish pro-amateur charity, and was an inductee of the World Golf Hall of Fame; and

WHEREAS, The hard work, sacrifice and dedication of Christy O'Connor, Sr., serve as an example to all; and

WHEREAS, His love of life and ability to live it to the fullest endeared Christy O'Connor, Sr., to his family members, friends and all who knew him, and enabled him to enrich their lives in ways they will never forget; and

WHEREAS, Christy O'Connor, Sr., was an individual of great integrity and accomplishment who will be dearly missed and fondly remembered by his many relatives, friends and admirers; and

WHEREAS, To his beloved family, Christy O'Connor, Sr., imparts a legacy of faithfulness, service and dignity; now, therefore

BE IT RESOLVED, That we, the Mayor and the members of the Chicago City Council, assembled this twenty-second day of June, 2016, do hereby commemorate Christy O'Connor, Sr., for his grace-filled life and do hereby express our condolences to his family; and

BE IT FURTHER RESOLVED, That a suitable copy of this resolution be presented to the family of Christy O'Connor, Sr.

Mayor

City Clerk

A resolution from the City of Chicago commemorating Christy O'Connor Snr, sent to his widow after his death

Viewing the plaque beside the third green at Royal Dublin, commemorating the birthplace of Michael Moran.

Bottom left: Similar in design to an old penny coin, the bronze plaque, 4.7 inches in diameter, was called the Widow's Penny. It was also known chillingly as the 'Dead Man's Penny', because of the circumstances in which it was acquired. Raised lettering on the right-hand side carried the name Michael Moran. A total of 1.355 million widow's pennies were issued to the next of kin of British service personnel killed in World War I.

Bottom right: Brian Purcell, captain of Royal Dublin, presenting the Moran Cup to the winner, Eamonn Brady, then of Clontarf GC, on the occasion of its special commemorative staging in 2018.

Design duo: Paul McGinley and Nick Bielenberg are pictured on the site of Luttrellstown Castle golf course, which they collaborated in designing.

Joe Carr displaying his sporting versatility on horseback in the yard of trainer Mick O'Toole, who stands close by.

This caricature of The Brad was created by the celebrated Scottish humorist George Houghton. It was among lots of art auctioned by Morgan O'Driscoll at his premises down in Skibbereen

First published in the *Liverpool Echo*, this image of Harry Bradshaw looking at his ball in a broken bottle was staged behind the professional's shop at Royal St George's, some hours after the actual event

An early picture of David Feherty (centre), who produced distinguished Open performances at Royal Troon in 1989 and at Turnberry in 1994, with Tommy Morris (Sales Director Window-Pak Ltd) and Roger Moore (Chairman Duraflex Systems)

OPEN CHAMPIONSHIP

1947
Hoylake, Royal Liverpool

Winner **F Daly**

F Daly *Balmoral, Belfast*	**73**	**70**	**78**	**72**	**293**
RW Horne *Hendon*	77	74	72	71	294
Mr FR Stranahan *USA*	71	79	72	72	
W Shankland *Templenewsam*	76	74	75	70	295
R Burton *Coombe Hill*	77	71	77	71	296
J Bulla *USA*	80	72	74	71	297
CH Ward *Little Aston*	76	73	76	72	
SL King *Wildernesse*	75	72	77	73	
A Lees *Dore & Totley*	75	74	72	76	
NG von Nida *Australia*	74	76	71	76	
TH Cotton *R Mid-Surrey*	69	78	74	76	
J Adams *Beaconsfield*	73	80	71	75	299
AH Padgham *Sundridge Park*	75	75	74	76	300
RA Whitcombe *Parkstone*	75	77	71	77	
F Bullock *Otley*	74	78	78	72	302
LB Ayton *Worthing*	69	80	74	79	
N Sutton *Leigh*	77	76	73	77	303
EE Whitcombe *Porters Park*	77	76	74	77	304
V Ghezzi *USA*	75	78	72	79	
A Perry *Reddish Vale*	76	77	70	81	
F van Donck *Belgium*	73	76	81	75	305
DJ Rees *South Herts*	77	74	73	81	
A Waters *Stand, Manchester*	75	78	76	77	306
J Burton *Hillside*	73	79	76	81	309
JA Jacobs *Lindrick*	75	80	76	79	310
JH Busson *Formby*	80	76	71	83	
A Havers *Moor Park*	80	76	79	76	311
B Shepard *Tehidy Park*	78	78	77	78	
K Bousfield *Coombe Hill*	78	76	79	78	
N Quigley *Windermere*	79	77	76	79	
TE Odams *Grim's Dyke*	80	76	79	77	312
W Anderson *Rye*	74	81	80	79	314
F Howie *Lees Hall*	75	80	80	79	
M Faulkner *Worlebury*	78	76	81	79	
WB Thomson *Grange Park*	78	76	78	83	315
JD Henderson *Ilkley*	78	78	81	79	316
T Gardner *Sandiway*	77	76	77	89	319
B Hodson *Chigwell*	79	77	84	84	324
D McEwan *Northampton*	77	79	87	84	327

In old unregenerate days at St Andrews running was beyond doubt regarded as part of the fun, a tradition to be hilariously observed. The young ladies and gentlemen of the University were leaders of the revels. I have a vision of a swirling mass of scarlet gowns rampaging up the course towards the second hole, while I proceed behind at a more leisurely pace, swearing gently to myself.

Some courses lend themselves to roping much better than others. One that is comparatively narrow and runs more or less straight out and home, as does St Andrews, is ideal. Still, as time goes on and golf becomes more and more popular, attracting a crowd that knows more of football and less of golf, I think that roping will become generally accepted.

COUNTRY LIFE (Bernard Darwin)

The winner, Fred Daly, was in the fifth pair to start, with Sam King. Their starting times for the two rounds were 8.40 and 11.10.

The programme carried the warning: *Bicycles must not be brought onto the links.*

From a total field of 293, 156 made the championship proper. Of these, 39 survived the cut after Daly had recorded the best second round of 70. He went on to win by a stroke for top prize of £150, from a fund of £1,000.

two years previously at St Andrews was sharpening his breathtaking skills.

Rafferty was suitably impressed. In fact, the 16-year-old from Warrenpoint chatted with 17-year-old Steve Nicklaus, the champion's caddie and had a few swings with some of the Bear's clubs. You could imagine their shared excitement as teenagers while Rafferty was storing away all the experience he could gather, in preparation for a career as a tournament professional.

'It's super to watch the way he strikes the ball', said Rafferty of the Bear. 'I was quite surprised by how light his clubs are, and it is the experience of being able to get so close to such a great player and his equipment that is making my visit here so much worthwhile.'

As it happened, the Irish youngster's practice was inhibited somewhat by split skin between the index and middle fingers of his right hand. He missed the cut after rounds of 75 and 76 but remained in Muirfield before departing Edinburgh, as arranged by the Golfing Union of Ireland, on the Monday morning.

Meanwhile, the impact of the Carrolls Irish Open, which was set to have its sixth staging a month later, was emphasised by Hubert Green, who would be tied sixth at Muirfield.

Reflecting on his victory at Portmarnock in 1977, tied 5th in 1978 and his plans for another visit the following month (when he finished third), he said:

> Portmarnock is something special. I really love it there. My wife also enjoys her visits immensely. We were engaged at the time of my first visit and she was pregnant when we came back in 1978.
>
> I have not yet received clearance from the PGA Tour for next month, but I don't anticipate any problems about that. If I don't win here, it would be nice to get into the top money at Portmarnock.

In fact, he picked up £4,475 in Dublin to complement his Open cheque for £7,250.

With two newspapers to service, the Muirfield assignment proved to be great preparation for my work in the *Irish Times*, which would span 21 years until June 2002. And I made the best of it, including an informative chat with 27-year-old Des Smyth, who carded a dispiriting 74 in a continuous downpour on the opening day. 'The course owes me three shots' (par 71), he said when we talked on the morning of the second round. That was when he set himself the target of 284 for a top-15 finish. 'I didn't putt well out there and accuracy on the greens is one of my strong suits.' When reflecting at the tournament's end on that target, I discovered that 284 would have left him tied 12th. Which meant his calculations weren't far off. As it happened, he actually finished in a tie for 79th and missed the second cut on the Saturday after rounds of 73 and 75 for 222.

But back to Friday and his thoughts entering the second round:

> As a professional golfer making a living from the game, I have got to take my luck as it comes. It would be silly of me to think that the best is now over for one year. Tournament golf is a constant challenge in which pride and conviction in one's ability has got to be the spur. Otherwise you may as well pack it in.

And so my pursuit of knowledge progressed relentlessly, guiding me to seek enlightenment from a richly promising source. 'All the teeth of this great links have been drawn', said Dr Golf himself, John Jacobs:

> In my view, the course was not playing as tough today [Thursday] as it would have been in dry, sunny weather in which competitors would have to contend with fast, bouncy ground.
>
> The only real problem about the rain is that it tends to make players disheartened if they have played a few holes badly and are wet and cold into the bargain. It requires a greater degree of concentration to keep going in those circumstances.

> On a dry, windy day, the greens can often become a quarter the size of what they appear when you're playing into them in those conditions.

Trevino also had very clear views on the weather. 'I go for flat bellies in off-weather', he claimed, even after opening rounds of 68 and 67. 'I just don't have the same mobility as Watson and other thin guys. At least the weather can't get any worse.'

Very different views came from Horacio Carbonetti, who held the course record for only 24 hours after a 64 on the Friday. 'I buy 12 newspapers and my picture is in every one', he told me proudly. 'I also speak to Radio Argentina on Saturday and they think I could be a big star.' Then, his face dropping slightly, he added: 'But not as big as [Guillermo] Vilas, the tennis player.' As it happened, his target fell to Isao Aoki, who shot a 63 on the Saturday and went on to be tied 12th.

There was time on the final day for a trip down memory lane. In the morning, Fred Daly, the 1947 champion, and Henry Cotton, who won his third Open at Muirfield the following year, played an exhibition nine holes. They commenced at the 10th before the first pairing of the day were due on the ninth green.

Daly enjoyed it immensely: 'It was a wonderful opportunity to take even a small part in such a great occasion', he said. When Daly's final putt, a six-footer on the 18th, appeared to be heading wide of the hole, Cotton bent down and sportingly picked up the ball. Whereupon they warmly congratulated each other.

Meanwhile, Dublin visitors to the Open got an unexpected bonus at their small hotel, The Mallard, in Gullane. The owners video-taped the day's televised golf coverage which meant that the Irish contingent, including golfers from Clontarf and Greystones, could watch a re-run of the day's play over dinner that evening – prompting comments like: 'Shush! Wait till you see the shot Watson played here.'

I reported that the only occasion during the four days when the eventual champion, Watson, showed any sign of inner turmoil was when he missed a 12-footer for a birdie on the sixth hole on Sunday afternoon.

Curiously, a section of the gallery clapped and even cheered his failure, and the player's response was to fix them with a withering stare.

Minutes later, the newly crowned champion was addressing the assembled press from countries as varied as Australia, Colombia, Japan, the US, Britain and the Republic of Ireland. Typically gracious, he thanked us simply for being there. 'Without the great work you do, golfers like me wouldn't be here today. And that's from the heart.'

Watson had to settle for a par after hitting two drivers to the 542-yard 17th and then managed to keep a rein on his emotions in the face of the acclaim which greeted him after a winning par on the last. He then admitted: 'If you took a picture of my insides right now, you'd see the extent of the emotional stress.'

Before heading for Germany and a very different golfing scene, my final observation on the 1980 Open was: 'Tom Watson was impeccably groomed. His low-key attire of white roll-neck sweater and blue cardigan made him look like a civil servant on holiday than a battle-hardened tournament professional.'

As a footnote to Muirfield, the adulation bestowed on the defending champion, Seve Ballesteros, seemed to do little to lift his challenge beyond the mundane. Rounds of 74,68,72,72 for an aggregate of 286 – two over par – left him in a share of 19th place with Bill Rogers (who would capture the Claret Jug a year later at Royal St George's), Bruce Lietzke and Norio Suzuki.

The 1979 champion at Royal Lytham had also been accorded appropriate prominence on the front and back covers of the Muirfield programme. As it happened, a full-page image of him on the back cover, advertising Slazenger clubs and balls, struck a particular chord with me a few years later. The Spaniard was about to enter a tumultuous period of his tournament career involving a serious dispute with the European Tour over appearance money. Among other things, it led to his absence from Europe's 1981 Ryder Cup matches at Walton Heath and from the Irish Opens of 1981 and 1982, after he had finished fourth behind Mark James at Portmarnock in 1980.

The impact of his absence, even for such a relatively short time, could be gauged from the excitement generated by his storming two-stroke comeback victory at Royal Dublin in 1983.

That was when I happened to be standing beside the putting green on one of the practice days when I was approached by Milltown's John Nestor, who would become a dear friend.

Seeing Seve's Slazenger golf bag lying on the ground, Nestor wanted a favour in his capacity as golf club manufacturer Mizuno's agent in this country. 'Could you find out what sort of irons Seve has in the bag', he asked. Not wishing to touch a professional's clubs in such circumstances, I turned to Peter Townsend, who happened to pass by at that time.

Whereupon I asked Peter if he could enlighten us by excavating the bag. Which he did. On examining one of the irons, we noted it had been crudely stamped with the letters S-L-A-Z-E-N-G-E-R. 'I can tell you what they're not', he said. 'They're not Slazengers.' On further inspection, he triumphantly declared that they were a set of unmarked Sounder irons, from the American company of that name. This was based on his own experience of playing the brand.

It transpired that Ballesteros was contracted to play Slazenger in Europe, Mizuno in the Far East and Sounder in the US. And rather than having to switch from one brand to another, depending on where he was playing, he hit on the compromise of having his Sounder set specially stamped as Slazenger.

All of which meant that the perennial pursuit of cash at the highest level had fast-tracked my golfing education a lot more quickly than I could ever have imagined.

11

New names on the leaderboard

'It's very different from what we play in the US, which can sometimes become a little monotonous.'

– Justin Leonard on the challenge of Royal Troon in the 1997 Open

● ● ● ●

Events in the Walker Cup at Interlachen in 1993 were brought sharply to mind by the leaderboards at Royal Troon four years later. Players who had captured our imagination as amateurs from both sides of the pond were now playing for pay in the 126th Open Championship. And for the most part, were making quite a job of it.

A notable exception was Ireland's Darren Clarke, who would have been an automatic choice for the Walker Cup at Portmarnock in 1991, had he not decided to turn professional after winning the Irish Close Championship the previous summer. But Pádraig Harrington, the player he beat in the 1990 final at Baltray, remained an amateur and was in the Interlaken line-up.

So was Justin Leonard, the 1992 US Amateur champion. His appearance at Troon, joint second with Jesper Parnevik and two strokes behind Clarke at the halfway stage, brought to mind a memorable remark from a rain-affected opening day in the US. 'I thought I was a good player until I met this guy', said 19-year-old Raymond Burns after being hammered 4 and 3 by Leonard in the first session of singles.

I can remember the disappointment of the opening morning when it took heroic efforts by the greens staff to make play possible after torrential overnight rain. Even at that, morning play wasn't possible, so it was decided to settle on day one for 10 rather than eight singles. On day two, four foursomes and another 10 singles would be played, which meant that the planned 24 games could be completed. Not that it affected the outcome, which left the Americans crushing winners by 19-5.

Leonard blitzed Burns by winning four of the opening five holes. And it was a tribute to the Ulsterman's tenacity that he managed to extend the match as far as he did. As it happened, Burns went on to win his singles on the second day by beating David Berganio on the 18th while Leonard thrashed Matthew Stanford by 5 and 4 in the anchor position. Harrington, meanwhile, halved his match with Brian Gay.

Having turned professional in 1994, Burns failed to qualify for Troon. By the time Leonard arrived there, however, he still retained one of the most distinctive movements in golf. It has been called the Mickey Mantle follow-through, after the famous Yankees baseball star. With his right arm finishing low across his chest, it allowed him to make a special impact on the tournament scene that season, not least in capturing the Open.

It was said that Leonard's swing reflected his overall approach to the game – straightforward and uncomplicated, but with a dash of boldness. And balance became his strong suit, both in the execution of golf shots and in a cool, mental approach to the business of handling newfound fame.

According to his one-time coach Randy Smith, Leonard remained pretty much the same golfer who came for lessons as a 10-year-old at the Royal Oaks Country Club in Dallas, back in 1983.

'Owing to his small size, Justin couldn't carry the ball 130 yards with his driver at that age', recalled Smith. 'But then, as now, he was a mature thinker who beat the opposition with smart course management, patience, concentration, discipline and playing the game one shot at a time.'

Smith's influence was very much in evidence in television images from Quail Hollow where Scottie Scheffler captured the PGA Championship in May 2025. And Scheffler was generous enough to declare: 'It's tough to put into words what he means to me. He's taught me everything about the game of golf.'

Most of the virtues imparted by Smith to the world number one were in evidence at St Andrews in 1997, when Leonard competed for the US in defence of the Alfred Dunhill Cup. Indeed, he gained the distinction on the opening day of carding a new record 65 for the lengthened so-called Millennium Course.

Even at that early stage in his career, Leonard was highlighted among the new breed of American players. With Tiger Woods, Phil Mickelson and Jim Furyk, he was among the twenty-somethings who were fancied to regain the Ryder Cup at Valderrama in September 1997, where they failed. And would be spearheading US hopes once more, at Brookline in 1999, when they succeeded, controversially.

Brookline was where Leonard fell foul of NBC anchorman Johnny Miller, who made an off-the-cuff remark that would have cut the Texan to the core. During Saturday's fourball session, Leonard and Hal Sutton were losing to the Spanish pairing of Miguel Ángel Jiménez and José María Olazábal. As it happened, Leonard was enduring a pretty bleak experience having lost his morning foursomes while partnering Payne Stewart. All of which prompted Miller to exclaim: 'My hunch is that Justin needs to go home and watch it on television.' Which, of course, would have removed him from Sunday's decisive, albeit outrageous, drama on the 17th hole.

As we sat down to talk at St Andrews, three months after Troon, I had with me the mental image of a remarkably composed young man, holding aloft the famous Claret Jug in his moment of Open triumph.

And he would go on to achieve admirable success in the shape of 12 PGA Tour wins, culminating in the FedEx St Jude Championship of 2008.

Then came a remarkable hiatus of 6,097 days until his next victory arrived on the weekend of 16b February 2025. Now 52, he ended the drought by winning the Chubb Classic on the Champions Tour with birdies on five of the last seven holes for a closing 68 and a four-stroke margin over Billy Andrade.

'I can remember most everything about Troon', he said in a soft Texas drawl:

> I didn't have a victory speech prepared, but the press secretary with the R&A gave me some note cards with names, like the R&A captain, the course superintendent and things like that.
>
> They had also written down the name of Barclay Howard [Scotland's leading amateur], whom I remembered from the Walker Cup. Then, once I got past the names that I didn't know, I put the cards in my pocket and just talked about the things I felt had made the tournament special for me, personally.
>
> You know, things like getting to play the final round with Fred Couples and the great tradition of the British Open. It's still very fresh to me, all the more so for being here, now at St Andrews, where I made my first appearance as a professional in the British Open two years ago.

Watching his intense, young face with not even the hint of a smile, it struck me how seriously he took his golf, perhaps life in general. Leonard went on:

> Being here in this atmosphere, playing such a famous links, brings everything back, crystal clear. And in terms of my development as a golfer, it's very important to be in this part of the world, playing in adverse conditions (sweaters and woolly hats). To be considered world-class, I believe you've got to be capable of competing in hostile environments. That's our goal.

With a final round of 65 at Troon, Leonard came from five strokes behind the third-round leader, Parnevik, to win by three from the Swede and Ireland's Clarke. It was a comeback that had previously been accomplished only once – by the English-born adopted American, 'Long' Jim Barnes, in 1925.

Wearing a baseball cap bearing the Hogan logo, Leonard had produced a round worthy of the most famous golfing Texan of them all, the player they called the 'Wee Ice Mon' when he captured the title at Carnoustie 44 years previously. The manner of Leonard's play of three critical holes certainly bore the Hogan stamp.

By single-putting the 15th, 16th and 17th, one for a par and the other two for birdies, he effectively placed both hands on the coveted trophy. 'The hair on the back of my neck stood up', he said, after the 30-footer found the target at the short 17th. At 25, he was the same age as Tom Watson had been when winning the first of five Open titles in 1975.

I put it to him that on first playing St Andrews, Bobby Jones hated the course so much that he tore up his card. The mask never slipped. 'I can't speak for Mr Jones', Leonard replied. 'I can understand why people consider the Old Course to be unattractive and unpredictable, because of the bounce of the ball. My response is that that's the beauty of it – not knowing where the ball's going to end up.'

And what of the placement of the bunkers, which seem to be random, rather than strategic? 'Yes, but they're very much in play' he argued. 'It's not like there's a couple of bunkers out there that you can simply blow the ball over, downwind. Because there's always another one waiting to trap you. I'm amazed to see how well the course stands up to all types of conditions.'

Very different from the target type golf to which he is accustomed? 'It's very different from what we play in the US, which can sometimes become a little monotonous', he replied. And once again, one imagined an anxiety not to offend anyone back home, as he added:

> Don't get me wrong, we play some really good golf courses but here, you have to use so many kinds of shots, so different from what we play in the States.
>
> I was small of stature growing up and I had to bounce the ball into the greens and play different shots to compensate for my size. Now, as a professional, I really enjoy coming over here and using those shots as a natural part of the game.

Those of us who attended the Walker Cup at Interlachen considered it something of an honour that Ireland's Raymond Burns had the distinction of facing Leonard in the first day's singles. When I informed Leonard of Burns's compliment, he didn't demure. 'I was more mature than most of my contemporaries', he said:

> There were a lot of guys out there at college level who hit the ball better than I did.
>
> In fact, I was probably middle of the road in that Walker Cup team as far as ball-striking was concerned and I was definitely a short hitter. But I knew how to get my game around the golf course and I was a good match player. I didn't let things bother me. That's probably what set me apart from the other players.

It certainly did. Apart from winning the highly competitive Western Amateur twice, shortly before turning professional two years later in 1994, he won the NCAA Championship with a 17-under-par aggregate of 271, to equal the record set by Phil Mickelson.

He went on to become one of the last of the leading US tournament professionals to use persimmon, which he eventually abandoned in May 1997:

> This titanium driver [which he declined to identify] is the first one that gave me the sort of control I could feel totally comfortable with.

> Now that I've achieved a great deal of success with it, I don't see myself changing. I believe I'm hitting my drives 10 to 15 yards further. The statistics probably won't show that, but after playing these golf courses, I know I'm hitting it farther.

He went on to describe his golfing father as 'useful, off seven or eight handicap, and can shoot 80 or 83. Those types of numbers.' Still, he seemed eminently capable of looking after himself, as he went on to talk of the golfers he admired most. 'I've gotten to know Bryon Nelson a little bit over the last three or four years and I admire him a great deal', he said.

> He seems to look out for me a bit. For instance, a few years ago, when I hadn't been playing well for about three or four months, he pulled me aside and sat me down for about an hour and just talked about the things I was trying to accomplish. He made suggestions as to how I might change my approach to getting there.
>
> We're not talking technical help but he's had so many great experiences in his own career and he remembers them all. Astonishing memory. Like he would talk about an amateur match play tournament he competed in when he was 17 and recall not only his shots but the shots his opponents played. And we're talking about more than 60 years ago. I find that amazing.
>
> And Hogan?
>
> I met Mr Hogan on two occasions but I didn't really get the chance to talk a great deal with him. I'm astonished at what he and his contemporaries accomplished and I have made a point of reading up on them. Very much so. I know Mr Nelson on a more personal level so I look up to him for the way he treats people and what a great citizen he is.

At this point, I couldn't help thinking of the first tee at Oak Hill two years previously when each Ryder Cup competitor, American and European, was introduced to Nelson before starting their singles match. Had he been at Valderrama, could the great man have altered the outcome of Leonard's match in which Thomas Bjørn got an unexpected and crucial half-point? A fascinating thought, he conceded.

Finally, I asked him the clichéd question as to which three people, alive or dead, he would most like to invite to dinner at his local golf club. Leonard replied in typically measured tones: 'Byron Nelson, Ben Hogan and my father.' And it struck me that here was a young man who clearly knew what he wanted out of life.

At the top of the leaderboard at Troon, he did the golfing equivalent of inheriting the earth, when he maintained American supremacy over the rugged Ayrshire links. Indeed, Leonard seemed to surprise everybody except himself, when a brilliant final round of 65 gave him the 126th Open by a three-stroke margin.

The 25-year-old's victory, on 272 – 12 under par – meant another cruel disappointment for Sweden's Parnevik, who led by two strokes going into the final round. Ireland's Clarke could afford to take a far more positive view of his share of second place, however, given the huge compensations that ensued. And with Harrington three places further back, it was the first time two Irishmen had finished in the top five of this event.

By sinking a 10-foot birdie putt on the 18th, where Parnevik bogeyed, Clarke raised himself from the third position to which he seemed consigned from mid-afternoon. So, a difference of £25,000 brought his reward to £150,000 – effectively the same as winning a £900,000 tournament on the European Tour.

It lifted Clarke to second place both in the Order of Merit and the Ryder Cup points table. But in career terms, it had the far more significant effect of qualifying him for a US Tour card for 1998.

While indicating that the projected earnings requirement for a place among the top 125 at the end of the 1997 season was about $170,000, a PGA Tour official promised: 'If Darren wants to play our tour, he's in.'

In the circumstances, Clarke performed heroically, especially given the confidence-wrecking potential of his experience on the second tee. After observing the boost of an opening birdie, I remember admiring his composure in choosing a three-iron off the tee for safety at the second, only to be horrified by a golfing unmentionable.

With the boundary fence only a few yards to his right and the beach beyond, the ball came off the shank of the club and squirted out of bounds. 'From then on I was frightened I was going to lose everything right', Clarke admitted afterwards:

> It was unnerving and clearly added to the pressure of the occasion. Before the start of the final round, I felt I could win. I then found myself gradually being forced to accept that I simply wasn't playing well enough.

So, he became the fourth Irishman to be an Open runner-up, following Fred Daly, in 1948, Harry Bradshaw in 1949 and Christy O'Connor Snr in 1965. And Parnevik faced even more acute pain than he had to endure after a bogey on Turnberry's 72nd hole in 1994, deprived him of a playoff with Nick Price.

'This is going to hurt a lot more', he admitted after three bogeys on the last six holes, including the 17th and 18th. 'The pressure today was a little too much. It seemed I had to scramble to save my life on every hole and when I saw that Justin had got to 12 under, the wind went totally out of my sails.'

Harrington's development in professional ranks had always seemed to be quietly measured. Unlike Clarke, who had been a European winner since 1993, he arrived at Troon with one international professional title to his credit, having captured the Spanish Open at Club de Campo 14 months previously.

From a share of 17th place overnight behind third-round leader Parnevik, the Stackstown man gathered in thousands of pounds with the passage of every hole during dramatic last-round progress at Troon. There was the sense of comfort at the nature of the challenge, which augured really well for future Open challenges down the road. A brilliant, four-under-par 67 for an aggregate of 280 earned him a share of fifth place for a reward of £62,500.

Interestingly, he discarded his accountant's hat when asked about money afterwards. 'I'll think about money later', he said. 'Now, my only thoughts are about how tremendous it is for me to finish in the top 10 of a Major championship.'

Meanwhile, there were Ryder Cup points to be considered. And his reward lifted him to 11th in the table, less than 4,000 points behind José María Olazábal in the critical 10th position. It would also mean an invitation into the PGA Championship at Winged Foot a month later. He was well and truly on his way among golf's big boys.

'My main objective coming here was to get into the top 15 for an exemption into next year's event', added the player who had finished in a share of 18th place on his Open debut at Royal Lytham 12 months previously. 'So, I've every reason to be happy.'

He had reason to be especially pleased with the quality of his shot-making, especially around the greens, which allowed him to out-score his celebrated playing partner Ernie Els by two strokes. Arguably the most impressive feature was Harrington's par at the closing hole. After pushing his drive into rough, he was in a right greenside trap in two. From there, he sent his recovery 10 feet past the pin which was at the back left of the green, only five yards in from the edge. His approach play was remarkably similar to that which would deliver a winning par on the 72nd in the PGA Championship at Oak Hill in 2008.

Though he didn't realise it at the time, the putt proved to be worth £15,500 – the difference between being tied fifth and tied sixth with two others. In the event, the ball was stroked unerringly into the cup, extending his right arm after the ball in exultation. 'That putt was really nice', he said. 'I very much wanted to finish the championship with a par at the 18th.'

He rated the final day at Troon pretty close to the Spanish Open win, though Club de Campo 'would have done more for my career, at the time. Essentially, I got my reward today for good chipping and putting and you've got to do that to score around here', he concluded.

In terms of the ultimate destination of the title, it was only when it was all over that one could recognise the number of red herrings that had been floating about since Saturday evening. And the biggest of them all concerned the prospects of highly regarded Tiger Woods, who claimed he could close an eight-stroke gap – and was believed.

As things turned out, Woods went in the opposite direction with a final round of 74. His chance was well and truly buried in one of the wonderfully strategic bunkers at the Postage Stamp eighth. The so-called phenom took two to escape and then three-putted for a triple-bogey six.

Meanwhile, 'Mr Excitement' was the heavily ironic description which one of the American scribes accorded to Leonard, who came to these shores for the 1993 Open at Royal St George's, as a reward for winning the US Amateur the previous year.

He then returned as a professional in 1995 when he went to Ladybank in attempting to qualify for St Andrews. 'Darren and I played together on that occasion', he recalled of Clarke. 'We both qualified and became firm friends after that.'

This most gracious of champions went on:

> I consider it a wonderful honour to win this title. I'm here on my own – well just me and my caddie. And I'm afraid I got a bit caught up out there [at the presentation ceremony], when I thought of my parents, my sister and my grandmother, back home in Dallas.
>
> I'm also thinking right now of how crazy the locker room must be at my home club of Royal Oaks. I certainly hope somebody has videoed it. And I'm thinking of how big my bill at the club is going to be when we start celebrating.

A distinguished list of winners at Troon became dominated by Americans after Arnold Palmer's triumph in 1962. It was followed by Tom

Weiskopf in 1973, Watson in 1982 and Mark Calcavecchia in 1989. But there was a particularly appealing dimension to Leonard's success.

In the context of Clarke's travails off the second tee, it was the rich irony of a coup de grace by the prospective champion later that afternoon. The Texan's three-iron tee shot on the 223-yard short 17th, was followed by a 30-foot putt which found the target. And he completed the assignment with admirable composure down the last, where a three-wood off the tee was followed by a 190-yard six-iron approach and two putts from 40 feet for a closing par.

While these critical shots were being executed, US Ryder Cup captain Tom Kite was at Prestwick airport having finished earlier that afternoon. On discovering what was happening back at Troon, 'He and his wife, Christy, turned the car around and came back to congratulate me', Leonard later recounted.

'Welcome to the Ryder Cup team' said Tom. It was a special moment with a special friend. 'Making the Ryder Cup team has been a goal of mind for the last two years.'

It was an occasion in golf when, as can sometimes happen, everything came together nicely.

12

A FORBIDDING TEST

'If Carnoustie was the only course I could play for the rest of my life, I'd quit the game.'

– David Feherty

• • • •

As a seven-handicap member of Portmarnock GC, Alan Swan has had the good fortune of being able to mix business with pleasure. This was especially true of his life in 1999 when, as managing director of Dublin clothing company John Swan Ltd, he sought to expand their brand Kartel through tournament golf.

With Pádraig Harrington already on the company's books, Swan had his eye on signing a quality British player. And the candidate who immediately came to mind was Scotland's Paul Lawrie, who, a month after his 30th birthday, had won the Qatar Masters in February of that year.

Conveniently, Lawrie was managed by Yorkshire's Adrian Mitchell, who was already familiar to Swan as Harrington's manager. So, an agreement was reached and the contract would be formally signed during Open week at Carnoustie in July.

With all the necessary paperwork finalised, pen was put to paper in remarkable circumstances. 'We were on the putting green at Carnoustie and, with Adrian bent over, myself and Lawrie signed the papers on his back', Swan recalled:

> And I remember that while all of this was going on, I was asking Lawrie what he thought of his prospects in the Open.
>
> Full of confidence, he told me that it frightened him how well he was playing. And with scare stories doing the rounds as to how difficult the course was likely to be, he assured us that not only would he hit every fairway, he would ensure that his drives finished down the correct side. And when I asked him if he fancied his chances of being the leading British player, his reply was that he was confident of beating everybody in the field.

All of which prompted Swan to phone his brother-in-law, Michael Hemp, in Dublin to check the relevant odds with Paddy Power bookmakers. Later, he got a call back informing him that Lawrie was 50/1 to be the leading European and 20/1 to be the leading Briton, with Colin Montgomerie among his most notable rivals. And he was 200/1 to be the overall winner.

Armed with this information, Swan decided to place a few bets. He had 50 punts each way on Lawrie being the leading British finisher; 50 punts each way on being the top European; and 100 punts on becoming Open champion. 'The upshot was that I won more than enough money on those bets to cover a two-year sponsorship deal with Lawrie', he recalled. Which, as things turned out, proved to be the duration of one of the most remarkable contracts in modern sport, certainly from an Irish perspective.

Prior to that July week, an abiding memory of Carnoustie for me was of the 1996 Scottish Open and the sight of Montgomerie coming into the media centre after being whipped by winds gusting up to 40 mph. A relentless battle with the elements was etched in the face of the not-so-jolly giant, whose boyish curls were flattened on his head, as if by layers of grease.

Before the course record-holder went into detail about a round of 81, he was asked by a scribe from the far side of the pond: 'Colin, was the wind a factor?' As if too numb to think, Montgomerie repeated in a seemingly thoughtless monotone: 'Was the wind a factor?' Then suddenly, as the reality of his torment dawned on him, he stormed: 'WAS THE WIND A FACTOR? WAS THE WIND A FACTOR?'

As we know, the wind was also a factor when Lawrie came from 10 strokes behind to win the Open, while the hapless Frenchman Jean Van de Velde crashed from three strokes ahead to squander his chance of victory. Both players were to become transient golfing heroes of mine – Lawrie for proving that an ordinary man can have his day in the sun, and Van de Velde for his remarkable graciousness in defeat.

The Frenchman's plight revived memories of the 1982 Open at Royal Troon, where Nick Price let the title slip over the closing three holes. After admitting that he 'backed into the title', Tom Watson went on to explain how pressure can manifest itself at the highest level:

> It's not about wobbly knees and trembling hands. It's about making the correct decisions when you're getting wrong messages from a mind that's in turmoil. Only a player with an exceptionally strong mind will recognise those messages for what they are, unless he has been in that position before.

It became patently obvious that the Frenchman made very poor decisions on a fateful 72nd hole. And instead of castigating him as did the numerous wiseacres on the ditch, rather should we sympathise with the fact that before he had the chance of learning how to win at the highest level, he was thrown into the white heat of battle, essentially as a novice. On the other hand, Lawrie showed himself to be made of significantly sterner stuff.

David Feherty once observed that if Carnoustie, with its treacherous finishing hole, was the only course he could play for the remainder of his life, he'd quit the game. And predictably, he offered his views on the 1999 Open set-up in typically colourful language. He wrote:

> With goat-choking weeds and fairways narrower than Adolf Hitler's mind, it was a test of how much of the Barry Burn you could swallow without throwing up.
>
> Jack Nicklaus once said that golf wasn't meant to be fair, but I believe it wasn't meant to be stupid either. That last bit was mine, not Jack's.
>
> Yet, whatever way you look at it, we had a perfect example of why this is the world's greatest game. What theatre! We had a playoff between three people (Lawrie, Van de Velde and Justin Leonard), two of whom felt like they had won the lottery just by being there and one who had the winning ticket under his beret but threw his hat in the air by mistake.

It seemed that just about every leading player felt obliged to offer his tuppence worth about this celebrated layout which was returning to the Open rota for the first time since Watson recorded the first of five triumphs in 1975. For instance, the 1985 champion, Sandy Lyle, had an early practice round which prompted the comment that the foot-high rough had rendered the course 'Tighter than a duck's backside.' 'What are the R&A trying to do to us?' he added.

Meanwhile, the vagaries of the Scottish weather had prompted Tiger Woods and leading American colleagues to consider no fewer than three modes of transport from their hotel base in St Andrews, across the Firth of Tay to this celebrated stretch on the Angus coast. Helicopters, you see, were considered too unreliable in the infamous Scottish haar (dense fog), which descended early in the week.

'I think the minimum ceiling for the helicopter is 200 feet', said Woods like an accomplished aviator. 'But we also have the option of a hovercraft, or to go by road. Obviously, it depends on what the conditions are and you have to allow time for back-up, too.' All of which made me feel decidedly more at ease about my modest hired chariot.

Still, El Tigre seemed to cope admirably, not least one imagines because of the delightful sojourn he and his colleagues had had in Ireland for most of the previous week. Woods played Waterville, the Old Head of Kinsale and Portmarnock before rounding off the trip with some fishing at The K Club. 'It was great, a lot of great brown trout that we really enjoyed demolishing', he enthused.

Regarding the visit to Old Head, one had to allow for the exaggeration of youth as he described the problems posed by fog of the West Cork variety, which he claimed didn't lift completely until they reached the 14th green. 'The hardest course we played was Old Head where we couldn't see more than 100 yards because of fog', he said. Having joined himself, David Duval, Mark O'Meara, Lee Janzen, Payne Stewart and Stuart Appleby as a remarkable six-ball on that memorable occasion, I can vouch for the fog having lifted by the time they reached the spectacular long 12th across an elbow of the cliff-face.

One imagines further dramatic effect was intended when Woods added: 'The cliffs are great until you walk up close to them, then you see there's a 300-foot drop off. It is not too hard to walk right off a cliff there.' I remember those among his golf-writing audience at Carnoustie, who were not familiar with Old Head, being suitably impressed.

In more credible vein, he went on to talk about the current form of Duval, who was with him in Ireland. Indeed, I was particularly taken by the closeness of the two of them when, in quiet moments, they could be seen chatting together animatedly and sharing each other's humour.

'I think David was playing the best of us in Ireland', said Woods. 'He was hitting the ball really well; controlling his traj [trajectory] really well.'

Meanwhile, none of the Old Head six-ball could have imagined what lay in store for a particularly celebrated member of their group. Stewart, who had captured the US Open at Pinehurst No 2 only the previous month in a glorious victory over Phil Mickelson, could look back on a memorable Open at Royal St George's in 1985 when a final round of 68 left him a stroke adrift of the winner, Lyle.

Now, he would be playing the Open for the last time in a challenge that never produced that memorable sparkle. Rounds of 79,73,74,74 for an aggregate of 300 left him in a share of 30th place alongside Darren Clarke and six others.

For his part, Woods had learned a lot from Stewart among his American rivals, though he was prepared to concede that this was only on their terms:

> I need to learn how to putt better in the wind, which requires a different technique, like changing the ball position and your grip pressure. I knew Mark O'Meara developed his own technique for the wind and he was able to share it with me, after he won the Open last year [1998 at Royal Birkdale].

Another demanding aspect of the Carnoustie experience was acknowledged to be the way conditions could change, almost by the hour. It was one of the great benefits Woods took from the Scottish Open experience and from this particular championship.

In his first look at Carnoustie in Open week, he played only four holes – the first, 16th, 17th and 18th – or the whisky line as he described them. But it was enough to convince him about the severity of the rough. Yet he expressed no great concern about the general conditions, no doubt in the belief that he had been playing well enough that season to take anything Carnoustie could throw at him. Five months previously, in February of that year, he had captured the Buick Invitational at Torrey Pines close to his birthplace in Cypress, California and though he wasn't pleased with an 18th-place finish in the US Masters, he had gone on to capture the Memorial Tournament in early June.

Then came the US Open at Pinehurst and a share of third place with Vijay Singh behind Stewart. And on the weekend of the Murphy's Irish Open, he had his third win of the season, taking the Western Open by three strokes at Cog Hill. Which added up to useful takings of $2,545,990 from 14 tournaments. And it was still only mid-July!

As for the championship itself, a grim opening day largely set the scene of what was to follow. The average score of 78.3 for the first round contained some very notable casualties. Among them was the recently crowned Murphy's Irish Open champion Sergio García, who shot a crushing 89, which was to be followed by an 83. Significantly, the lead was set by Australian journeyman Rod Pampling, with a level par 71 in only the second group on the course. And nobody managed to match him for the remainder of the day.

Eventually, the championship managed to encompass a remarkable sweep of emotions ranging from controversy to farce and ultimately to raw courage, before Lawrie captured the title in extraordinary circumstances. He did it in a playoff against the 1997 champion, Leonard, and the hapless Van de Velde, who had earlier squandered his chance in heartbreaking fashion.

After a six-over-par aggregate of 290 and figures of level par for the four playoff holes, Lawrie became the first champion born and living in Scotland since Willie Auchterlonie way back in 1893. Tommy Armour, though Scottish-born, was a naturalised American when he won at Carnoustie in 1931, while the 1985 champion, Lyle, was English-born of Scottish parents.

Ten strokes off the lead in the eighth last pairing of the day, Lawrie posted the clubhouse target after a best-of-the-day final round of 67. But despite his pre-championship predictions to Alan Swan, he didn't dare hope it could give him anything more than one of the minor places. Indeed, he admitted after 72 holds: 'I'm a couple of shots too many, but I'm really happy with what I've done.'

Three hours later, he was honest enough to proclaim: 'I can't believe this has happened. No way did I think I could win, but I managed it somehow.'

A measure of his achievement was that he had broken an American stranglehold on the world's greatest championship since John Daly triumphed at St Andrews in 1995. And he became the first player since Kel Nagle in 1960 to win this title without first having a tournament breakthrough on US soil. Lyle won in Kapalua prior to his Open triumph of 1985.

Lawrie did it by covering golf's most treacherous 17th and 18th holes in a stunning aggregate of three under par: his finish to the championship proper was birdie, par, and in the playoff he crushed the opposition by playing the same two holes in birdie, birdie.

Indeed, the final hole was executed in a manner worthy of a distinguished champion. After splitting the fairway, Lawrie had the courage to play the shot of the championship, a 221-yard four-iron which came to rest within four feet of the hole. And there wasn't the hint of nerves as he stroked the ball into the cup for a closing three.

Yet, deep down, he knew he should never have been given the chance. Standing on the 72nd tee, Van de Velde was three under par and three strokes clear of his closest challengers after Leonard, in the previous two-ball, had finished with a bogey by hitting his second into the serpentine Barry Burn.

But where a bogey, or even a double-bogey, seemed an eminently attainable target, the hapless Frenchman crumbled to a wretched seven while onlookers almost squirmed with embarrassment at his torment. For 17 holes he had shouldered the pressures with remarkable calm, but at the climactic moment, the magnitude of the occasion simply overwhelmed him.

'I had 185 yards to the green and the lie was so perfect that I felt I had to hit a two-iron', he said with admirable good humour afterwards. 'Maybe hitting that shot for the British Open was too much for me, but there are worse things in life. Next time I hit a wedge and you'll all say I was a coward.'

A crucial, ominous sound heard on the broadcast was Van de Velde's two-iron second shot smashing against the grandstand, and then bouncing into deep rough, still a long distance from the green. As one seasoned observer remarked:

> That was one of those things where fate was against him, because the ball could have bounced off the grandstand and gone further

> right, or stayed in the grandstand, and it would have been a free drop. It was, objectively speaking, about as bad a golf shot as a professional could play in the circumstances. He's hit two shots and not one of them has landed on the hole yet. But at least he went for it!

Van de Velde then hit his third shot from a terrible lie, where he had to negotiate tall grass and bunkers to reach the green. And a water hazard. 'I don't understand what is happening', remarked Peter Alliss, the BBC's voice of golf, in a rare struggle for words. 'What on earth are you doing? Oh, Jean, please', he pleaded as Van de Velde removed his footwear with a view to entering the Barry Burn. 'Would somebody kindly go and stop him? Give him a large brandy and mop him down.'

While Van der Velde stood like a tragicomic figure in the shallow water, weighing up his options, Alliss added:

> I've never seen anything like it before. And to attempt to hit the ball out of there is pure madness, because he could hit the wall, go back in, the ball could hit him. He could end up not finishing in the top 20.

Meanwhile, the player's wife of nine years, Brigitte, hardly knew how to react and at one point seemed to break into slightly hysterical laughter. As Watson had observed 17 years previously at Royal Troon, the Frenchman was making a series of poor decisions. After being extremely fortunate to escape the Burn from a blocked drive off the 18th tee, he lacked the prudence to take safe options from then on while using the shots he had in hand. Ideally, from a position within the coils of the Burn, over on the neighbouring 17th, a safe bogey should have been his target.

Instead, with the challenge of clearing the hazard, he went for a grand finale, aiming for the clock on the hotel wall, behind the green. But the shot was blocked and through a series of almost comic bounces, hit the front of the grandstand, was deflected back over the Burn and came to rest in thick rough.

Now Van de Velde had to pitch over both Burn and bunker to reach the green 30 yards away. But his arms failed to deliver the necessary power to the sand wedge and the ball popped into the water. Would he try to play it with disastrous results, or would sanity somehow prevail in the shape of a penalty drop? Perhaps it was the coldness of the stream covering up to his ankles which restored some semblance of focus to his addled brain.

In the event, the drop was made, the Burn was safely traversed, but the ball failed to carry all the way to the green. Rather did it come to rest in the sand where his playing partner, Craig Parry, had already landed. How much more drama could the situation possibly produce? Parry stepped into the trap and duly holed the bunker shot for a closing birdie that would have been worth millions to the Frenchman.

For his part, Van de Velde played a fine recovery to seven feet past the target. Never can onlookers, whatever their affiliation, have said such heartfelt prayers for a successful conclusion. With remarkable resolve, he eased the ball towards the left half of the cup; it turned as he had hoped and found the target for a triple-bogey seven.

Some observers expressed the view that Van de Velde had fallen victim to some kind of Carnoustie curse. For in the 1931 Open, a 4,5 finish would have given the Argentinian José Jurado this coveted title. Instead, he carded 6,5 and Tommy Armour was champion.

Up to that fateful final hole, Van de Velde had carded no worse than a bogey, whereas among those who effectively gave up the chase was Woods, no less, with a double-bogey six at the 12th, where he had to take a penalty drop from a second shot into gorse. El Tigre's problems stemmed largely from lack of success on the greens, as he had feared. In fact, he played an extraordinary sequence of 35 holes without a birdie from the 14th on Friday. And it was ended by his only birdie of the final round, again on the long 14th where he recovered from a greenside bunker to 12 feet and sank the putt.

Parry also had a spectacular tumble. The Australian was tied for the lead with Van de Velde at two over par when they left the green at the short eighth. And he led the championship on his own when the Frenchman bogeyed the 11th.

Lawrie, meanwhile, was removed from all this drama while carding six birdies in the company of Patrik Sjöland. The most important of these was a 20-footer at the 17th, which he followed with a brilliant up and down from a bunker on the last.

As a chilly, overcast day drew to a close, rain added to the discomfiture of the attendance of 32,000 when the four-hole aggregate playoff, which was then unique to this championship, got under way. Starting on the 15th, it seemed like a continuation of the Van de Velde farce of the 72nd hole, when all three players drove into trouble down the left.

Almost predictably, the Frenchman came off worst, by taking a penalty drop on the way to a double-bogey six. All three bogeyed the short 16th, which meant that Lawrie and Leonard were level on two over par, one ahead of Van de Velde, on the 17th tee.

Here, Lawrie struck a telling blow with a two-iron approach, followed by a 15-foot birdie putt. Though Van de Velde also birdied the 17th from 18 feet, the Scot held a priceless one-shot lead going down the last. And there was rich irony in the Frenchman's closing bogey, which would have made such a huge difference 90 minutes earlier.

Meanwhile, an even greater irony was to be found in the fiercely demanding course, which brought widespread, scathing criticism of Carnoustie greenkeeper John Philp, and the R&A championship committee. Little could they have imagined that while frustrating the leading American challengers, with Woods tied seventh, they would open the door for a remarkable home triumph.

Meanwhile, a greenkeeper can rarely have been so vilified. At a time when veterans could still compete, Gary Player returned to the scene of his 1968 Open triumph to card 81,83, the same aggregate as another former champion, Bob Charles (83,81). And Tony Jacklin, the 1969 champion, returned rounds of 85,82.

'I hope I don't ever encounter these conditions again', said Duval, the recent world's number one.

And he seemed to have an ally in the great Peter Thomson, a five-time Open champion, who had predicted: 'If Tiger Woods doesn't win, or come close to winning this week, some sort of silliness will have been perpetrated.'

Still, there were others who thought greenkeeper Philp had done a splendid job in preparing the famous links for the Open. 'You won't find a better-presented links course than this', enthused Colin Montgomerie, who finished tied 15th. And outgoing R&A secretary Michael Bonallack said: 'We are delighted with the course.'

Some months later, Woods and Duval received official confirmation of these views, from the British establishment no less. Among the list of sports people, including Tommy Horton, who were awarded an MBE in the New Year's honours list for 2000, there was the redoubtable Mr Philp who got the nod for 'services to golf'. Throughout its rich history, the royal and ancient game had rarely witnessed happenings of such great moment.

Ten days after the drama of Carnoustie, I found myself thinking of the old Edith Piaf song 'Non, je ne regrette rien' when I met with Van de Velde on the putting green at The K Club, prior to the Smurfit European Open.

Indeed, there were clearly no regrets when the tour's favourite Frenchman was greeted by a stream of fellow professionals, some commiserating, some welcoming him back to action, all of them clearly supportive.

Derrick Cooper, one of Carnoustie's many victims in a final round of 85, was among the well-wishers. So was Darren Clarke. And Van de Velde talked animatedly in Spanish with the Argentinian Ángel Cabrera, who had finished in a share of fourth place in the Open with Australia's Parry.

Then, with typical antipodean boldness, Greg Turner stepped forward. 'I don't think you made a bad decision on the 18th, Jean', said the New Zealander. 'There's no safe way to play that fucking hole. People like things to be logical but sport is not like that.'

Van de Velde smiled the same gracious smile he had somehow managed to muster when entering the media centre late on that fateful Sunday evening, vanquished but unbowed. 'You know I read the newspaper like you all did this morning and some terrible things are happening to other people', he had said. 'And you know, as I say it is a golf tournament, it's a game and I gave it my best shot ....'

There was an inescapable irony about his arrival at the front of the clubhouse only seconds after Open champion Lawrie had gone inside to make a television commercial for his new Irish sponsor, Kartel. Among other things, Carnoustie had created a gap of several million pounds in their respective financial wellbeing, quite apart from an actual prize money difference of £165,000.

But the Frenchman seemed unconcerned by such matters, having spent the previous week with his parents at their home in Mont-de-Marsan, about 80 kilometres from Biarritz. 'It was good that I had to come here, otherwise I would still be opening letters and taking phone calls', he said.

How was he?

> I'm good, very good. And I'm happy to be here. Lots of people have been saying how sorry they are for me. And that's OK. If people liked the excitement of the finish, fine. I did it my way, but maybe next time I will try to put the finish together properly.

For that particular week's tournament, he was a guest in one of the splendid houses overlooking the short fifth hole at The K Club. And the extent to which he had already come to terms with a crushing disappointment was reflected in his willingness to talk about it all:

> In a way, the golfing public discovered me at Carnoustie. Before that, not many people would have been aware of my existence.

> I know that people have their own idea as to how I should have played the 72nd hole. And I suppose it will be normal for a while for people to come up to me and tell me how sorry they are. But these things happen. All the guys [his fellow professionals] said it could happen to anybody. Gary Player came to me afterwards and said that something similar had happened to him at the Masters.
>
> It also happened to Arnold Palmer in the US Open, where he was seven ahead of Billy Casper with nine to play and still lost [at the Olympic Club, San Francisco in 1966]. They were great players. Me, I'm not the best player in the world, so why should it not happen to me?

Then came the only admission that he might have done things differently:

> I would do everything the same except for the third shot. It was a very nasty lie and instead of trying to go forward and clear the burn, I realise now that I should have gone left. Even if I didn't hit the fairway, the lie would have to have been better.

When considering everything that happened on that fateful hole, especially the freakish bounce which deflected the ball off the grandstand and back over the ubiquitous burn, was he tempted to look on golf as a cruel game? 'No', he replied. 'In fact, it has given me a lot.'

He continued:

> After all, by my performance at Carnoustie, I will be playing in the US PGA Championship in two weeks. And I will be in next year's Masters. So I don't have any reason to feel sorry for myself.
>
> I prefer to think of the great second round of 68 I shot on a most difficult course to lead the British Open by one stroke at the halfway stage. Then there was my 70 on the Saturday, which gave me a five-shot lead entering the final round. And in the greatest tournament in the world! That has to be worth something.

> I know there is a feeling that I will not recover from the way things ended, but I don't believe that. In fact, I am convinced that I can recreate the same position again.

As he digested those words, the idea seemed to appeal to him enormously. And once again he was the flamboyant, if somewhat eccentric, Frenchman, taking off his shoes and socks to follow his ball into the Barry Burn.

'I know what I will do', he said with one of his special, wicked smiles. 'If I am leading by three shots on the 72nd tee at St Andrews next year, I will play the last hole with my putter. That way I cannot get into trouble, no?'

Indeed not. Provided, of course, he successfully negotiates the Swilcan Burn ....

Behind Lee Westwood, Van de Velde was tied 35th with Ian Woosnam, among others, for this European Open. And there were other occasions when he continued to command our attention for the wrong reason as tournament observers. Almost seven years after Carnoustie, he recorded a notable one-stroke victory over England's Lee Slattery in the Madeira Island Open. But his closing 68 was not without drama on the 72nd hole.

This is how Norman Dabell, who reported the event for the *European Tour's Yearbook*, described the finale:

> His finish was not exactly poetry in motion, as Van de Velde found what he described as 'the nastiest piece of grass on the whole course', using up all but one of the three shots he had in hand over Slattery at the final hole.
>
> But it was no longer hard lines for Jean. His arduous voyage was over.

This time, unlike Carnoustie, the Frenchman's ball proved to be unsinkable and it delivered a fourth professional tournament victory, less than two months prior to his 40th birthday.

13

A TRADITION DELIVERS

'The longer you play, the better chance the better player has of winning.'

– Jack Nicklaus

• • • •

Late on a Sunday afternoon at Carnoustie in July 2007, Ireland found a new golfing hero. Dating back to Michael Moran at Hoylake in 1913, a protracted chapter of spirited, if largely unavailing, challenges for a coveted crown had reached a thrilling conclusion in another century.

We were more than happy to settle for the fact that Fred Daly's Open triumph of 1947 had finally been matched. But a modest champion, who readily acknowledged frailty among his undoubted strengths, had set his sights on further glory at Royal Birkdale the following year without ever imagining it would happen so soon.

In early autumn 1983, a 12-year-old lad with a shock of black hair darted among the gathering of about 700 at Stackstown GC, hardly aware of the golfing giants who were plying their craft to mark a special occasion for the club. 'As a prelude to our first invitation Open Week being held to celebrate the official opening of the course and clubhouse, an exhibition was held on Sunday, September 11th between two of the most renowned and respected names in world golf.' These words were written in a commemorative booklet by the honorary greens officer, Paddy Harrington, who happened to have acted as match referee.

Paddy's son found it difficult to remember the occasion by the time he had embarked on a professional career. 'I imagine I was more interested in chasing rabbits', Pádraig Harrington recalled. 'Though I was aware of Christy's [O'Connor Snr] prominence in Irish golf at the time, I knew nothing of Peter Thomson.'

So he would have been blissfully unaware of the key role Royal Birkdale played in the career of the great Australian, who won his first and fifth Open titles there. Nor of the fact that O'Connor had been tied second behind Thomson on this majestic strip of Lancashire duneland in 1965, before going on to produce further sparkling golf there, as a partner for Peter Alliss in the Ryder Cup the same year.

Nor would he have known anything of the marvellous two-iron approach shot of 213 yards which Tom Watson had hit to Birkdale's 18th green on the way to victory in the 1983 Open, two months before those celebrations at Stackstown.

Twenty years on, the occasion took on a fascinating, fresh relevance in the wake of Harrington's playoff triumph in the Deutsche Bank Open in Hamburg. Among other things, it brought delighted surprise to Thomson. It being May, he had yet to move to his summer residence in St Andrews, so I phoned him at his Melbourne home and thought it best not to remind him of the outcome of the exhibition in which he was soundly whipped 82–75 by Himself on a wild, windy day which became almost typical of Stackstown.

We spoke instead about that young observer, who by this stage in 2003 was occupying eighth place in the world rankings.

Thomson, who had seen Harrington get within a shot of a playoff for the Open title at Muirfield in July 2002, had noted the player's progress since then and was fully aware of the victory in Germany:

That was a fine win, but unless a player can distinguish himself on a really big occasion, he can't claim to have reached the top of the tree. And if Pádraig is looking to win a Major title, he can gain confidence from the knowledge that the opposition are now no better than he is. With his athletic built and warm smile, I believe he would be a popular, saleable champion. I like players who aren't afraid to smile.

On the Tuesday of Open week at Birkdale '08 – a world removed from Open Week for the modest handicappers at Stackstown – the Association of Golf Writers held their annual dinner in the Royal and Ancient marquee. And during the course of the evening, they presented their annual award to a player who had distinguished himself on a really big occasion. As the Open champion of 2007, Harrington became only the fourth Irishman – after Joe Carr, Harry Bradshaw and Christy O'Connor Snr – to be so honoured by the scribes. By a charming coincidence, the man the AGW chose to present the award was none other than Thomson. On reflection, one could be forgiven for thinking that strange forces were at work.

Meanwhile, the winds that sweep over Stackstown, on its hilly perch to the southwest of Dublin City, had played a crucial part in shaping Harrington for the test which lay ahead. And while he was coming to terms with an injured right wrist while planning his assault on a second, successive Open title, other words of Thomson's came to mind:

To win the Open, you don't have to be perfect. You just have to be a little better than the rest of the field over four, specific rounds.

There is no easy way, however, of finding out whether you have what it takes. In my experience, it demands determination and a pretty smart brain. A fellow must know what he's doing all the time. You could describe it as a combination of brain power and muscle power. Unless a player can distinguish himself on the really big occasion, he can't claim to have reached the top of the tree.

Late on the following Sunday evening at Birkdale, when the crowds were departing one of the most absorbing Opens in recent memory, I stood beside the 72nd green speaking to Harrington's mental coach, Dr Bob Rotella. He spoke with obvious affection and admiration for a player who wasn't afraid to test himself. A player who met Thomson's requirements as 'a good learner'. And Rotella added: 'He's incredibly honest with himself and with me. His parents taught him well, and he had the good sense to listen to them.'

As we talked, I became aware of how cool and calm the weather had become under a bright, blue sky, as if nature were now mocking those hapless challengers who had been overwhelmed by conditions which ranged from punishingly difficult to downright horrific over four days. There were glorious memories of an event in which Greg Norman had us thinking that it just might be possible for a player to win a Major championship at the venerable age of 53. But, of course, we remembered Harrington most of all, and his execution of what came to be known as the perfect shot on the 572-yard 71st hole.

With a helping wind, the yardage of 272 was perfect. The club, a favourite of the player's, was also perfect for a situation of extreme pressure. And, most remarkably, the downhill lie was perfect in that it would send the ball on a low, wind-cheating trajectory. In such circumstances, the fact that he made perfect contact illustrated the heights to which Harrington had risen as a master of his craft.

When the ball came to rest three feet behind the pin, the defending champion rolled in the downhill putt for a glorious eagle. In that instant, we knew we had witnessed something quite special; a memory which would live down through the years. And when the Dubliner went on to become the first European to retain the title since James Braid in 1906, there was an awareness of Ireland now having a world-class sportsman of rare vision and determination.

Carnoustie had been only a stepping stone.

Glorious stretches of links terrain along the Lancashire coast have long been familiar to this country's purists, who were drawn there initially by the British Amateur triumph of Jimmy Bruen in 1946. Then, only a season later, Fred Daly made the great breakthrough when capturing the 1947 Open Championship at Hoylake. But it was only in 1965 that rank-and-file Irish enthusiasts became familiar with the rather special appeal of Royal Birkdale, through Thomson's fifth Open triumph.

Since then, there have been the thrilling memories of 1976, when a tied fifth-place finish by Christy Jnr, behind Johnny Miller, earned him the distinction of becoming the first Irish professional to compete in the US Masters, a year later. His great friend Eamonn Darcy finished in the same position behind Ian Baker-Finch to dominate the Irish interest in 1991.

All of which set nicely into perspective the scale of Harrington's performance at Birkdale in 2008. With a display of stunning quality and courage, the Dubliner became the first player anywhere to successfully defend the title since Tom Watson at the same venue in 1983. Now, in 2017, his return there in the company of fellow Irish champions Rory McIlroy and Darren Clarke illustrated the extent of Irish progress over the previous 70 years.

Recalling his exploits on the 71st hole, Harrington said: 'I had just hit the five-wood off the tee. I was unbreakable at that very moment, and it was my favourite club. As much as it was a great shot, I was in a great place [mentally] to hit it.'

The green was later repositioned slightly and its contours softened, but where was the club? I tracked it down at Royal Birkdale, where I was informed that two Harrington clubs are on display in a glass case in the clubhouse. One carries the inscription: 'Wilson Staff lob wedge. Donated by Pádraig Harrington 2008 Open Champion.' Beneath it is the famous fairway wood with the inscription: 'Wilson Staff 5 wood on loan from Pádraig Harrington. This club was used by Pádraig Harrington for his second shot on the 71st hole to set up eagle and go on to win the Championship.' The head cover lay on the bottom of the case.

While the wedge was 'donated', I thought it particularly interesting that the wood was 'on loan' – which is no more than one would expect with such a precious implement.

'There's a certain wildness, a ruggedness about Birkdale which represents the traditions of the game,' Harrington claimed:

> There's a huge push at the moment to make the game very ordered and very fair, even perfect, if you like. But the game was never meant to be that way. It was designed to be a game of managing your wits and your temperament; your capacity to handle good and bad breaks.
>
> Like you look at pictures of the original game and note how they played the ball as it lay. That was it. There was no relief for anything, not even footprints in bunkers. The game has become more sanitised over the years but the Open remains different. I'm not saying it hasn't moved with the times, but there's still nothing predictable about it.
>
> Every single person going into an Open Championship is thinking, you know, 'I could get the wrong side of the draw here. Mayhem could happen.' That's the excitement of it. I just love the idea of being tested mentally, as you are at the Open. It could be a wedge shot that's as difficult as any you've ever played, or it could be a long-iron shot where the ball kicks beautifully towards thee pin. That's the magic of it.

In January 2008, when he was less than four months into a professional career, Rory McIlroy visited Harrington's home in Rathmichael, County Dublin, for a magazine photoshoot. When asked if there was anything in the trophy-laden abode that he would like to take away with him, the 18-year-old pointed with a half-smile to the Claret Jug, which had giant-sized, artificial ladybirds on stems sticking out of it.

Harrington had won the grand old trophy at Carnoustie the previous July and would still have it more than a year later, after retaining the Open at Birkdale.

Carnoustie also proved to be a very significant Open debut for McIlroy, quite apart from his role as a babysitter for four-year-old Patrick Harrington during the playoff for the title. Only two months past his 18th birthday, he soared right up among the Irish challengers with an opening 68 and went on to capture the amateur medal, just as Jimmy Bruen had done 68 years previously.

Arguably more telling was the impression he made on one of the game's leading caddies. JP Fitzgerald was working for Ernie Els when he first took notice of his future employer. 'On television during the 2007 Open, I saw Rory hit a two-iron second-shot into the wind to the last', Fitzgerald recalled.

'What really impressed me was that with 230 yards to go, he hit it so high up in the air that it stopped on the green almost where it landed. I later made a point of saying to him: "That was a special shot."'

Before the end of the following year, Fitzgerald had become McIlroy's caddie and they went on to share several tournament victories, including the 2011 US Open, the 2012 and 2014 PGA Championships, and the 2014 Open.

You felt their partnership endured largely because Fitzgerald had the good sense to acknowledge who was in charge. Like in the wake of the PGA victory at Kiawah, where the bagman was asked if he had brought a last-round charge by Ian Poulter to his employer's attention. 'You don't have to bring those sorts of things to this fellow's attention', Fitzgerald memorably replied. 'Believe me, Rory knows everything that's going on. You might say he's a bit of an anorak in that regard.'

McIlroy also prompted enduring loyalty from his long-time coach, Michael Bannon, who once told me:

> When I thought of Gerry and Rosie, Rory's parents, and the great responsibility they gave me, it often filled me with trepidation. It made me conscious of telling him not simply the right things, but things that would be right for him. Imagine if I told him the wrong thing ....

Which brought to mind McIlroy's Augusta National debut in 2009 when Bannon happened to bump into Michael Bonallack outside the fairway ropes.

On being warmly complimented about McIlroy's stunning technique, the coach modestly acknowledged: 'He's doing all right.' To which Bonallack responded: 'You can certainly say that', before adding: 'Don't, don't let anybody touch him.' Nor did he.

McIlroy's wilful nature also led him to effectively manage his own destiny, after a spell with Chubby Chandler's ISM was followed by a move to Horizon Sports Management, which culminated in a protracted legal battle. And it explained how he remained faithful to JP Fitzgerald, who came in for considerable criticism after the player's collapse in the 2011 Masters, and to his enduring friendship with Harry Diamond, his current bagman.

The 2008 visit to the Harrington home confirmed the player as being extremely bright and one of the most likeable among the world's young sportsmen. Harrington said:

> Every time you meet him, he keeps exceeding your expectations, over and over. You're waiting for him to act like he's a top player; you're waiting for him to change. But he doesn't, except maybe to become even better as a person.
>
> At the moment, Rory's a young man, playing like he really enjoys his golf. He's excited; experiencing the novelty factor. And in the longer term, he'll have to watch out for injuries, just like the rest of us. But a real threat to his golfing career is that he'll get bored. He's wise to reduce his schedule if it means that every event he turns up for feels like it's precious. But if he's turning up and it doesn't feel precious ....

All the while, McIlroy would have been keenly aware of the impact Bob Rotella was having on his Irish colleagues. He would have seen firsthand the American's influence on Harrington's Open successes at Carnoustie and Birkdale, to be followed by Darren Clarke's remarkable triumph at Royal St George's in 2011.

Though temperamentally, McIlroy and Clarke came across as very different people, Rotella could see common fundamentals where their mental approach to golf was concerned. 'When Darren's a little off, he looks like he's a different player', the American said. 'But when his head's in the right place, he's fantastic. The point is that the talent and the skill are still in there. All that has to happen is that he gets out of his way sufficiently to let them out.'

Then, while McIlroy was going through a bleak patch, Rotella said: 'I believe Rory could be put right quite quickly. I remember an occasion when Darren and I sat down together for a two-hour chat and at the end of it he said "I've just had a huge weight lifted off my shoulders." And he went on to describe a light going on, he felt so much better. Rory's got to clear his head the same way.'

Darren Clarke

In mid-November 1990, a quiet passing of the baton took place in Irish professional golf. Three days after Darren Clarke had secured a European Tour card in the Qualifying School at Montpellier, Fred Daly died.

Though we couldn't have known it at the time, we were witnessing the emergence of a player whose international successes, especially in WGC events in the US, would help fill the enormous void left by the island's lone winner of the Open Championship. And Daly's demise lent further emphasis to the revolutionary changes which had been taking place here, in the development of young talent.

Behind the 72nd green at Royal St George's on Sunday 17 July 2011, Clarke's mind guru for a momentous week talked about contagion in an unusually positive sense. 'When you look at your country', said Bob Rotella, 'do you think the top players aren't identifying with each other and thinking "he's from Ireland and can do this; I'm from Ireland so I can do it too"? Sure, contagion is there. Oh God yes. No question.'

Mindful of the psychologist's words, you notice that only a year after Daly became the first home winner of the Irish Open in 1946, his great friend Harry Bradshaw captured the title. And when the Portrush man savoured an Open triumph at Hoylake in 1947, Bradshaw went close to doing the same at Royal St George's two years later, losing a playoff to Bobby Locke.

In this context, we can but speculate as to the impact an Open win by Christy O'Connor Snr might have had. The Brad, who knew him better than most, expressed the view to me that, deep down, O'Connor feared that winning the Open would change him into an international player, so dragging him away from the native patch he loved so well.

This would also explain why he declined to play in the US Masters where he had a standing invitation from 1955 to 1973 as a current Ryder Cup player, though contemporaries such as Peter Alliss, Harry Weetman, Bernard Hunt and even Neil Coles, who hated flying, made the trip.

Rotella's words could also be heard echoing loudly in the background of a chat I had with Graeme McDowell after he had missed the cut on his US Masters debut in 2005. 'I've been trying to put myself in [Pádraig] Harrington's way as much as possible,' said the future US Open champion. 'Pick his brains. I love the way he goes about things. For me, he's the guy who has it all worked out. He's the guy I want to be.'

As it happened, the seventies was a rather bleak decade in the Irish amateur game. The glory days of Joe Carr, Tom Craddock and Jimmy Bruen were at an end and a dearth of talent could be seen in only two Walker Cup representatives over the 10 years – Roddy Carr in 1971 and Pat Mulcare in 1975. And, of course, it was a time of great torment in the North, when The Troubles were at their height.

Attempts at achieving some sense of normality through golf were admirably positive, however, with players crossing the Border for championships in both directions. But there were exceptions. Like in 1974, when the Interprovincial Championship, which should have had a Northern venue, was switched to Royal Dublin and the Home Internationals, scheduled for Royal County Down in 1979, were abandoned altogether.

From two Walker Cup players during the seventies, Ireland delivered no fewer than six a decade later, in Philip Walton, Ronan Rafferty, Arthur Pierse, Garth McGimpsey, John McHenry and Eoghan O'Connell. So, what happened in the meantime?

'As far I'm concerned, the big change occurred when Joe Carr became captain of the Irish team in 1979', said McGimpsey. 'I first played for Ireland in 1978 and when Joe took over, he brought a freshness and a modern approach to Irish golf.' Which was, perhaps, entirely to be expected, given how progressive Carr had been during his own playing days in terms of practice, physical fitness, diet and mental preparation.

McGimpsey went on:

> Up to Joe's captaincy, the Irish amateur scene wasn't taken all that seriously. But Joe instituted squad training trips to Spain, which were very significant in the development of young players such as Rafferty and Walton. And I was lucky to be part of it, too. Before that, you were looking at trials in the depth of winter in places like Carlow and Malone whereas Joe took us away to the sun, where we could play 36 holes a day for six days in a row while developing a keen sense of team spirit.
>
> I happened to be on one of those trips in 1981 when Rafferty set a course record 67 around Sotogrande Old and Enda McMenamin had a hole in one on what is now the short 15th at Valderrama. It was called Las Aves back then, with the nines reversed. That same year, Walton broke new ground by capturing the Spanish Amateur Open title at Torrequebrada, eastwards on the Costa del Sol.

McGimpsey also pointed to Irish players embarking on scholarships to American universities. Walton, for instance, went to Oklahoma State where he was mixing with such promising American talent as Scott Verplank, Bob Tway and Jeff Maggert; McHenry went to William and Mary; and Clarke had a spell, albeit a short one, at Wake Forest where O'Connell later did a full degree course.

'I remember Philip joking that he came back with a degree in finger-painting', McGimpsey went on. 'The important thing was that he became a seriously good player who helped my thinking, along with my putting stroke. His development contrasted sharply with my own, in that I was

23 when I first came on the scene. The upshot of it was that Ireland won the European Team Championship at Chantilly in 1983.'

By then, the era of the full-time amateur had arrived in Irish golf. From a time when the top players were career amateurs, our youngsters began to view a professional career in a much more favourable light. No longer would it be necessary, as in the days of Daly, Bradshaw and O'Connor, for a player to have the financial security of a club job before trying his luck on the tournament circuit. Amateur internationals Des Smyth, John O'Leary and John McHenry made the move, while Eddie Polland, Eamonn Darcy, David Feherty and David Jones progressed through assistant professional ranks.

Then, as a logical follow-up to squad training in the sun, the GUI appointed former English Ryder Cup player John Garner as the country's first national coach. To understand the significance of this move, one had only to be at Royal St George's on that memorable Sunday in 2011, listening to Godfrey Clarke relate how the newly crowned Open champion received his first golf lessons from Garner.

Recalling those heady days with Clarke and Paul McGinley, Garner said: 'Darren came to me back in 1983, when he was a three handicapper on a boys' squad in Belfast and was with me for three years.' Asked if he ever sensed he was working with a future Major champion, Garner replied that while he could see undoubted talent, his primary objective was simply to nurture the players in his care. Around the same time, Michael Bannon, runner-up to Rafferty in the 1980 Irish Amateur Close at Royal County Down, was acquiring a reputation as a gifted coach at Holywood GC, several years before a youngster named McIlroy would become his most celebrated pupil.

When Garner moved on, the GUI appointed as his successor another English coach, Howard Bennett, who established such a close relationship with Harrington during the amateur years that he was included among special guests at Pinehurst in 2024, when the Dubliner was inducted into Golf's Hall of Fame.

With his appointment as head greenkeeper at Dungannon GC in 1983, Godfrey Clarke opened the door for participation by himself and his son in inter-club matches. As he pointed out at Royal St George's, his son's golfing future became a committed effort by a working-class family who had to make sacrifices, just like Kenny and Marian McDowell and Gerry and Rosie McIlroy would do in later years.

Of those Dungannon days before his dad moved some years later to Ballycastle GC, the son recalled: 'We didn't really have a chance of winning a provincial pennant. The height of our ambition was to give the club a boost by winning a couple of rounds, but I looked upon it as terrific fun and great experience.'

Ireland's young amateurs of the 1980s had the best of two worlds. With no lack of competition from their peers, they could also test themselves against gifted career amateurs such as McGimpsey, Pierse, Declan Branigan, Adrian Morrow, Mark Gannon and Barry Reddan. And as a priceless by-product, they were making their own special contribution to north–south relations some time before the peace process secured a treasured prize.

'I consider myself to have dual nationality, British on one hand and Irish on the other,' said McGimpsey. 'There's no way around that. But there was nobody more proud of playing for Ireland than I was. Through 226 senior international matches, I was proud to be part of winning Irish teams, and I never had a problem in standing for the Irish national anthem.'

He added:

> I consider myself lucky to have had the opportunity of playing great courses throughout this island; places like Baltray, Lahinch, Portrush and Rosses Point on an annual basis. Our courses are better than anywhere in the world, which must also be hugely influential in moulding top-class talent.
>
> After Darren's win, people emphasised Northern Ireland because its smallness had the effect of magnifying the achievement all the more. It makes an attractive statistic. But an equally attractive statistic, in my view, is 11 Majors from Ireland in the last

18 years. That's unbelievable – a cause for celebration throughout the whole of the island.

Clarke's entirely predictable debut for Ireland came at Lahinch on 11 September 1987, the last day of the Home Internationals. And with a half-point in his singles against Scottish veteran George Macgregor, he contributed to Ireland's first Triple Crown triumph. After a 1990 season in which he captured the Spanish Amateur, North of Ireland, South of Ireland and Irish Close titles, going through 25 matches unbeaten, he felt there was nothing further to prove. So, he turned professional.

By that stage, the GUI production process was being finetuned year on year, while former amateur rivals found themselves playing side-by-side in professional ranks. Like in the World Cup at Erinvale, South Africa, in November 1996, when Clarke and Harrington teamed up for the first time.

On the eve of battle, Harrington bowed to his partner's seniority, acknowledging Clarke's decisive victory over him in the Irish Close final of 1990. 'I was totally in awe of Darren at that stage', he said. 'He was a fantastic player, totally unbeatable in my view.'

Fifteen years later, at Royal St George's, Clarke turned to Rotella and asked: 'How does Pádraig approach a Major?' The American replied: 'He has a very quiet mind. And you, Darren, have to have a very quiet mind.'

Clarke followed the Harrington lead, and won by three strokes from Phil Mickelson and Dustin Johnson. Which suggested the image of this huge jigsaw into which Joe Carr was putting the first pieces in place, more than 30 years previously.

Rory McIlroy

On the Saturday morning of the 2013 Open, Rory McIlroy cut a lonely figure on the practice ground at Muirfield. With rounds of 79 and 75, he had missed his first cut in six appearances in the Open.

Yet he had no plans to seek the help of Bob Rotella, even though the renowned psychologist had let it be known that he would be only too happy to receive the call. The troubled 24-year-old remained determined to work his way out of what had become a six-month slump.

'I'd love to have Rory say he wanted to see me, but he hasn't', Rotella told me. 'I'd find the time, I'll tell you that.' Then he added: 'There would be no point in my making the approach. I don't walk up to people and tell them to come and see me. It doesn't work like that. They have to be ready to want to talk about this to me.'

When I wondered what precisely he could offer McIlroy, he said with typical directness: 'Peace of mind. That's all. He knows how to play. He's a great player and he'll be a great player again. But I'd have to find out what he has to say before I'd know what to offer him.'

Which wasn't going to happen. When I asked McIlroy on that Saturday morning if he planned to make the call, he replied: 'It's something I haven't really thought about yet.' Was it likely to happen? 'Probably not.' Then, significantly, he added: 'I believe I can work it out for myself.'

Later, I suggested to him that he was different to Tiger Woods in his approach to his chosen pursuit. 'Oh yeah', he replied. 'For sure. I can't bring the intensity he brings to every week. I try to bring it to the big events where I want to do well. But I would find it very difficult to do that every week.'

Committed club practitioners must find themselves questioning how a great player with total control of the golf ball could begin spraying it in all directions. Didn't muscle memory and repeating swings offer protection against such lapses?

'I explained in my book that muscle memory doesn't exist', said Rotella. 'If it did, the ball would keep going like a dart, even if your mind was in a bad place. It wouldn't matter where your head was. A clear mind is a beautiful thing but when there's even a little bit of a cloud in there, it's not the same.'

He went on:

> I'm saddened observing what Rory is going through. I can't help but feel that way because I like him as a person and I admire him as a golfer. But it's all part of the process. There will be some

benefits for him from what he's going through at the moment and he will be fine again. But it will take time, despite the fact that there's really a very fine line in getting it back to being simple.

Could it be achieved without intervention? 'Yes, but ideally you want to get out of it as quickly as possible. You could do it like Ben Hogan and take 25 years to figure it out, or you could bypass that painful process by learning how it's done. That's all.'

By way of bypassing the painful process to which Rotella referred, McIlroy turned to the game's greatest competitor of them all, Jack Nicklaus. The outcome was stunning rounds of 66,66,69,71 for a wire-to-wire victory in the 2014 Open at Royal Liverpool, Hoylake, 12 months later. With a 17-under-par aggregate of 271, he completed the third leg of the elusive career Grand Slam, which would cause him serious torment for close on 11 years.

'To me, Jack Nicklaus certainly had a big impact on Rory's play', said McIlroy's manager, Sean O'Flaherty, looking back on a glorious experience at Hoylake in 2014. The champion's right-hand man had sat in on the meeting with the Bear a month previously, during the week prior to the US Open at Pinehurst.

He remembered the Bear's emphasis on putting oneself first, in which context he highlighted the support of his own wife, Barbara. 'He insisted that there was no other way of doing it', said O'Flaherty. 'And I could see Rory's reaction to being told he didn't have to win every Major by eight shots. Nicklaus pointed out that only four of his were the result of playing brilliantly; the other 14 were the product of being able to get the ball around the course without playing his best.' Which is precisely what McIlroy did in a closing 71 at Hoylake.

Naturally, Nicklaus was very pleased with the outcome. Complimenting Sergio García and Rickie Fowler for the manner in which they rose to the challenge of confronting a six-stroke lead, the Bear expressed admiration for the way McIlroy did 'what he had to do', by way of response.

'Rory's short game was fantastic', he went on:

> How many times when he pitched did he hit it up there, a foot from the hole? It was the best I've seen him swing the club in a long time. I was very interested and very excited to see such good golf in the last round of a Major. All of a sudden you get challenged, and you meet the challenge. It gives you a tremendous amount of confidence.

Asked what distinguished McIlroy from his peers, Nicklaus typically shunned hyperbole when replying:

> What makes him special is that he's just good. He drives the ball a long way, hits it up in the air, which is very important to have the ability to do. Long is good, but when you're long and high, you can take advantage by doing that. It's amazing the guy does not have a larger stature. I also think he believes in what he can do.

Did he take personal credit for any particular aspect of the champion's performance? 'I saw some things we talked about that he used', he said.

> It seemed like he was working on what we talked about. I saw it all four days and whether it was from his own teacher, that's very difficult to answer. But I loved his golf swing. I thought it was really good. He didn't have some of the things I've seen cause him problems.
>
> He was very impressive in every challenge he had all week, especially his second round. He must have got 9,000 questions about how bad he was [on Fridays], and he handled it beautifully, very impressively, by shooting 66. I was very, very proud of him.

Interestingly, McIlroy had turned his back on advice from Nicklaus only a few years previously, yet was welcomed back, largely because of the great man's enduring affection for him. And it is clear that Rotella maintained a similar attitude towards him, given how far removed their relationship was at the 2025 Masters, compared with the 2013 Open at Muirfield.

And why such interest in a lad from Holywood, Co. Down, on the other side of the Atlantic? 'I happened to take a liking to him,' said Nicklaus, who was aged 74 at the time. 'We met the first time in the Gardens Mall [West Palm Beach] when he was 19. He was driving a Honda car, and he had a mop of hair. He stopped and was very pleasant and I enjoyed him. He came back a year later and had lunch with me. He's a really nice young man.'

With a driver off the first tee and a target of reaching 20 under par for the Championship, McIlroy approached the final round with an aggressive attitude similar to that of García and Fowler. And given that they finished first and second in average driving distance over the four days, it is intriguing to compare the clubbing of the two Europeans, especially given their status among the game's finest ball-strikers.

As it happened, they used the same club off the tee only five times in the final 18 holes: 201-yard 6th – six-iron; 197-yard 9th – eight-iron; par-four 12th – three-wood; par-four 14th – three-wood; par-five 16th – driver. On the driving holes, McIlroy varied from driver to three-wood, two-iron, four-iron and six-iron (372-yard 4th) while García used driver, three-wood, five-wood, three-iron, five-iron and seven-iron (4th). All of which reflected the careful planning which went into negotiating one's way around punishing fairway bunkers and dogleg configurations.

McIlroy's superior length was probably best illustrated by their play of the 577-yard, par-five 16th where he followed a driver off the tee with a 218-yard seven-iron to 45 feet from where two putts delivered a birdie-four. From his drive, García needed a six-iron shot of 244 yards which finished 30 feet from the hole, also leaving two putts for birdie.

'Looking back on the Majors, his win in the US Open [2011] came at a time when his career was very much on an upward curve', added O'Flaherty:

> Then came the PGA Championship [2012] after a bit of a lull involving four missed cuts in 12 tournaments. Since then, he has

had to endure the greatest backward step of his career. Two years might be a short time for most players in pursuit of Majors, but for him, it must have felt like an eternity.

His standards are so much higher than anybody else's. So there's a huge sense of achievement from what he did at Hoylake. He got the reward for putting himself first and giving his golf the attention it deserves.

Des Smyth

My first sight of an Irish player in serious contention for the Open was at Troon in 1982. It was also where I gained a priceless insight into the key ingredient which went into the making of a Major champion.

Des Smyth was our man, playing in his sixth Open at a time when he was twice a Ryder Cup representative and a four-time winner on the European Tour. At local level, there was also a stunning victory in the Irish Dunlop Tournament at Headfort, where a 27-under-par aggregate of 261 gave him victory by the crushing margin of 16 strokes over Peter Townsend, no less.

Events at Troon, however, were to illustrate to him the considerable gap that he had yet to bridge with the game's top players. Enlightenment came on the back nine of his final round. 'In hindsight, I felt myself in the mix, but quite a bit behind', he recalled. 'I remember having a birdie on the 11th which was then a par five (481 yards) and one of the on-course leaderboards told me I was minus four for the Championship.

'Going down the 12th fairway, I remember turning to my caddie and saying that I thought I should go for flags from there on in. This could be an opportunity I might not get again.' He soon realised that it was the wrong decision to make, given that the pins, for the most part, were tucked away into corners on that fateful homeward journey:

> I short-sighted myself twice and made bogeys at the 12th and the short 14th. Too late, I was to discover that minus four would have been good enough. On the short 14th, I remember the pin was over

on the left and I went for it and got plugged in a bunker underneath the face. I paid the price. Guys confronted with that situation on a regular basis would have read it better than I did. Quite simply, I didn't appreciate the degree of difficulty of that finishing stretch, where pars would have been a great result for those in contention.

Nick Price, who was in a commanding position on that fateful afternoon, fell into the same trap. With a two-stroke lead on the homeward journey, Price squandered his chance of victory with a double-bogey six on the 457-yard 15th and a bogey four on the treacherous, short 17th (223 yards).

In the event, Tom Watson won by a stroke from Peter Oosterhuis and Price in a share of second place and Smyth earned £11,000 for a share of fourth place a stroke further back with Nick Faldo, Tom Purtzer and Masahiro Kuramoto.

Memorably, Watson admitted afterwards that he thought he would need a birdie on the final hole to get into a playoff. But as Smyth has since acknowledged, it would have been too risky to attack a pin which was tucked inside a greenside bunker on the right. He would need to sink a putt of 20 to 25 feet from the centre of the green. Which didn't happen. But a closing par for 70 and an aggregate of 284 was good enough. Smyth concluded: 'I learned that day that you made your score going out and you then hung onto it on the way back. Still, I really enjoyed the experience.'

Christy O'Connor Jnr

Irish players always seemed to relish the special challenge of the quirky fairways at Royal St George's. Like in 1959 when Royal Dublin's Noel Fogarty took an embryonic Golden Bear to the 19th, before losing a fourth-round tie to 19-year-old Nicklaus in the British Amateur. And in the 1985 Open, when Christy O'Connor Jnr communed with the gods in a course-record opening round of 64.

The existing record of 65, which gave the Dunlop 65 golf ball its name, was set by Henry Cotton en route to his Open triumph of 1934, when Sandwich measured a substantial 6,700 yards. And the great man was present at the back of the media centre when O'Connor came in for interview 51 years later.

'Not a bad score for 17 holes, young man', he mischievously piped up, much to the delight of the assembled scribes. 'Thank you so much, Mr Cotton', was O'Connor's respectful reply. The Galwayman was entitled to be pleased, having spread-eagled the field with a run of seven birdies from the fourth. That was when a British colleague, Ron Moseley, turned to me in the media centre, having seen a mass of red numbers on the scoreboard, and exclaimed: 'Look at what Christy is doing.'

Dave Musgrove, who was with Seve Ballesteros for an Open victory at Royal Lytham in 1979, caddied this time around for Sandy Lyle six years later, when they were with O'Connor in the third-last pairing of the final round. Describing Sandwich as tough and ruthless, Musgrave recalled: 'When we stood on the 10th tee, Christy turned to us and said "Whichever one of us can score two under for the back nine, will win."'

As it happened, Lyle finished two strokes clear of the Galwayman, despite a bogey at the last, where he appeared to mishit a chip. 'It wasn't a duff', insisted Musgrove. 'Another yard and it would have been perfect.' In the event, Lyle then putted from the fringe to two feet and, to his eternal credit, sank the next one for victory.

O'Connor shot a closing 72 to Lyle's 70 for a share of third place with David Graham, Bernhard Langer, Mark O'Meara and José Rivero. And after O'Connor's opening 64, his close friend Eamonn Darcy had the lowest score of the second round with a 68 and was eventually tied 11th.

Eamonn Darcy

A further six years on and the Open had us at Royal Birkdale where the cheering started for a popular Irishman when he was still 150 yards from the 18th green. Wave upon wave of the most thrilling sound swept on the wind from the grandstands, filling him with emotion.

On 20 July 1991, Eamonn Darcy experienced an enduring sense of how it must feel to become Open champion.

But this was Saturday. Granted, the Irishman had led the championship at one stage of a dramatic afternoon, but, after 54 holes, he ended the day a stroke adrift of joint leaders Ian Baker-Finch and Mark O'Meara.

He and a virtually unknown Australian referred to in a section of the British media as Ian Baker-Who, had been down this particular road before, when golf's most coveted prize beckoned. That was when Baker-Finch had led by three strokes at the halfway stage at St Andrews in 1984 and was tied for the lead after 54 holes with the defending champion Tom Watson, before it all fell apart in a final round of 79.

'I enjoyed it so much that I remember thinking I'd love a really decent run in the Open', recalled Darcy. 'I wanted to have the chance of getting right up there with the leaders, as The Brad [Harry Bradshaw] did in 1949 and Senior [Christy O'Connor Snr] did on a number of occasions.'

He went on:

> To be honest, I thought Sandwich would be my best bet in view of my record there [as runner-up to Arnold Palmer in the PGA Championship of 1975] but now, here I was at Birkdale, walking down the 18th fairway on the Saturday afternoon.
>
> I remember how good it felt to have so many people showing their appreciation of the score I had battled hard to achieve. I couldn't believe it.
>
> There had been great excitement at Muirfield Village four years previously when I sank that putt against Ben Crenshaw in the Ryder Cup. That was a very special moment. But it was special mainly because of what it meant to the European team.
>
> At Birkdale, the applause had a much more personal impact. I felt at the very height of my career and this was for me, in recognition of my third-round 66. These were golf people who knew the game and appreciated my efforts purely as an individual player. And I was to learn afterwards that there were many of them who genuinely believed I could go on and win.

I remember not wanting to think about such things with a round still to be played. But I felt very comfortable in myself, even if I was a bit surprised at being up there within a stroke of the lead.

Darcy played the last round with another Australian, Mike Harwood. And the magic stayed with him, particularly on the greens where he had reaped a rich dividend the previous day. 'I remember that after knocking it out in 31, I discovered at the next leaderboard that I had actually fallen further behind', he said.

This was due to a sparkling outward 29 by Baker-Finch who had become, at that time, only the tenth player in Open history to break 30 for nine holes. Meanwhile, Darcy's challenge was effectively ended by a wretched double-bogey seven at the long 15th. 'I went for the green with a one iron, only to pull it into serious trouble on the left', Darcy recalled.

From there, he needed two hacks to get the ball onto the green and two putts completed an ugly seven. Though he went on to birdie the long 17th, it was sufficient only to lift him to a share of fifth place with the American Jody Mudd, who broke the course record with a closing 63.

Still Darcy learned, much to his delight, that nearly men can also have rich memories from the Open.

Feherty and the fear of failure

There were other profitable adventures by Irish players before Harrington's breakthrough changed the entire complexion of the event from our perspective. Ronan Rafferty missed the cut for a share of 95th place as a 16-year-old at Muirfield in 1980.

Nine years later, a return to Troon saw David Feherty make his mark with rounds of 71,67,69,72 for a share of sixth place with Fred Couples behind the surprise winner, Mark Calcavecchia, after a playoff.

That was when Greg Norman, after a record-breaking final round of 64, re-lived the pain of several disappointments in Major tournaments with the words: 'I've had them taken away from me. I would just love to sit here and have one given to me.'

Which, not for the first time, didn't happen.

For his part, Feherty returned to the limelight at Turnberry in 1994, when his best Open performance delivered a share of fourth place with Mark James and Sweden's Anders Forsbrand behind a resurgent Nick Price.

Yet the Bangor man was honest enough to actually question his right to be there, which was potentially ruinous to his natural competitive instincts. Feherty publicly admitted that when he found himself in challenging positions for the Open, like at Troon and Turnberry, 'there was one pivotal moment when I always messed up.' He added: 'I just didn't have the mental capacity to go all the way.'

Rafferty, meanwhile, had to settle for a share of 11th place at Turnberry, despite middle rounds of 66 and 65. But Irish aspirants were set to undergo a profound change, though it would be some years before this became a competitive reality.

Their thinking would eventually be changed by Harrington, who talked very differently about competitive failure at the highest level. 'You find yourself in the public spotlight, leading a tournament by one and you mess up, say with a double-bogey on the 17th', he said. 'Going down the 18th, you're going to be feeling as bad as can be.'

But he insisted: 'There is no way I would choose to be in any other position. Standing on that 18th one shot behind, there's nothing you could offer me that I would swap it for, however low I might feel. I would still want that chance to win, because that's what I do. That's the reason I'm there.'

14

More than a bag-carrier

'He told me he caddied in the same group with me in the Hot Springs Open. That's why I voted for him, because he was a caddie.'

– Former US Open champion Tommy Bolt on American president Bill Clinton

• • • •

Thinking back to the dramatic happenings on the 72nd hole of the 2007 Open at Carnoustie, I imagined what I might have done in Pádraig Harrington's situation. I eventually decided that I would have been so overwhelmed with embarrassment that I would have abandoned everything and headed speedily for the nearest exit.

Interestingly, in various reflections since then, Harrington has admitted to having had very similar thoughts. And that a desperate situation was saved only by the positivity of his caddie, Ronan Flood.

'I'd hit two of the worst shots of my life', Harrington said of his drive into the Barry Burn and a five-iron third shot into a further segment of the hazard:

> I was feeling terrible. My caddie literally had to talk me around. It was 150 yards of a conversation that I didn't want to have and he just kept at me.
>
> I've never felt that bad on a golf course. I felt embarrassed. My caddie kept at me, kept telling me to play it out, one shot at a time, see what happened. By the time I hit my chip shot from 48 yards as my fifth shot on that hole, I hit it like a teenager showing off. I was back in the zone.

For Flood, however, the agony was far from over. 'At the time in my head, I was kind of thinking, "Oh God, it's nearly five feet"', he said. '"God, what a disaster! If you miss this, what a disaster!"'

'But when we talked about it after, to him it was a tap-in. He only realised how long it was when he saw it on the replay. He thought that he had just knocked it up nearly stone dead, whereas I remember standing by the hole as it came up and thinking, "sit down, sit down". It went that dodgy distance by, all right, but thankfully [it was] a tap-in for him.'

For both player and caddie, the key to Harrington's eventual triumph was Flood's incessant chatter after their first visit to the Burn.

'Pádraig had played great, unbelievable, like the best I've ever seen him play for 17 holes on the Sunday', Flood added.

> He was six under par [for the day] through 17 and he could have been probably eight or nine under.
>
> It was the walking referee who told us the third shot was in the Burn. And Pádraig he just went quiet and, yes, I was thinking about Van de Velde [who had a similar disaster on Carnoustie's 72nd in the 1999 Open]. I'm sure he was thinking about Van de Velde, but over the years we've had different times when things have gone wrong, so I just started talking to him just the same as we would normally, just telling him that the hole wasn't over, a lot of clichés about we'll just wait, get through this hole and see what happens.
>
> I just kept talking to him and looking for him to give me a response, just say anything. And I kept saying, 'come on, you hear

me,' whatever. Eventually he was like, 'yes, ok, yes.' He wasn't answering me for probably two thirds of the walk down and then he started talking and getting into it.

He started answering me back more, talking a little bit before we got to the ball, so at least it was kind of somewhat out of his head. By the time we got down there, he'd worked out the yardage, he'd dropped his ball and he was back into playing golf. So he was fine at that stage.

Harrington later described his pitch on 18 as one of the two greatest shots he has played in his career, together with the stunning five-wood into the 71st hole that effectively secured a successful defence of the Open at Royal Birkdale the following year.

Forty years previously, in the 1967 Open at Hoylake, another caddie faced a very different challenge in getting his player over the finishing line. Scotland's Willie Aitchison was guiding the fortunes of Roberto de Vicenzo through a similarly testing climax.

During a sojourn I had at Harbour Town in the US in the spring of 2005, I had the great pleasure of meeting up with the legendary Willie. He happened to be in Hilton Head visiting his daughter Catherine, who worked there as a nurse. And he talked about the possibility of a caddying comeback – at 77.

'Another daughter of mine, Isobel, has a son Gary who will be attempting to qualify for this year's Open Championship', said the veteran Scot. 'And if he makes it, I've promised to carry the bag.' It seemed that the young man, Gary Shepherd, had been doing admirable things back home as a member of Erskine GC and would not be overawed by the prospect of playing at St Andrews.

For his part, Willie, who last carried a bag on the Old Course for a ceremonial four holes with Lee Trevino in 2000, looked in terrific shape for his age. Predictably, he was delighted about the Open returning to Hoylake, given the special memories it held for him. He was given to believe that something special was being arranged for himself and de Vicenzo.

Which would have been to mark their partnership of 1967 when the Argentinian, then aged 44 years and 93 days, became the oldest winner of the Open on the occasion of its last staging at Hoylake.

'We played with Gary Player in the final round, a group ahead of Jack Nicklaus, and the bookmakers made Roberto the outsider of the trio', he reflected in 2010. With remarkable recall, Willie continued:

> By the time we got to the 15th, the crowd was massive. Soon we were on the 16th tee, looking at these chestnut fences which flanked the fairway, nothing like the ropes we have these days. Anyway, as Roberto was on the backswing of his drive, these guys jumped back off the fence and went 'Wheeee.'
>
> In the circumstances, my man did well to hit what was a reasonable drive down the long 16th [529 yards]. Not a good one, but OK. This was the famous par five with its internal out of bounds and I knew it would probably decide the championship. So, I went down the fairway to figure out what Roberto should do from there. Going out of bounds right would spoil everything.
>
> I had no yardage. We sized up shots the proper way in those days. Anyway, after I had eyed up the distance and judged the wind, I had a gut feeling. So when Roberto turned to me and said 'Willie, which way?', I just took the cover off the three-wood and handed it to him. 'Hit it,' I said. 'To lay up?' he asked. 'No', I replied. 'To hit the green.'
>
> He never hesitated. For a carry of 230 yards into a light wind, I knew it had to be hit 100 per cent. As the ball was in flight my stomach was turning over and I prayed it would be right. Eventually, I heaved a sigh of relief as it bounced on the green. Two putts and we had our birdie.
>
> After a par on the 17th, I could see the emotion beginning to get the better of Roberto. Trying desperately to control himself, he succeeded in hitting a fine three-wood down the 18th fairway. But by the time he got to his ball, his face was covered with tears.

> 'Willie', he said, 'I can't see the green. Give me a club that will get me there for two putts.' I handed him an eight iron and when he hit it, we walked the rest of the way to the green with everybody in the stands rising to acclaim the new champion. 'Viva Roberto!' they kept calling. 'Viva Roberto!' I later learned that Henry Cotton had been behind this salute. It was the most sentimental thing I've ever seen in golf.

Warming to the memory, he went on:

> I had been with him barely 18 months at that time, having previously worked for Tony Lema, who was killed in an air crash in 1966. Roberto and I got on really well together, though he was a highly emotional man. Even with the lead from the middle of the third round, he believed the fates were against him because of his age.
>
> With a closing 70, he finished two strokes clear of Nicklaus and by that stage, there wasn't a dry eye to be seen. For Roberto and me, there would never be another moment quite like it.

Aitchison paused. 'I last saw him here at St Andrews in 2005 and, do you know, he barely recognised me. I was disgusted.' Then he laughed heartily.

Caddie stories are almost as plentiful as golfers. But none of the hackneyed stereotypes can be applied to a partnership which has become one of the most celebrated in the game. The fact is that Pádraig Harrington and Ronan Flood are different: close friends who became remarkable working partners.

There is an obvious empathy, even in the way they talk about each other. And as the husbands of sisters, Caroline and Suzie née Gregan, their mutual understanding is further strengthened by shared socializing, away from golf events.

A downside of this closeness, of course, is that Flood will feel more acutely the pain of Harrington's setbacks. But at the other end, there is a corresponding heightening of joy at an outstanding success. Like in a second successive Open Championship triumph at Royal Birkdale in 2008. After Harrington had extracted a rich dividend from a course whose fairness reminded him of Portmarnock, player and caddie walked together down the 18th fairway for the last time. They turned to each other, smiling. 'Well done!' said Flood. 'You can enjoy it now.'

'Well done!' said Harrington to his friend. It could hardly have been more different from Carnoustie, 12 months previously.

This time, they simply embraced every glorious element of a marvellous occasion. 'We exchanged a few words about how great a walk it was, but for the most part we just took in the scene', said Flood. 'Huge crowds lining the fairway. The grandstand. Sustained cheering and clapping. People shouting Pádraig's name. The best walk in golf.'

Flood went on: 'Can you think of any other tournament in the world where you are going to experience such an atmosphere? And to know that your player is about to win the Open ... I simply concentrated on enjoying every second of it. The merging of sounds. The spectacle of a great, great occasion.'

In May 2004, Flood was deskbound as an assistant bank manager in the corporate section of Allied Irish Bank's headquarters in Ballsbridge, Dublin. A month later, he was treading the world's fairways as Harrington's caddie, having taken leave of absence from his job. Two years further on, he informed the bank there was no point in their holding his position any longer. He wouldn't be coming back.

He and Harrington had been friends from their days as juniors at Stackstown GC, where Flood acquired a decidedly useful game which would ultimately give him a two handicap. And it was there that he met Suzie, whose father, Dermot, brought his daughters there as members.

As we talked of Birkdale, one could imagine his immense value to Harrington. His calm assurance. How they seemed to be of one mind in everything the player did with club in hand. And his refusal to sacrifice honesty by investing a working situation with convenient drama and significance for the benefit of listeners.

Like the 13th hole of the final round, where the sinking of a 15-foot birdie putt seemed to spark off Harrington's victory surge. 'There was no trigger, no spark', insisted Flood.

> There was no thought like 'Oh my God! This is it. He can win from here.' You're looking for something special but for me, Pádraig simply played the 13th very well, just as he had played the hole before, and the one before that.
>
> There was nothing special about it. He hit a nice tee shot at 13 followed by a lovely five iron, and a good putt which happened to drop in. But it didn't have me thinking 'Right. That's it.' For Pádraig and myself, it meant we just kept doing what we had been doing since the round began.

He then said pointedly:

> If you want to know when I thought we'd retain the Open, it was when we were heading to the first tee on Sunday afternoon. From the outset, I figured that Pádraig was one of only a small number of players capable of winning. So, I wasn't surprised we were in the last group. And before his first tee shot; before that great up and down for an opening par, I was convinced he was playing well enough to win. To be perfectly honest, as far back as on the plane going over the previous Sunday, I thought he could win. Though you obviously need certain things to happen, the guy is good enough to win any tournament in which he tees it up.

Still, almost as an indulgence, he took me through the closing holes, recounting a very good tee shot at the short 14th for what proved to be a comfortable par. A solid tee shot at the long 15th allowed him to go for the green in two, as he had done on the Saturday. And he proceeded to make birdie there for a third successive day.

'I had been watching the leaderboards so I knew exactly where he stood, the whole way round', Flood went on.

> Pádraig doesn't look at them. I remember thinking it was nice, having Greg Norman and his caddie Linn [Strickler] with us. In that situation, however, in the final round of a Major championship, there wasn't a huge amount of chat. While Norman got on and did his own thing, he made sure to compliment Pádraig on the good things he did, but it wasn't as if the two of them were shooting the breeze. They were engaged in serious business.
>
> After Pádraig had found a good position from his five-wood tee shot (306 yards) on the 17th, he said to me: 'I must be three ahead, am I?' He'd assumed Norman was second, but I knew Ian Poulter had finished on seven over, which meant that Pádraig had a two-shot lead on him with two to play. Though I was more than happy for him to go for the green (272 yards) with another five wood, I wanted him to know how he stood before he hit it.
>
> Then, as soon as the ball left the clubface, I was sure this shot was about to win him another Open.

This was when Flood broke from his normal routine. Instead of waiting for the ball to land before saying anything, he exclaimed 'Great shot!' not long after it had soared into the air. His reaction so surprised Harrington that the player actually made a point of mentioning it during his post-championship press conference.

'I wouldn't have listened for the sound of club on ball as an indication of the purity of the strike', said the caddie:

> I don't ever feel the need to analyse. But I could see from the flight that it wasn't going to be in any trouble. He hit it towards the grandstand on the left and I probably said 'Great shot!' when it had drifted in enough to carry the first bunker and was going to be inside the second one.
>
> The worst he was making was five, while the odds were on a four. But I never expected it to finish where it did [three feet above the hole], which was brilliant. Now I'm thinking, 'he can't be caught. It's nearly all over. The job is pretty much done.' I knew Pádraig

wouldn't have to worry about making a four down the last. Even if Norman eagled 17, we still had a couple of shots in the bag.

These thoughts would have been influenced considerably by the nature of Birkdale's 473-yard 18th. Even with a menacing pot-bunker down the right and a narrow entrance to the green, it didn't have anything like the card-wrecking potential of the 18th at Carnoustie and its treacherously serpentine Barry Burn.

Down the final hole, a five-iron approach of 212 yards was hit on a similar flight to the five wood at 17 – towards the grandstand on the left, inviting the wind to ease it safely onto the green. Which had millions screaming approval. Two putts later, and the job was officially done.

It seemed odd in a way that an accountant and a banker should have discovered a common bond on fairways rather than in finance. 'We've always been good friends', said Flood. 'I don't know if that helps on the golf course. It's hard to pinpoint when we went beyond simply being friends to becoming a strong working partnership.'

He continued:

> Back in the days when I was working in the bank, my concern was that I mightn't be among the spectators when he started winning Major championships. That's how convinced I was of his talent. Then I found myself saying to Pádraig's brother that I was the luckiest man alive, having a ringside seat and enjoying watching him play.
>
> We all get on very well, which is great. And he's such an ordinary guy who hasn't really changed over the years. He's so generous; so ready to help people. And polite. Of course, there's a tough side to him. You can't do what he's done without being tough. But it doesn't mean throwing the head and refusing to talk to the press, or things like that.
>
> His job happens to be a very exciting one, because he does it so well. But he's essentially a normal fellow who happened to become one of the best players in the world. I was thrilled for him winning

the Open the first time round, if only as a reward for all the hard work he had put into his game. Then he became a multiple Major winner, and there aren't many of them around.

Flood concluded: 'He's such a talented guy that if he went out there carrying his own bag, he'd still win tournaments. The only difference would be that he'd be a bit more tired from carrying the bag. I've no doubt about that.'

Like the kid who ran away to the circus, Flood was the banker who found fulfilment in a game he happened to play pretty well. Except that it worked out differently to how he had imagined it. As the American caddie Ernest 'Creamy' Carolan once remarked: 'There's something haunting about getting up at dawn and walking a golf course, checking pin placements. It's easy to lose track of reality.'

Very different from the sometimes-straitened occasions in the world of finance.

Willie Aitchison was 85 when he died on 4 January 2015, in his home city of Glasgow. My last chat with him was in July 2010, prior to the 139th Open at St Andrews.

It was an occasion when legendary golfing partners looked out on the famous 17th hole, which was becoming more sodden by the minute. Trevino kept insisting he was prepared to brave the elements, but Aitchison, his one-time caddie, was especially grateful that the Champions Challenge had been cancelled.

It meant he could spend Wednesday afternoon at St Andrews, mulling over old times with a man who was both employer and close friend during their 27 years together. And with the heavens chucking it down outside, the comfort of Trevino's suite in the Old Course Hotel was all the more appealing. Particularly over a pot of tea.

By that stage, the celebrated venue, which would hail a new beginning with the victory of Louis Oosthuizen four days later, had become more accustomed to endings. As in the swansong of Arnold Palmer in 1995; of Jack Nicklaus in 2000; and the Bear's encore curtain call in 2005.

And of Tom Watson's goodbye on this occasion. Yet there was something deeply poignant about a caddie's farewell.

'I knew Fred Daly very well', said Willie:

> He was a very jolly fella. Everybody liked Fred. We played practice rounds with him. He was very confident; very aware of what he could do and he wasn't frightened to tell you. A very different character from [Harry] Bradshaw, who I saw play as well.
>
> Brad, of course, had a different physique. If it came to a crunch, I think I would back Fred every day to beat Bradshaw. Still, they were two good Irishmen. Joe Carr was another good friend of mine. I caddied for Michael Bonallack when we beat Carr in the semi-final of the [British] Amateur. They were the two main men in amateur golf at that time. They were very different men. Joe was very charismatic whereas Michael was quiet.

Now in his eighties, Aitchison had hoped for a final meeting with de Vicenzo, to mull over their experience of 1967 at Hoylake. But he couldn't be too selfish. A few hours with Trevino was way beyond his expectations while being driven from his home in Glasgow that morning by his son, Willie Jnr.

This was their first meeting since 2000 and both men suspected it might be their last. And as respective eyes assessed the physical impact of the intervening years, there was a conscious effort not to allow emotions to take over. As the caddie told me later, it would have been so easy to dissolve into tears.

Instead, they talked quietly about their yesterdays; about the triumphs, disappointments and, most of all, the fun they had together. They recalled their first St Andrews Open in 1970, when Trevino led after 54 holes, and then witnessed playing partner Doug Sanders ruinously push a putt for the championship of less than three feet past the hole on the 72nd green.

Then there was the joy of Trevino's successive triumphs at Royal Birkdale in 1971 and at Muirfield a year later. Glorious times when both men were at the peak of their formidable powers. Finally, their Open swansong came in 2000 when Trevino, with Aitchison by his side for the last time, bade a competitive farewell to the Auld Grey Toon with rounds of 80 and 77.

The Champions Challenge was actually inaugurated on that occasion when the caddie also renewed acquaintance with de Vicenzo. He had hoped to do so again when the Open returned to Hoylake in 2006, but the Argentinian declined the Royal and Ancient's invitation to make the trip, because of failing health.

'When Lee and I settled down for a chat in his suite on the Wednesday in 2010, his first concern was whether I was all right about him having his son, Daniel, caddie for him on this occasion', said Aitchison. 'Of course, I didn't mind. It would have been pure joy for me, simply walking the four holes with them.'

With no attempt to hide an inner glow, he went on:

> I'm now the oldest of the old-time caddies: the last survivor. I caddied for [Sam] Snead and [Gary] Player. And I caddied for [Tom] Watson in the Irish Open at Woodbrook in 1975, after he and his regular man, Alfie Fyles, had a bit of a falling-out over money.
>
> Since I started in the British Amateur at St Andrews in 1951, caddying has been my life. There was no accommodation locally for caddies at that time and I slept in a greenkeeper's hut behind the 15th tee, where the toilets are now.
>
> 'Even after all the years, there can still be great moments. Like what happened to me at Royal Portrush when I was there with some friends a few years ago. When the local caddies recognised me they did me the honour of doffing their caps, which was a very humbling experience.
>
> 'I feel very privileged that my friendship with Lee has lasted 40 years. I told him how my children used to be terrified of stepping out of line, for fear I'd report them to him. They looked on him as a sort of god.

He continued:

> In the hotel on the Wednesday, my son and two grandsons were present at the start, having photographs taken. But after a few minutes, they left the two of us together. I was wondering how I was going to handle it but once we started talking, I was fine. Mind you, I don't know if I could have contained myself if we had walked up the 18th together.
>
> That green has wonderful memories for me. Back in 2000, the R&A gave special permission for my wife and family to join me on the 18th with Lee. And the sight of them all prompted Lee to remark: 'Willie, I've all the money I'll ever need, but you're the luckiest man in the world to have your family around you like this. I envy you.'

Willie's wife died in 2002, leaving him on his own in a maisonette in Cumlodden Drive on the north side of Glasgow. 'I've been in this street for 78 years and Aitchisons lived here for another 25 before that', he said, with a directness which must have given him priceless clarity while among the top flight of tour caddies. And he remained immensely proud of his son and six daughters.

All too soon, three hours had slipped by and it was time for old friends to part. When they embraced, emotions remained in check. Then, as Aitchison headed for the lobby, his thoughts again drifted towards Roberto.

Suddenly, as if pre-ordained from on high, the 88-year-old Argentinian and his caddie of 1967 were walking towards each other. 'He seemed as surprised as I was, but we instinctively gave each other a big hug', said Aitchison:

> For years, I had imagined how our reunion might be, if we were to meet again. When it happened, we were so taken aback that we really didn't know how to react.

We were together no more than a few minutes. In that time, however, I had a flashback to the scene on the 18th at Hoylake all those years ago. I remembered Roberto hitting a fine three-wood tee shot down the middle of the fairway and then turning to me with his face covered in tears. 'Willie', he said, 'I can't see the green. Give me a club that will get me there for two putts.' For Roberto and me, there would never be another moment quite like it.

Later on that Wednesday evening in 2010, in the quiet of his Glasgow home, the emotion of an extraordinary day could be contained no longer. 'I had a wee sob in private, thinking I'll probably never see them again', he said. 'I suppose it's natural to have those thoughts when you get to my age.'

Much has changed in golf since Aitchison was at the peak of his craft. Money was modest, yet there was the satisfaction of working with some of the top men of their day, players who expected a caddie to be an on-course psychologist as well as an astute decision-maker.

Great players like Trevino and de Vicenzo trusted Willie to pull the club which could win a Major championship. Job satisfaction can hardly come much better than that.

15

All about Lowry

'Pressure is for tyres.'
– 2019 Open champion Shane Lowry

As eager fans streamed in record numbers into Royal Portrush for the Irish Open at the end of June 2012, local officials considered the words of Pádraig Harrington, an honorary life member of the host club. 'Let's put it this way; it's more of a reality than people might think', was how the Dubliner assessed the possibility of the Open Championship returning to the County Antrim links.

Harrington's optimism provided a timely lift, coming as it did the week after the announcement of Royal Troon for the 2016 staging. Apart from his status as a two-time Open champion, his words were viewed in the context of regular contact with chief executive Peter Dawson, as an official ambassador for the Royal and Ancient, whose emblem he carried on his left sleeve.

Harrington further suggested: 'Staging the Irish Open here this week was an inspired decision which could lead to other things down the road.' And at the mention of 'other things', there was a knowing raising of his eyebrows.

Having already endured the long wait since 1951 to get the Open back on the Dunluce Links, it could be that the eventual reward for Royal Portrush might be greater than their wildest imaginings. One recalled that when Royal St George's had a 32-year gap between their Opens of 1949 and 1981, it was followed by a remarkably quick return there in 1985, to justify the R&A's heavy financial investment on infrastructure.

A cumulative four-day attendance figure of 112,000 for the Irish Open, despite wretched weather, set a record for the European Tour, while demonstrating that the Northern Ireland public were prepared to enthusiastically support an important international sporting event. From an infrastructural standpoint, however, R&A observers would have noted that much work still had to be done if Portrush was to measure up to the highest level as a Major championship venue.

In this context, absolutely no relevance could be applied to the 1951 staging won by Max Faulkner.

One of the more obvious ways of dealing with large attendances these days is through grandstands spread throughout the layout, each holding up to 2,000 spectators. In the event, the host club and the European Tour (DP World Tour) gained priceless experience from staging the Irish Open.

When the tents departed and the Dunluce Links was returned to its members, the cost to Royal Portrush of staging the 2012 Irish Open was estimated at around £200,000, largely the consequence of lost green fees traffic.

It was an investment, however, that the club were more than happy to make. They knew that if they happened to land the ultimate prize, lucrative streams of overseas visitors would be assured for generations to come.

Apart from contributing more than £100 million to the local economy, the Open would secure the club's future for the next generation, according to past captain Sir Richard McLaughlin. 'Even in the depths of the Troubles, the 1951 Open continued to bring people here', he said.

'And there's no doubt that the Irish Open became a complete turning point in getting it back.'

Ever the pragmatist, one of this island's leading golf club administrators captured beautifully the essence of what this meant to her revered establishment. 'My marketing budget has now been reduced to zero', said Wilma Erskine, then secretary/manager of the Co. Antrim links, who retired the position after the 2019 Open had been hailed a resounding success. Indeed, the very idea of such status was enough to send pulses racing among peripatetic golfers worldwide.

In this context, the importance of the record-breaking attendances of 2012 couldn't be overstated. It was all there in an interview which Dawson gave to the *Scotland on Sunday* newspaper, earlier, in January of that year. 'We will be very interested to see how the course copes commercially and in terms of spectator movement when the Irish Open is held there later this year', he said. 'So we are taking it seriously.'

Local figures also played their part, notably the 2011 Open champion, Darren Clarke, who badgered the R&A relentlessly in pursuit of the grand prize. He could recall the somewhat dispiriting start of a nine at the first hole on his competitive debut over Dunluce, as a 15-year-old. 'I would consider it tighter than most of the other Open courses', he said. 'Stand on the ninth tee out there and you've got to hit the fairway, which is a big ask. It is simply a very demanding course.'

Architect Stan Ebert said:

> It is hard to argue against this being the finest piece of linksland on which the Open Championship is played. No other venue, in my view, has such pure links undulations through its 18 holes. Then there's the great skill the original designer, Harry Colt, had as a master in traversing such difficult terrain to bring the best out of it.

On a memorable Tuesday, 12 July 2005, a par finish from the 16th would have ensured Rory McIlroy a course record 63 in the second qualifying round of the North of Ireland Amateur Championship. Two months past his 16th birthday and from the very back tees of a course measuring 7,134 yards, he responded to the challenge with birdies on the 17th and 18th for a stunning 61. In fact, he finished with a run of five birdies which began at Calamity in a stunning homeward 28.

Birdies at the second, sixth and ninth brought him to the turn in 33. This was followed by an eagle and six further birdies. There were eight pars but no bogey on the card. Dunmurry's Stephen Crowe, an awestruck playing partner, retains a particular recollection of the long 17th where McIlroy got up and down for yet another birdie. 'I couldn't hit my shot', Crowe said, due to the dramatic increase in spectator numbers. 'I had to say to people, "Excuse me, do you mind moving back." The situation wasn't getting out of control, but it would have been no harm to have had a marshal there.'

Another fascinated observer, Kenny Fahey of Connemara, had arrived home from the University of Rhode Island. 'If that's what good looks like, I definitely cannot do it', he said. 'It was more like silence around the clubhouse afterwards. Rory didn't even go on to win the North [he lost in the second round] and no one cared. When a thoroughbred shines and you get a chance to be around, it's really special.'

The choice as architect of Ebert, a partner in the design practice of Mackenzie and Ebert, was based on a lengthy association with the club going back to their preparations for the 1993 British Amateur, when he worked with Donald Steel. An acknowledged links expert who did splendid work in Ireland at Enniscrone, Steel also happened to be a great admirer of Harry Colt.

Yet there were those who considered any tampering with Colt's masterpiece as nothing short of vandalism. In which context, it should be noted that the eighth and ninth holes were, in fact, designed by prominent club member Sir Anthony Babington and erstwhile club professional PD 'Stevie' Stevenson, prior to the 1951 Open. The planned removal of the 17th and 18th holes would make the 442-yard 16th, with its out-of-bounds beckoning on the left and bunkers at 260 to 271 yards off the tee, a daunting new finishing hole.

When looking over the area of the proposed new seventh and eighth holes, I thought of Darren Clarke's claim that 'if it's a beautiful setting you're looking for, I can't imagine anything to stir the heart like the fifth at Portrush, sweeping down to the White Rocks and the ocean beyond.'

Effectively, the fifth and sixth of the Valley would be re-created into a par four and a par five. So, when you finished the short sixth on Dunluce, the seventh would be located in the area of the existing sixth on the Valley (237-yard par three) and the fifth on the Valley (336-yard par four) would form the basis of the new eighth.

As we saw at Hoylake for the return of the Open to Royal Liverpool in 2006, there is nothing new about making logistical changes to established courses for the staging of Major events.

Meanwhile, it is clear that the men-only, or single-sex issue, formed part of the discussions with Dawson, who was assured that Royal Portrush is most definitely a mixed club, though the lady members have long had their own separate clubhouse, where I happened to enjoy 'elevenses' as a guest, some years ago.

The club's constitution states: 'Membership of the club shall be in the following classes – Ordinary members, life members, honorary members, temporary members, clubhouse members, weekday members, student members, Great Britain members, members of the Ladies Branch.' Women pay their fees to the club which oversees them. Other categories, incidentally, include residents of the Republic of Ireland.

At a time when tournament performances are being increasingly influenced by scientific factors, Shane Lowry stands apart as a disarmingly simple practitioner of his craft, a soft hands player of the highest quality. In fact, it was this innate simplicity which made a remarkable success possible for him on the PGA Tour in truly torrid circumstances at Firestone back in August 2015.

The climactic stage of the WGC Bridgestone Invitational contained all the ingredients for a reflective discourse on pressure in sport. Yet Lowry was conscious only of an enveloping calm which allowed him to accomplish a memorable triumph.

It brought to mind a charming story from his coach, Neil Manchip, on seeing him as an 18-year-old in a trial for the European Boys Championship at The Island in May 2005. When Lowry sank a difficult four-footer on the 18th, a bystander remarked: 'You were under a bit of pressure there.' Which brought the response 'pressure is for tyres' in a rich Midland accent.

When based as a teaching professional at Royal Dublin, Manchip was recruited by the Golfing Union of Ireland in the autumn of 2004. After six weeks' trial, agreement was reached whereby he would work a specific number of days each year, for a set fee per day. 'From an early stage, it was clear that he and Shane got on really well together', Shay Smith, the former GUI general secretary, recalled.

Around the same time, the GUI also considered it appropriate to bring on board a coach with an international reputation, to embellish Manchip's input. 'This led to me making contact with Pete Cowen', said Smith. 'I remember picking him up at Dublin Airport where he stipulated that his fee was one thousand sterling per day, plus expenses.

'At those sort of numbers, we limited his involvement to one weekend, but everybody, including the players, seemed to be delighted with him.' That, incidentally, was when he first set eyes on Lowry and spoke afterwards of the tremendous potential of 'the tubby kid with glasses.'

'I saw Shane as a really good golfer', Manchip later observed: 'At 18, he was someone who walked along the grass and hit the ball a whack; then he walked further along the grass and chipped or putted it, or whatever. Shane is a naturally talented guy and there's not a whole lot complicated going on there. No arsing around.'

'Himself and Shane struck a great relationship from the outset', said Shay Smith. 'Shane was on the Boys International panel and Neil was able to play them and beat them. That's where the respect emanated from. In time, he and Neil became quite close.' Under Manchip's guidance, the GUI won the European Team Championship in 2007 and again in 2008.

Ten years on, Lowry smiled at the memory. 'You heard that thing about pressure from Neil, didn't you', he said. 'And to be honest, I don't think pressure meant anything to me at that time.'

Heat was departing from a bright August sun as we sat in late afternoon a few days after Firestone, behind the 18th green at Whistling Straits, where Lowry was clearly at peace with the world.

'I know that getting over the line is always important', he went on, 'but I don't tend to sit down and think about things. I don't analyse what happened. Like when I was a kid playing amateur golf, I would always be looking forward to the next week rather than what had happened the week before.

'I was conscious of having something which made me able to win, especially in my last few years as an amateur. Which is massive in this game.' When I reminded him that two months after those events at The Island, he won the Leinster Boys Championship at Skerries, he proudly listed later victories, like the Irish Close (2007), and the West of Ireland and North of Ireland Championships of 2008. That last one, of course, had been at Royal Portrush.

Destiny now beckoned Lowry once more at a place of splendid achievement. This time, his sights were on the very pinnacle of the professional game, which he was ready to grasp over majestic duneland that had been expertly revised for the 148th Open.

With a superbly crafted third round of 63, the 32-year-old native of Clara, Co. Offaly, sent hearts racing as he opened up a four-stroke lead on the Saturday over England's Tommy Fleetwood.

The day had begun with Royal Portrush as a sight to behold, with flags along the grandstand behind the 18th green, fluttering in a fresh north-westerly. Later, the wind abated, rendering a reshaped stretch decidedly vulnerable, yet it retained the visual beauty which had been gaining universal accolades since the first ball was struck on the previous Thursday morning.

Conscious of a game in excellent order and with a mental attitude to match, Lowry had the confidence to deliver arguably his finest round on Irish terrain. Especially notable were short-game skills, which had characterised his play back in teenage years of lavish promise.

A decisive move clear of his closest challengers had been sparked by a run of three birdies from the 15th, the middle of them, a glorious two at Calamity, where a nine-foot putt was stroked unerringly into the centre of the cup. This stamp of a master, with the endorsement of Northern caddie Bo Martin, was followed by a stunning pitch to three feet at the 17th, before a two-putt par at the last completed the magic.

Given the circumstances, it was a deeply moving climax to a great day's sport, where hearts gladly opened to a brilliant representative of Irish golf. And as tension slowly eased, he was more than happy to reciprocate with the warmest of smiles.

'Honestly, this has been the most incredible day I've ever had on a golf course', said Lowry, who had the same 54-hole lead when winning in Abu Dhabi earlier that year. 'In the circumstances, I thought I dealt with things very well. People literally a yard away, while I walked from green to tee, roaring in your face as loud as they could. And tomorrow is going to be a stressful, difficult day, but I'm mentally prepared for it.'

On the Sunday, Dr Kevin Flanagan drove from Portrush back to his home at Rosses Point, having watched extraordinary events in the Open. It had been a wonderfully warm experience for the former Ireland selector and captain, because of his relationship with Lowry.

In fact, the newly crowned 'Champion Golfer of the Year' was happy to acknowledge: 'I'll be forever grateful to Kevin for what became a huge stepping-stone in my career. God knows where I'd be if Kevin hadn't been so supportive.'

All of which hinged on a chance meeting they had in an Offaly filling station back in the spring of 2009. 'I was on my way home from Tullamore', said the jubilee captain of Co. Sligo Golf Club. 'Shane explained to me that he desperately wanted to play in the Irish Open at Baltray and wondered if I could make it possible.'

The problem was that the professional event clashed with England's Brabazon Trophy, which would have been the obvious option for Ireland's number-one player in a Walker Cup year. Through Flanagan's intervention, however, arrangements were changed to allow Lowry become one of the GUI's nominated players at Baltray.

Three days after making history as the first amateur winner of the blue riband of Irish golf, Lowry brought the trophy to GUI headquarters at Carton House. There, he expressed his thanks to general secretary Shay Smith for everything the Union had done for him, while revealing that he was about to turn professional.

There are tournament professionals who view their amateur days as some sort of unfortunate disease which needs to be eradicated at the earliest opportunity. For Lowry, however, the experience could hardly have been more fulfilling. Significant trophies were accompanied by representative honours at boy, youth and senior levels. And there was the opportunity of meeting a coach and mentor, who played a key role in his challenge at Royal Portrush.

On a personal level, I loved the phrase 'arsing around', which is so typical of Manchip, whom I first got to know as a paying pupil. The arrangement was made by my wife, who thoughtfully believed that he might ease the pain a merciless game was inflicting on me.

It was probably too late for him to significantly change my skill level – 'compress the ball' – but I was fascinated by his general approach to teaching. Direct and uncomplicated, I could see how he would appeal to Lowry, who came to golf from pitch and putt, from where, according to Flanagan, every pitch and chip was executed by a trusty 63-degree wedge.

'That was when he first played in the West of Ireland in 2006', he went on. 'On hearing he was good, I went out to watch him play a few holes. He had a lovely, natural style and around the greens, I would describe him as the ultimate soft hands player. And unlike most of the boys who had their dad or a relative carrying the bag for them, he came with a proper caddie, which was unusual.'

It was an occasion when golf meted out its first seriously rough lesson to the lad from Clara. 'I remember being pleased with myself after an opening 73, even though it was six strokes behind a remarkable 67 by England's David Horsey', Lowry recalled:

> As it turned out, I was set to lead the qualifiers until it was discovered that I had signed for wrong figures in a second-round 66.
>
> While the total was correct, it included an eagle on the long fifth and a par on the sixth, whereas I had actually birdied both holes. I had turned 19 less than two weeks previously, and though it wasn't to be an ideal memory of my first West, it proved to be a very valuable lesson.

There was further pain for him only a month later. 'On a really rough day for the final rounds of the 2006 Irish Amateur Open at Portmarnock, Shane carded a really outstanding 74, to put himself in contention for the title', said Smith:

> Unfortunately, he neglected to sign his card, and I sensed how disappointing it was going to be for him, coming so soon after what had happened at Rosses Point. I was the one who had to give him the bad news, which remains one of the most awful things I've had to do in golf. But his reaction was remarkable. 'That's my own fault', he admitted. And with that, he proceeded to try and calm his father, Brendan, who was even more upset than Shane.

At this point, the question arises as to whether the golf devotee who would take up two terms of residence at 1600 Pennsylvania Avenue in Washington DC remembers Lowry from an event to which he made literally a flying visit. It was the representative match against the Metropolitan Golf Association (MGA), played at Trump National on Long Island.

When the singles got under way, a striking figure, who had just disembarked from a helicopter, proceeded to walk out on the course with a singles match which happened to involve Lowry. On reaching a particularly demanding par three, where Lowry hit a glorious three iron, the future president of the United States was prompted to exclaim to nobody in particular: 'That's one of the sweetest shots I've seen. That guy's a helluva player.' A few holes later, the chopper returned and Donald Trump was gone.

In the course of internationals at boys, youths and senior levels, Lowry gained a reputation as a popular player who liked to address colleagues by their surname, as in Kearney, Shaw and Caldwell. 'He was a responsible person', added Smith. 'When we had a day off in New York, I dropped them into Manhattan. And I entrusted Shane with the spending money for the team.'

'I have found that doing the right things in life has a lot to do with being with the right people', said Lowry. 'If you ask me what I've learned from Pádraig [Harrington], I can't be specific. But I believe that simply doing different things together has made me a better person going about my business. You just learned.

The Open of 2019 imposed very special pressures on Greystones professional Paul Dunne, who happened to be experiencing a lean time on tour back then and was in Spain on a holiday that particular week. So, in attempting to follow Lowry's every move, his only source was his mobile phone.

He hoped his own situation would be only a temporary loss of form. 'I didn't expect to go through my whole career plain-sailing', said the 2017 British Masters champion back then. 'Some times are going to be more difficult than others. I haven't been hitting the ball quite as well as I'd like and I haven't been getting myself successfully out of trouble. It's just a bit of everything.'

Sadly, problems have persisted for a player who, from an early stage in his tournament career, had got used to moving in elite golfing company, like 12 holes' practice with Harrington in Switzerland, along with a chipping and pitching challenge.

'Until I can do it myself, I'm going to be the only one at that dinner table without a Claret Jug, which is a little bit frustrating', he said with a smile. 'Watching Shane at Royal Portrush, I wasn't necessarily thinking I'm going to take this for my game and run with it. I was just genuinely happy for him. We're very close.'

He went on: 'While there's a lot to be learned from different people, though for me, maybe not so much from Rory. You learn more from the people you can relate to. I'm not sure there are many people who can relate to the way Rory plays. He's just so good.'

Yet thinking, no doubt, of how he resisted a late surge from McIlroy to capture the 2017 British Masters at Close House, Dunne pointed to one of the most encouraging aspects of golf. 'No matter how good anybody is, you can always beat them over a few days' golf', he said. 'Which is different to tennis, say. You could never beat Rory at tennis, but anyone who holds a card on any tour could beat him over a day's golf.'

He continued:

> I learned more from Pádraig, especially his positivity. He's just constantly positive. That, and his unwavering self-belief. Like anyone, his beliefs can change over time, but at a given moment, his belief is absolute.
>
> Most of all, he loves golf. With a lot of people who get to his age and have been a professional as long as he has, you can see they're doing it because they really don't know what else to do. But Pádraig still loves it, which must be a great blessing. I hope I still love the game at that age.

Meanwhile, Dunne's admiration for Lowry reached new heights when they represented Ireland in the World Cup in Melbourne in November 2018. 'I'd never seen a display of iron play like it', he said:

> It was like nothing I'd ever witnessed. I've never seen Tiger [Woods] up close, but I can't imagine he could be any better.
>
> So his win in Abu Dhabi a few months later didn't surprise me. Nor did winning the Open. Some of the shots he hit at Portrush .... His tee shot at 16 [Calamity, par three]. I know he had a big lead [six strokes] at that stage but the wind was in off the left and it's raining. And he's hitting a three-iron nonchalantly into the middle of the green. Fantastic.

He went on:

> The scenes around Shane were incredible. Knowing the golf course, I could see the moments that kept his momentum going; from his bogey putt on the first in the final round. Give me a four-shot lead in an Open and I don't imagine I'd relish going out on the Sunday to face the hardest drive you could have off the first tee.
>
> Even some of the shots coming in, right to the 17th. The difficulty of that drive from an elevated tee to a tiny fairway is underrated. It would have been so easy to leak it on the breeze. It wasn't until he hit it that I could feel it was all over. That drive really showed how much he was in control of what he was doing. It brought back memories to me as a kid, watching Pádraig when he won at Carnoustie, except that I went on to develop a relationship with Shane.

At the end of that memorable day, when Dunne's flight got into Dublin at around midnight, there was a message on his phone as to where the party was. 'My girlfriend had to be in work early the following morning, so I went with a friend', he said. 'I met Shane in the bar in Dawson Street at about 2:00 a.m. and stayed a few hours.

'It was very good. Good singing. Well, I'm not really sure if the singing was good, but I know I did my best in that regard.'

With a winning aggregate of 15 under par, the Open champion for 2019 earned $1.935 million for capturing the fourth and final Major of the year. That represented an increase on the 2018 figure of $1.89 million awarded to the Carnoustie champion, Francesco Molinari.

Victory also came with an exemption into the event until he reaches age 60, along with a five-year exemption on the PGA Tour, five-year exemptions into the Masters, PGA Championship, US Open, and Players Championship, and a 10-year exemption on the DP World Tour.

Meanwhile, reflecting on that chance meeting between player and national captain in Tullamore back in 2009, Kevin Flanagan recalled: 'When Shane talked about playing the Irish Open, I told him he should tell Colin Dalgleish, the Walker Cup captain, that he would be missing the Brabazon Trophy.

'He was our best player, but I could see he was really keen to be in Baltray. I gather he went home that night, high as a kite, telling his parents they wouldn't believe who he had just met.' Reflecting on events at Portrush, Flanagan added: 'I met Shane's parents there, and his brother Alan. I didn't meet Shane. That will be for another time.

'I always knew Shane was very good. Capable of winning a British Open? I don't know. But I could see remarkable potential, just the same.'

Thinking of a simple stepping-stone which would ultimately take on huge significance, his one-time mentor smiled: 'You could say that the rest is history.'

16

Eddie Jordan and golf: A tribute

'God said to Faldo, as he once said to Nicklaus, "You will have skills like no other." Then He whispered to Ballesteros, as He whispered to Palmer, "but they will love you more."'

– Tom Callahan in the Washington Post

● ● ● ●

On getting to know Eddie Jordan, the feeling grew that any challenge, whatever the circumstances, was to be relished. Even if it came to impromptu shots with a strange driver while wearing street shoes on the practice ground at Valderrama.

So, the idea of challenging a three-time Open champion shouldn't have surprised. Especially when given a motor-racing environment.

I especially remember a chat I had with Jordan in 2009, four years after he had sold his Formula One team in January 2005. He was returning to the motoring limelight in Australia, as a member of BBC Television's presentation team for the grand prix season, offering his 'expert insight and passionate perspective.'

Even in quieter times, there was never the danger of Jordan becoming anonymous, given his connections in golf, which included the distinction of caddying for Paul McGinley on the European Tour. Small wonder the 2014 Ryder Cup captain was devastated by the news of Eddie's death at 76, in late March 2025.

'Heartbreaking to lose one of my very best friends to the curse that cancer is', McGinley wrote of his fellow Dubliner. 'Heaven will be some craic now you've arrived.' Reflecting on a happier time when Jordan had caddied for him in the BMW International Open, McGinley said:

> Eddie was great all that week and I couldn't have asked for a better caddie. In fact, I could see why he had been so successful as a Formula One team boss. As a long-time friend, I thought I knew him very well, but I saw another side to him in Munich, which thrilled me so much. I'm not going to say what it was. It will remain a secret.

This was the man who thought nothing of bribing Nick Faldo to acquire car-testing time at Silverstone. And who invited Tiger Woods to a stay at his Wentworth home, only to impose a charge of £30,000 which he then gave to charity.

Still, he considered it something of a mixed blessing to have gained international celebrity through motor-racing. 'While it has allowed me to meet some of golf's greatest players', he acknowledged, 'there's always the problem that while I want to talk golf, all they've wanted to talk to me about has been grand prix cars.'

'I have to admit that there has been the odd, special exception', he went on:

> Like 1996 at Club de Campo in Madrid, where I played with the defending champion, Seve Ballesteros, in the Spanish Open pro-am. Eric Peugeot, a very good one-handicapper, was also in our team and we ended up being mesmerised by Seve's extraordinary short game.

Mind you, it was one of those days when he needed to be sinking putts. Off the first tee, for instance, his drive was so far left as to be almost two fairways offline. But for him, the score was all that mattered and when he finished with a 66, I learned how important it is to keep a tally of your putts.

That was the week, incidentally, which marked Pádraig Harrington's breakthrough victory on the European Tour.

Jordan continued:

Then there was the Irish Open pro-am at Mount Juliet, where Nigel Mansell and myself were in Greg Norman's team. Mansell, incidentally, is probably the toughest competitor I have come across in amateur golf. But that occasion became memorable because of the finest long-iron shot I have ever seen. It came from Greg on the long 10th [546 yards], where his drive was a bit too far left for a straight shot at the green, down the right corridor. To make matters more difficult, the wind was blowing right to left. Anyway, Greg took out this two iron and played the most glorious cut-shot imaginable. The ball soared up and over the trees and then held its line while fighting the wind. And, of course, he got the distance perfectly. In fact, he was unlucky not to make an eagle.

Jordan's deal with Faldo came early in 1996 when the chief Jordan designer at the time, Gary Anderson, was anxious to do some urgent pre-season testing. However, a phone call to Brian Pallott, the track manager at Silverstone, did not deliver the expected response. 'Can't be done', the man with a long-time business attachment to Silverstone was informed. 'The track is taken up. A private day.' Intrigued by this, Jordan wanted to know who had booked it, but Pallott wasn't saying.

In typically persuasive fashion, the motoring chief persisted until he was eventually informed that Faldo had taken over the track to put a newly purchased Porsche 959 through its paces. This, incidentally, was the same ultra-exclusive car which Faldo's American girlfriend at the time, Brenna Cepelak, severely thumped with a nine iron after the pair split up in October 1998. As she intended, the damage was extensive and quite costly to repair.

In the event, the upshot of Jordan's persistence with Pallott was that a compromise was reached. If Faldo would allow the grand prix car on the track, his reward would be a drive in it. And that's what happened.

Jordan recalled:

> We had to take the seat out to allow for Faldo's size [6ft 3ins], but it meant there was room later for Anderson to have a spin and then for singer Chris Rea [whose ballad 'Driving Home for Christmas' is an all-time favourite] to drive it. The pay-off for me was an invitation to play a round with Nick at Sunningdale a short while afterwards.
>
> Now, I've had the good fortune of playing quite a bit of golf with guys like Mansell, Alain Prost and the useful Jacques Laffite, but to play a private round with the winner of five Major championship [Faldo had yet to win his third Masters at that time] would be something else.
>
> I knew that ideally, Nick preferred to play with low-handicap amateurs, but he was willing to indulge me off 12. When it came to talking, however, all he seemed interested in was cars, just like Nick Price, Greg Norman and Frank Nobilo had been in similar situations. Still, I'll always remember that round with Faldo, if only for the crazy circumstances which brought it about.

Having liberated himself from the weekly crises associated with running a grand prix team, Jordan experienced the special joy of caddying for a close friend in Munich, at the end of August 2005. That was when McGinley finished on 20 under par in sixth place to book a slot in the World Match Play Championship at Wentworth, three weeks later.

For his part, Jordan was deadly serious about the undertaking. 'Paul had retained one of the nicest swings in the game and was playing amazing golf at the time, and I was determined we needed to capitalise on that form, as a team', he recalled:

> So it was no jaunt. In fact, I kept telling him that I wasn't going to be content simply to carry the bag and take the necessary care with yardages and so on. It was about us trying to win. I wanted to be part of a winning combination. So I was really, really tough on him. Each evening, we sat down and went through his round and I didn't spare him where I felt he had made silly errors.

Little more than a year after caddying in the BMW, Jordan had another memorable golfing experience. In the week prior to the 2006 Ryder Cup, he had Woods and his caddie, Steve Williams, as guests at his Wentworth home, which was located on a corner where the end of the garden looked out on the fourth, fifth and sixth holes of the famous West Course.

'Steve was a massive fan of Jordan Grand Prix and he told Tiger about us', said Eddie:

> The upshot was that I offered to put them up during the World Match Play. The two of them, along with a chef and other members of Tiger's team, stayed in the house while myself and Marie [Eddie's wife] moved into the annexe.
>
> In the evenings, Tiger used to go out my back garden and practise on hole five where he would acquire quite an audience by the time he reached the green. Then he'd slip away into the trees, with people probably thinking he was going to the loo. Instead, he was heading for the back entrance to my house.
>
> We thought he would leave when he was beaten by Shaun Micheel in the first round on the Thursday, but he stayed in the house for a full week. Then came the really interesting bit. Though Tiger's management company, IMG, had offered to pay us £15,000 for the week, I later told them the price was double that. Then I requested that two cheques be written for £15,000 each, one made out to the Tiger Woods Foundation and the other to my charity,

CLIC [Cancel Leukaemia in Children]. When I told Tiger what I had done, he thought it was classic. A great move. He loved it. Then I explained that this was normal practice in motor racing.

Little more than a year after caddying for McGinley, Jordan was indulging his Irishness once more as a spectator at the 2006 Ryder Cup. 'I thought The K Club did a wonderful job', he said. 'In fact, it's hard to see it being surpassed as an Irish sporting spectacle. My only complaint was that Ian Woosnam, Darren [Clarke] and the boys should have learned from Michael Schumacher how to spray champagne more elegantly.

'Great credit was due to the Irish government for their investment and belief in the project, and to Michael Smurfit for giving us such a great venue.' And he played his own part as a sponsor of amateur and professional golf in Ireland through the Eddie Jordan Classic.

'When I think of some of the conditions we faced in the difficult, early days of the Classic at The K Club, the course looked absolutely amazing', he recalled:

> Then there was the privilege I had of playing at various times with almost every member of the European Ryder Cup team.
>
> You cannot come to Ireland and expect seven days of sunshine. But the welcome was stunning. They reopened a couple of rooms in the Shelbourne Hotel for the Ryder Cup and I was fortunate in being one of those who stayed there to witness this great old institution reclaim its former glory. And Dublin on the Saturday night was wild, making Valderrama [1997] look decidedly muted by comparison. I've seen some big shows in my time, and the 2006 Ryder Cup stood comparison with the biggest of them.

Given his rental deal with Tiger Woods, it could have been described as a very memorable fortnight for Jordan, whose work for charity was remarkable.

There was the occasion when a friend of Kathy's, my wife, had a son battling for survival with cystic fibrosis. On meeting Eddie during a function in Dublin, she told him of the youngster's plight. Pointing to me, whom he knew as a newspaperman with the *Irish Times*, he promised to help Kathy's friend provided I was told nothing about it. So it was that a deal was done which involved a considerable amount of donated money from Eddie, apart from all sorts of motoring memorabilia. Sadly, the youngster didn't survive, but his grateful mother still retains Eddie's kindness close to her heart.

For his work with the BBC, Jordan grandly described himself as Formula One's Gary Lineker, relishing the public exposure. Interestingly, his initial reaction to the offer was that they couldn't be serious and he still said no when they asked him a second time. It was his wife, Marie, who eventually persuaded him to sign. He told me:

> I'm doing all the big interviews; the difficult ones. I suppose the BBC see the value of my experience of the pits and the team principals' meetings and other key aspects of the grand prix scene. What it's like to be with the stewards every other week. Not that I will be doing a major expose of the sport, but I'll try and explain the ins and outs of it as best possible.

In that moment, I could imagine his excitement at re-living the roar of high-revving engines and the intoxicating whiff of high-octane fuel. Bedroom slippers and Ovaltine were still a long way down the road for Ireland's favourite motorman.

And there was always golf. He wanted to know if I still remembered Old Sotogrande all those years ago (1994), when himself, Marie, JP Fitzgerald and myself played the final hole in total darkness, having started a fourball round in the late afternoon. It was an occasion we liked to remind each other of from time to time, as if to cement the sort of relationship Jordan seemed to delight in maintaining with long-standing contacts in the media.

I can't remember who won that particular battle. All I can recall is that Eddie was my partner and with the 18th green engulfed in darkness, he insisted that the winner would be determined by sound. In other words, the rattle of a putt against the pin would be decisive. And while I can recall such a sound, I genuinely can't remember who made it.

Typically enthusiastic, Jordan went on to talk of current happenings, about the fun he and his wife enjoyed as members of Sunningdale. Marie, a former Irish basketball international, became a very impressive five-handicap golfer. Indeed, she and McGinley's wife, Ally, became the Surrey foursomes champions and they also reached the grand finals of the *Mail on Sunday* Classic in Spain in November 2008.

Referring to the former professional career of her partner, Marie remarked: 'Allison was a top golfer and still plays off scratch despite being busy bringing up a family. She is my star.' Meanwhile, Fitzgerald, the other member of that Old Sotogrande fourball, was a regular houseguest of the Jordans and kept them up to speed with current happenings on the European Tour, when caddying for Rory McIlroy.

'Tournament golfers are a lot like racing drivers in that they're involved in a one-man sport', said Jordan:

> According to JP, McIlroy does everything right. I just hope he can learn the importance of good psychology, which is certainly in Harrington's locker. What's so nice about Pádraig is that not everybody is in love with his swing. But down the stretch, he's resilient and tough and is feared by his rivals because of what he can drag out of himself. Just like Tiger does. I'm so happy for JP. I told him I didn't think there could be another caddie in the world who had won with more diverse players. He's had tournament wins with McGinley, Thomas Bjørn, Darren [Clarke], [Ernie] Els and with Rory. He must be making ten times as much carrying bags as he might ever have made had he decided to turn pro.

He went on:

> I enjoy my trips back to Ireland, like my recent one to Doonbeg for a game with Keith Wood. That was nice, though I'm afraid my golf hasn't got any better over the years. I also played golf with

Des Smyth in Barbados [in February] and had dinner with Paul [McGinley] before he went to the AT&T with Dermot Desmond.

I'm ecstatic about what's happening in Irish golf, especially how well Pádraig has done. Down the stretch, he has shown himself to be tough and wonderfully resilient. Mentally, he has moved to a level that is beyond most of his rivals. Time will tell whether other Irish players have it, but it's certainly impressive what Rory has done. Now he needs to push on.

The timing of our latest meeting, after a glorious rugby victory over France, revived other Jordan memories for me. Like in the early 1970s, when in desperate attempts at getting a business career off the floor, he sold smoked salmon to French rugby fans from a stall at the top of Grafton Street in Dublin. The man always had style, a fact which invariably made the annual launch of a Jordan Formula One car a special experience.

After years of struggle for Jordan in the 1990s, I especially remember 1998, when a quintessentially British institution was filled with the plaintive note of the uilleann pipes. It was Jordan's way of putting his personal stamp on the launch of the Jordan Mugen Honda 198, at London's Royal Albert Hall. There, a 20-minute spectacular display of acrobatics from Cirque de Soleil ended with the new, yellow-liveried car being lowered on a platform from 50 feet above the assembled media numbering 600.

Among other things, it emphasised the remarkable resilience of a businessman who, since breaking into the ridiculously expensive world of grand prix racing in 1991, would solemnly describe each new season as 'a make-or-break year in which I've got to deliver.'

'Yes, they were great times', he mused. 'I happened to be in the Theatre Royal in Drury Lane recently and there was a picture of one of our launches with Riverdance. I always liked to give these occasions an Irish context.

'Happily, I didn't make many enemies in Formula One, possibly because I showed no favour.' He paused. 'I robbed everybody', he said casually, with a sly grin. Then, by way of emphasis, he added: 'Not just a few.' With that little stab of self-deprecation, he chuckled heartily:

> To be honest, it's part of how I was brought up. As a nation, we Irish don't tend to take things too seriously. We enjoy life because of our awareness that we're on just one short, little trip. I have met some great people and not-so-great people. That's been the beauty of motor-racing for me. You won't find the sort of tribalism you have in football, for instance. Had I been a football manager, I would have found it difficult not to put some noses out of joint, whereas you could be in a pub as a Jordan fan and have a sociable drink with devotees of Ferrari.

With a rare touch of gravity entering his voice, he went on:

> The ability of Jordan Grand Prix to hold onto its big sponsors over the years was especially gratifying, and I like to think they got value for money from our small private team where the owner, me, held 100 per cent of the equity. In the last 25 years, only five teams have won multiple grands prix – Ferrari, Jordan, McLaren, Williams, Renault/Benetton. Powerful teams like Toyota, Honda and BMW have failed to do so. And it's unlikely they'll succeed in the foreseeable future, given the dominance of Ferrari and McLaren right now.

Later Jordan launches made quite a change from the modest gatherings I remembered from the earlier years at his Silverstone factory. Bearing a hornet on its nose – 'Ready to sting the big boys!' – the 1998 car represented a triumph for the engineering skills of Jordan designer Gary Anderson, who was forced at short notice to adapt to the most radical technical rule changes for 15 years.

Federation Internationale Automobile (FIA), the sports ruling body, believed that cornering speeds had become dangerously fast. As a consequence, grooved tyres and reduced down-force would mean less adhesion, forcing drivers to slow down. There was also a narrowing of the chassis from two metres to 1.8 metres, while changes were made to the side pods so as to withstand the increased loads of the revised FIA side-impact test.

'In the interest of safety, it came down to a choice between changing the circuits or changing the cars', said Anderson. 'Obviously it's very much cheaper to change the cars.'

The scale of this London showpiece emphasised the remarkable resilience of Jordan. Seven years on from his entry into grand prix racing, he was still without a victory. But 1998 was to change all that, thanks to the coup of landing the 1996 world champion, Damon Hill, along with a works engine deal with Mugen Honda.

There was no hiding Jordan's delight at the presence of Hill on the launch platform close by Hirotoshi Honda, whose father founded the Japanese giant. In the event, Hill would form a partnership with 22-year-old Ralf Schumacher, whose older brother, Michael, raised a storm of controversy by deliberately crashing into champion-elect Jacques Villeneuve during the European Grand Prix in Jerez the previous October.

Jordan's expectations were high.

'We're paying Damon more than a full season cost us in 1991', he said of a reported £10 million, two-year deal with the Killiney-based driver. Then, employing a musical analogy, he went on: 'He's the most expensive lead guitarist in the world. And far better guitarists than him have played here.'

So as to finance a driver with 21 grand prix victories, Jordan employed all his formidable trading skills. He created a vacancy for Hill by collecting $3 million in compensation from Benetton for Giancarlo Fisichella. And he had previously got $4 million from Ferrari for Eddie Irvine along with undisclosed amounts for the contacts of Michael Schumacher and Jean Alesi. So, expensive though it undoubtedly was, the Hill contract did not see Jordan strapped for cash. 'Selling drivers has kept us in business', he claimed.

Meanwhile, by way of cementing their driving partnership, Hill informed Ralf Schumacher with boyish enthusiasm that the prince who lent his name to the Albert Hall was a German who married Queen Victoria. Meanwhile, Hirotoshi Honda gently rebuked Jordan for brazenly wearing a Ferrari watch.

All this and a French circus made for one of the better Jordan productions.

My return to London for the 1999 launch was especially memorable. This time, the host venue was the London Palladium, where Jordan addressed 500 scribes with remarkable humility. 'You had the opportunity to kill us in the first half of last season and you were very easy on us', he said. 'At the time, that's what we needed and I thank you for your patience.' It was a nice touch, which his audience clearly appreciated.

This would be the first time in their history that Jordan Grand Prix would have two drivers with grand prix victories to their credit, now that Heinz-Harald Frentzen had joined Damon Hill. Then there was Jordan's position as one of the so-called top four teams, an elevated status achieved for the first time in the 1998 constructors' championship. Which lent a piquant touch to the choice of a Pakistani illusionist as the feature entertainer. 'Now that we have tasted victory, I feel psychologically stronger', said the owner. 'Indeed, spin doctors would probably call this car the "New Era Jordan".'

Later, the illusionist's *pièce de résistance* was to wrap an entire dance troupe behind an emerald-green sheet. And presto, the sheet was removed to reveal the spanking new grand prix car – with an appropriate heightening of the decibel level, naturally.

Jordan's fortunes had changed utterly by events in Round 13 of the 1998 schedule at Spa-Francorchamps. On 30 August, having had his highest finish of fourth in the two previous races, Hill swept to victory in the Belgian Grand Prix. And, oh happy days! Ralf Schumacher followed him home for a Jordan 1, 2.

Lingering doubts were instantly removed about the value of a reported £20 million in sponsorship which Benson & Hedges was now investing in the team for a fourth successive season. And if he had a mind to, Jordan could have done some determined arm-twisting of the motoring media, with the £40 million he was reported to have received from equity investor Warburg Pincus.

Significantly, there was no mention at the 1999 launch of erstwhile Jordan technical director Gary Anderson, who designed the triumphant car in Belgium before a parting of the ways saw him move to Stewart. Granted, it was acknowledged that the new car, from a design team headed by Anderson's successor Mike Gascoyne, was largely a development of the 1998 model.

For the technically minded, the 199 had a six-speed longitudinal gearbox with a significantly modified layout. And Hirotoshi Honda informed us that while the new engine was smaller, it had a lower centre of gravity and an increased power output in excess of 725 bhp.

Interestingly, Frentzen had driven a Reynard-Mugen for Jordan as a colleague of Eddie Irvine's in the 1990 Formula 3000 Championship. Since then, the 31-year-old German had 81 grand prix starts, including a victory at Imola in 1997. 'I feel at home with Jordan', he said. 'Several of the mechanics I worked with in 1990 are still here, including my number one mechanic, Andy Stevenson.'

Two more grand prix triumphs, in the French and the Italian, were delivered in 1999 before Jordan achieved his fourth and last victory in Brazil in 2003. Two years later, he sold out for a reported £75 million. He had done so as a uniquely 100 per cent privately owned outfit in a notoriously expensive sport.

In a dismissive attempt at explaining his success, he repeated something he had told me in an earlier conversation. 'I was consistent in that I robbed everybody, so I didn't tend to make enemies', he said. 'And we both know that this life we live is just one short little trip that flies by.

'Motor racing has a unique appeal, which means that you meet some great people, varied and wide. So it's hugely important how you treat them.'

When I expressed the hope for him that his money was safely lodged in the local post office, he replied: 'There's a lot of money in motor-racing and a big mix. Once you've gone to Synge Street and emerged the other end as I did, you acquire an understanding of how to get through life. And I still have that education.'

Then, almost as an afterthought, he added: 'Of course we all have enemies, but I generally managed to hold onto my big sponsors. That was the key.'

17

Finale: On to Portmarnock

For the title of this book, I'm indebted to the child's imagination of three-year-old Paddy Harrington. On first studying the Claret Jug when his father captured it at Carnoustie in 2007, he decided it would be a perfect receptacle for his toy ladybirds. Little did father or son realise that Pádraig's success would spark a significant upsurge in Irish influence at the highest level of the game.

This transformation, or contagion as Dr Bob Rotella famously described it, included the return of the Open to Royal Portrush in 2019, when Shane Lowry secured a thrilling victory. And after only a six-year gap, it has been back there again in 2025. And it is fascinating to contemplate the prospect of a further Irish staging at Portmarnock during the coming decade.

When details of the British Amateur at Portmarnock were being announced for 2019 to celebrate the club's 125th anniversary, it wasn't a stretch to think of Gavin Caldwell as a considerable influence on securing it, given his status as the outgoing captain of the R&A. It is also acknowledged that the concept of an Open Championship coming to Portmarnock would not have got off the ground but for Caldwell.

All of which prompted reflections on a previous amateur staging in North Dublin which have inevitably grown dim in the memory. This was the British Amateur of 1949, which had been captured by Belfast's Sam (Max) McCready in extraordinary circumstances. In fact, it was to become part of one of the great political scoops of the twentieth century for Hector Legge, editor of the *Sunday Independent*.

With de Valera's *Irish Press* Group representing the political interests of Fianna Fáil, it was perhaps inevitable that newspaper production on the other side of Dublin's River Liffey would lean very strongly towards the Fine Gael party, of which John A. Costello was leader in 1948. Costello also happened to be Taoiseach and a member of Portmarnock GC, which, given its status in the Irish game, was always conscious of its responsibility towards the staging of major golf events. And its single-gender status would not have been an issue back then. It is also likely that as the chief holder of the nation's purse-strings, Costello would not have been averse to making a contribution to the Portmarnock enterprise, just as his successors have pledged down the road.

To borrow the immortal words of Sam Goldwyn, so many people have passed water under the bridge since then, that it's hard to imagine that the head of state of this part of our divided island was King George VI at the time of dramatic events in the autumn of 1948.

That was when Taoiseach Costello declared this country a republic, while on an official visit to Canada in the company, incidentally, of the bold Hector Legge, who reported the event for the *Sunday Independent*. Seven months later, the Republic of Ireland Act became law on 18 April 1949 and, as a consequence, the country's membership of the Commonwealth ended automatically and the President of Ireland became, finally and unambiguously, the Irish head of state.

Which prompts a fascinating thought. Had the event under consideration by the R&A at a time when the Irish Free State was part of the British Commonwealth been the Open, or the British Open as it was then generally known, would it have been an acceptable location for the British Open? It could have been argued, after all, that the term 'Open' precluded any political restriction, especially for the original of the species.

When I made this suggestion to Pádraig Harrington some years ago, he could see the logic of it. During a press conference sometime later, however, he gently accused me of misleading him, presumably having been enlightened by a new-found closeness with the R&A.

Meanwhile, some wonderful memories, many of them charmingly mischievous, were revived of 1949. Special interest centred on Dublin-born journalist and general toff the Honourable Patrick Campbell, 3rd Baron Glenavy, who had a remarkable fourth-round victory over international Dr Billy O'Sullivan.

As a valued columnist, Campbell appears to have had a *laissez-faire* attitude to *Sunday Dispatch* deadlines. The Championship started on a Monday and ended the following Saturday, yet the *Dispatch*'s man saw fit to transmit his copy for the week on the Wednesday evening, prior to Thursday's meeting with Dr O'Sullivan. So it was that in Sunday's paper the editor felt it necessary to tail the offering with the paragraph: 'Patrick Campbell beat Dr O'Sullivan in the fourth round, but was knocked out by KG Thom in the fifth – and we have not heard from him since.'

In the event, the honourable scribe applied himself to the challenge with a system he called 'Crushing Power'. This involved sessions on the practice ground 'off the top of which the American competitors have already shaved a couple of inches.'

He wrote:

> I asked a distinguished golf correspondent to watch me playing a couple of shots. 'Just', I said, 'to get them really drilled at the hole.' I played seven of my best and two of the ones that leave the elbows numb but not broken. 'Well', I asked him, 'how does it feel?' He sucked his teeth carefully. 'It feels', he said, 'like someone rubbing a knife on a plate.'
>
> 'But the smooth lurch', I said. 'The hands and the stomach and the kneecaps sweeping through?'
>
> 'You might be keeping goal', he said, 'at lacrosse.' After a moment, he added: 'Mixed lacrosse.'

Undeterred, Campbell proceeded, as he put it, 'to rebuild the thing from the ground up, bringing a group of muscles into play which I'd last used while being stunned by a blow on top of the head from a PT instructor during a boxing lesson.'

For all the self-mocking, he did considerably better than more fancied Irish contenders and had reason to feel suitably buoyant after wrapping up a third-round victory by the 14th. 'I am a winner', he enthused, 'with no one cheering more loudly than myself.'

Of his 10:30 a.m. assignment with O'Sullivan, he continued: '... if I'm to run out on the first tee tomorrow morning in racing shorts and Girl Guide's beret, almost before the first two eggs have bounced off the stop-netting, it will be difficult to tell how I'm to face up to the first six-inch putt.'

'There's just one point I'd like to make clear,' he further informed his readers. 'Should I beat Dr O'Sullivan in the morning, and subsequently smash my way through to the final, and then tear the raspberry mousse [sweater] off Frank Stranahan, I am not available for the Walker Cup. This summer, I'm thinking of embroidering a fire-screen.'

There was also tremendous fun off-stage as it were, in the well-aimed swipes of *Irish Times* columnist Myles na gCopaleen at his waspish best. Though the highly regarded golf correspondent JP Rooney insisted the event should be designated as the 'Amateur Championship', Myles thought otherwise. And after some appropriate research, he wrote on Monday, 30 May 1949:

> Well, yesterday's London papers either don't know about this or don't agree. Let me quote:
>
> 'Irishman Sam McCready won the British Amateur Golf Championship at Portmarnock yesterday.' – *Sunday Express.*
>
> 'Max [sic] McCready beat the American amateur champion, William Turnesa, in the final of the British Amateur Championship at Portmarnock.' – *The People.*
>
> 'Sam McCready won the British Amateur Golf Championship at Portmarnock yesterday.' – *Sunday Chronicle.*

The only paper accessible to me which calls it 'the Amateur Golf Championship' is *The Observer* and that, of course, may be a mistake on the part of that dread Tory eructation.

Henry Longhurst, meanwhile, experienced a notable change of heart from earlier criticism of the R&A's choice of Portmarnock. Outdoing Myles in his waspishness, our Henry had written on 31 October 1948 a reaction piece to the change of our political status:

> ... I ally myself with those who trust that the Championship Committee will, in the light of current events, revise their decision to take the British championship to Éire, and take it instead to either of the great seaside links of Northern Ireland – Newcastle, Co. Down or Portrush.
>
> Far be it for me in this humble corner on a Sunday morning to get mixed up with politics but it would seem strange that we should play a British championship in a country which is making every legitimate step to inform the world that it is, as it were, 'under entirely new management', and will have no truck with the word British.

He went on:

> I have always taken the view with my friends in Éire that this is wholly their own affair. I do not presume to suggest to them what their attitude should be, and am careful when in their country to talk of being 'abroad'.
>
> In one respect, with the best will in the world, I differ from them. They are fond of saying: 'Ah! Golf knows no boundaries!' Golf does know boundaries, and the boundaries for the British Amateur Championship are the boundaries of the United Kingdom.
>
> If we are to play at Portmarnock, interesting precedents will be established. Not only shall we for the first time be playing abroad, and may thus look forward one day to holding the championship

at Le Touquet, but we shall also for the first time be compelled to arm ourselves with passports or even documents required for the identification of aliens.

Referring to this piece from the previous October, Myles saw it as justification for giving considerable attention to 'Mr Longhurst.' 'Only to remind everybody who entertained him at Portmarnock, that some months ago, he published in the *Sunday Times* [this] nasty and bitter little article, all the worse for its urbanity of style, protesting against the decision to have the championship on the Portmarnock course.'

Myles proceeded to draw his readers' attention to what can only be described as a remarkable change of heart from dear Henry when reporting on the actual championship. About which Longhurst wrote: 'The morning round was played in glorious Technicolor. The white tents and newly painted red and white clubhouse gleamed in the sun, the sea glistened on either side of the course and the Dublin mountains shimmered purple in the background.'

And there was more. 'The larks sang fit to burst and a lizard sunned itself on my sleeve as I watched the ninth hole – all in splendid contrast to the pouring rain one learned there was in England', he continued. Then, as a little bonus, he saw fit to write of Portmarnock: 'For those who have not seen this great links, I may perhaps add that when the Irish Open Championship was played here two years ago, with a special prize of £200 to be divided among those professionals who broke 70, only one man did it. That was Fred Daly who later went on to win the British Open.'

The cynic in me is tempted to conclude that these fine words were penned after Henry, whom Joe Carr referred to humorously as 'Henry Longthirst', had been treated to several sessions of gin in the members' bar! Anyway, we will give the final words to the irrepressible Myles, who once memorably remarked that a certain individual 'is to be avoided like the pledge.'

Regarding the 1949 British Amateur, he concluded: 'I will say no more on this embarrassing topic save to remark that it is just as well that Mr

Longhurst personally risked the contamination of Portmarnock. Indeed he is probably still there.'

The mood among Portmarnock's members as to their attitude towards the possibility of staging the AIG Women's Open and Open Championship was best reflected in a vote of a special general meeting of the members in April 2025. By the crushing majority of 96 per cent, they expressed themselves behind the project.

Effectively, they were giving their approval to structural changes to their links proposed during a year's work by architect Martin Ebert of Mackenzie & Ebert, who are acknowledged as the current experts in this area. As a consequence, the future of the project now rests with the government, which has promised up to €40 million in funding, and the R&A.

This doesn't mean that the pace of progress, however, has been advanced. I understand that the mood in the R&A has changed significantly since Martin Slumbers was replaced by Mark Darbon as their CEO in July 2024. It is not that Darbon is less enthusiastic than his predecessor about the project; it is simply that the pressures of his appointment have deflected him in other directions.

Still, a final decision is expected before the end of 2025. And current thinking is that this could probably mean a Women's Open in 2029 and the Open sometime in the following decade, possibly by 2035.

So, would this mean a next Irish staging of the Open taking place south of the border at Portmarnock, though it would be ten years since Portrush hosted it for a third time? My understanding is that this could be very much the case, from the reaction of a certain section of Portrush members who believe they have done their bit, for the moment, by staging the event twice in six years.

My colleague, Brian Keogh of the *Irish Independent*, has been very much on top of this story from the time it gained serious traction in the wake of the British Amateur at Portmarnock in 2019. And regarding the proposed changes to the course, he wrote that they include 'making the par-four second a par-three, playing to the same green and modifying the proposed fifth hole by building a new green and moving the tee back 40 yards.'

He went on:

> This would eliminate safety concerns as the fifth green is in the line of players driving at the 398-yard third. The 17th would become the 18th for the Open, with the 18th becoming the first hole. Several new back tees and bunkers will also be built to make the course a better challenge for the game's best players. The par-three 12th green will also be softened to allow for more pin positions, while the practice range will be reformed.

I also understand that further adjustments will be necessary to the course, as in a service road traversing it and the building of compounds in outer areas where dunes would be softened to create open areas for TV compounds, etc. These changes would need to be made some time in advance of the event, to facilitate the movement of heavy structural equipment.

The estimated cost of this work is €1.5 million, which will be covered entirely by the R&A. As a separate issue, however, the club is conscious of the need to seriously upgrade elements of their clubhouse, such as plumbing and electricity, which have gone into disrepair. And an upgrading of the professional's shop will be necessary. Then there is the water supply from Portmarnock Village, which is considered inadequate. These internal issues would be handled at the club's own expense.

Meanwhile, despite the pressures of office, Darbon views the project with real optimism:

> We're in the midst of a planning process right now and that is focused on a detailed feasibility study to get under the skin of how we can stage an Open Championship at Portmarnock. We're really optimistic about that prospect. We're working closely with the local authority and the government to support us in undertaking that feasibility work. We're not quite there yet but it's a

> process that is gathering some pace and we are optimistic about the future.
>
> We have to finish the feasibility work to begin with, but we're really optimistic about bringing both the AIG Women's Open and the Open Championship here.

Current concentration is on work outside the club's entrance gates. The road from Portmarnock Village onto the peninsula needs to be widened significantly.

This is in the hands of Fingal County Council who, in conjunction with the R&A, have put together a plan, not only for Championship week, but, as I have indicated, to facilitate getting articulated lorries on site in the run-up to the event.

When Portmarnock was proposed as a venue for Ireland's first staging of the Ryder Cup in 1993, a key component was considered to be the construction of a Bailey bridge from Baldoyle Road. This has since been rejected as a workable option.

Still, in his capacity as Minister for Housing, Local Government and Heritage, Darragh O'Brien confirmed that between €35 million and €40 million of public money would be invested in infrastructure outside the gates of the club, apart from the expenditure on the links itself.

'It will mean a massive investment', the Minister said. 'The prestige of hosting this event will be absolutely colossal. I'm delighted to have it supported. I've met with the R&A and Portmarnock Golf Club and they deserve incredible credit, as do Fingal County Council, for securing this really world-famous event.'

Meanwhile, it must be acknowledged that the hosting of an Open Championship had only a relatively small bearing, possibly as low as five per cent, on the decision by Portmarnock's members to relinquish their single-gender status. It has been pointed out to me that the transition has become an unqualified success, to the extent that Portmarnock has emerged as the only fully integrated club in the country, with its women members, for instance, playing in the captain's prize. It has been a resounding success.

So, will the big event happen? As is generally the case in such matters, it will all come down to money.

If an agreement is reached, it will be very similar to what happened with Royal Portrush prior to 2019. They supplied the course where changes were made, which involved the elimination of the old 17th and 18th holes and the recreation of a new seventh and eighth. The R&A then computed their overall costs and handed the bill to the Northern Ireland Executive with the message, 'if you want the Open, this is what it's going to cost you.' When they got their cheque, the deal was done.

In effect, the responsibility for staging the Open has now gone from Portmarnock GC to the R&A and the government. All three have had suitably productive meetings involving civil servants under the authority of the Minister for Sport, Patrick O'Donovan. As I have indicated, however, the process was slowed down by the retirement of Martin Slumbers and by this country's general election in late 2024.

Another, personal element to the process concerns Pádraig Harrington, our most successful Open competitor, with back-to-back successes in 2007 and 2008. These made him exempt until he's 60 and he has admitted that saying farewell to the event in Portmarnock in 2032 would be a splendid way to bow out.

'It would be very nice if it was to be my last year in 2032 that the Open came to Portmarnock', he said. 'Hopefully, that can happen. It would be my last one ... I'd be 60 that year.'

Indications, however, are that his 60th birthday will come a few years too early to fulfil that ambition. The problem could be overcome, of course, through a special exemption, which has been done before.

It's about money as far as the R&A are concerned and, at this stage, the expectation would be that up to 245,000 tickets to the Open could be sold per staging. So, three Irish stagings combined with at least one AIG Women's Open could result in a cumulative gross economic impact of €338 million.

From their experience with the 1991 Walker Cup and the 2019 British Amateur, quite apart from observations of the 2006 Ryder Cup and various Irish Opens, the R&A will be keenly conscious of Ireland's reputation as a world-leading golf destination.

What really impressed Slumbers, however, was the 2019 Open. 'I think you need to look at what happened in Portrush', he said:

> I mean, Portrush [2019] was amazing. What Portrush did – it's a very interesting piece of the equation – is that the vast majority of the people who came to Portrush had never been to an Open Championship before.
>
> It was a different audience. There were more Americans. But it wasn't dominated by Americans, it was about 20 per cent from the United States. So it opened up a new market. And that's good for business and good for golf.

Two years after Portrush, St Andrews played host to the 150th Open, on which an independent study was commissioned by the R&A. Through VisitScotland and Fife Council, it established that the event generated almost €350 million in economic benefit for Scotland.

With that sort of revenue floating around, it is hardly any wonder that the political implications of staging the Open outside of the UK for the first time haven't been mentioned. Just think of all the gin it would have bought for dear old Henry, back in 1949!